THE SHOPPER'S
GUIDE TO PARIS

Lucia van der Post has edited and mainly written the 'How to Spend It' column of the *Financial Times* for the past 14 years where thousands of readers have learned to trust her judgement. Born in South Africa, Lucia fell in love with London on a trip to England and has lived there ever since. Following five years on the *Sunday Telegraph*, she joined the *Sunday Times* Look team, and then moved on to the *Financial Times*. Lucia's first trip to Paris was in 1963; she spends as much time there as she can. She is married to Neil Crichton-Miller and has two grown-up children.

LUCIA VAN DER POST

THE SHOPPER'S GUIDE TO PARIS

MICHAEL JOSEPH

LONDON

First published in Great Britain by
Michael Joseph Ltd,
27 Wrights Lane, London W8
1987

British Library Cataloguing in Publication Data

van der Post, Lucia
The shopper's guide to Paris.
1. Stores, Retail—France—Paris—
Guide-books 2. Paris (France)—Description
—Guide-books
I. Title
914.4′3604838   DC708
ISBN 0-7181-2715-3

Typeset by Cambrian Typesetters, Frimley, Surrey
Printed in Great Britain by
Butler & Tanner, Frome, Somerset

The author and publishers would like to thank the
following for permission to reproduce copyright
photographs in this book.
Barnaby's Picture Library: *pages* 42, 45, 132, 136
Chanel: *page* 21 **Hermes:** *pages* 28, 189 **John
Harris:** *pages* 140, 151 **Photo Jean Ribière:** *pages*
14, 46, 62, 72, 95, 130, 163 **Topham:** *pages* 66, 74,
96, 160, 172, 175, 198, 214 **Trevor Humphries,**
Financial Times: *pages* 8, 10, 11, 12, 17, 18, 30, 32,
34, 37, 38, 39, 55, 57, 61, 71, 81, 82, 85, 87, 88,
89, 92, 101, 107, 109, 110, 112, 114, 119, 123,
124, 134, 138, 147, 149, 155, 158, 165, 169, 170,
177, 180, 183, 190, 191, 194, 204, 207, 210, 213,
217, 218, 222, 230

CONTENTS

INTRODUCING THE SHOPPER'S GUIDE

Why another guide to Paris? Is not this lovely city already more than adequately endowed with guides to this and directories to that? The answer, surprisingly, is no. There are indeed many guides but almost without exception they concentrate on advising their readers about such matters as which restaurants serve the finest *quenelles*, which hotels offer the plushest bathrooms, which museums the most distinguished pictures and which winebars the finest wines. Few seem to reflect the fact that for many people nowadays shopping is or could be one of life's great pleasures.

Shopping today, in Paris of all places, should be about more than just tracking down the cheapest of life's necessities — it should be fun. Paris, after all, belongs to us all, and has long been known as one of the great centres of civilised living.

This guide aims to restore the art of shopping to its rightful place and to guide the reader to the small markets, the little specialist shops, the interesting boutiques, the stores and the grand establishments of the city.

It doesn't aim to be comprehensive. Do not look to it for a list of every shop in the whole of Paris — you will not find it. What you will find is a strictly personal, highly selective, idiosyncratic guide to the Paris that I have discovered, to the shops and services that I think are the best of their kind that Paris has to offer. It is, if you like, prejudiced.

Remember above all that Paris is a living, vital, changing city. Paris is not what it was, nor should we wish it to be. It has not escaped some of the ravages of over-enthusiastic modernisation. Shopping patterns are changing. Where once almost every Parisian woman did her food shopping daily in her own *quartier*, today she may well go out to work and make big, less frequent forays to supermarkets further afield. There is a fad at the moment for giant covered arcades and shopping

precincts. Areas like Les Halles and the Marais are today in a constant state of flux and shops come and go with surprising rapidity.

But beneath it all, Paris is still a surprisingly old-fashioned and conservative city. A city that it takes time and knowledge to get to know. A city full of surprises.

You can walk off a great boulevard and find yourself in a cobbled street. Just minutes from busy intersections are quiet courtyards behind which lurk *ateliers* and houses which can scarcely have changed since the Middle Ages.

There are still small, delightful shops where you can track down a handmade shoe, a quirky antique, an exceptionally finely-cut coat or a rare wine. Haute couture still flourishes. Parisian women, at their best, still know better than any other how to make an outsider feel dowdy.

Paris is many things to many people. Nobody can discover it all or know it all. What this guide hopes to do is to introduce you to some of its delights and to encourage you to discover a Paris of your own.

ESSENTIAL INFORMATION

I have tried to make this guide as easy to use and follow as possible. It is divided into two parts. The first part takes you on a walkabout tour through each of the five main shopping areas, so that you don't have to backtrack too much if you are looking for several things at once. The second part is ordered alphabetically, for ease of reference, and develops the scope of Part I. For instance, if you are looking for that exclusive fashion item on the Right Bank, you need to look through the section 'Haute Couture' as well so that you can go straight to the *maisons* of your choice. Most of the section headings in Part II are self-explanatory: under 'Something for Monsieur', for instance, you will find most of the important suggestions for shops that might interest the male of the species, although of course he is also likely to be interested in some of the other sections as well, in food, wine, antiques, department stores and so on. Those chapters, too, are clearly labelled. There is some inevitable overlapping (some shops which might also interest *monsieur* will be found in the chapter headed Right Bank and so on) but a careful use of the index should guide you to all the shops that might interest you.

Though all cities are subdivided in various ways, Paris is perhaps unique in the organisation of its twenty *arrondissements*, which are arranged numerically in a spiral, starting with the 1st *arrondissement* in the centre on the Right Bank near the Louvre and spiralling round twice before ending up on the eastern side of the city with *arrondissement* number 20.

Paris is a far more compact city than most and visitors will find that the areas which provide the most interesting and rewarding shopping are by and large to be found in the inner core of Paris — with one important exception, the 16th *arrondissement*. For those who like to savour the atmosphere of a district and suss out the shops in a favourite part I have decided to concentrate on five main shopping districts: the Right Bank, the Left Bank, Les Halles, the Marais and the 16th. Each has its own pleasures, its unique character and you will be able to wander happily through them, making discoveries of your own as well as following mine.

This isn't to say that there aren't any fine and interesting shops in some of the out-of-the-way districts — of course there are — but on the whole these are the *quartiers* which are currently buzzing and will prove the most rewarding. These are the *quartiers* where those who want to discover what

today's Paris is all about should head for; where the old-established *ateliers*, the time-honoured emporia and the modern boutiques have made their base. Those whose time is limited would, I think, have more fun getting to know one of these districts in some depth rather than trying to dash about them all.

So arm yourself with a good pair of walking shoes, some handy credit cards, a good map and let's start.

WHEN TO GO?

Each to his own season. I love it in August when the city acquires a mature tranquillity that is usually conspicuously absent. This is the time of year when many small shopkeepers, all the *beau monde* and much of the bourgeoisie decamp to the mountains, seaside and other fashionable watering-holes, leaving Paris wonderfully hassle-free for you and me. *But* it does mean you risk your favourite restaurant being shut, your friends being out of town and the general summer lassitude offering a ready excuse for anything that is either closed or doesn't work. July combines (usually) good weather with lots of jolly *fêtes*, as the school and universities disgorge their highly-disciplined inmates. Just before Christmas is frenetic but satisfyingly filled with heady anticipation and shopping fever. The time of the big exhibitions (Prêt-à-Porter in February and September, the Air Show in June and the Motor Show in October) is another hectic time: your favourite restaurants will be booked up, the hotels full and the general air of chaos great. If you want to visit Paris during Christmas, New Year or Easter — which are after all the most popular times for everybody — remember that these are holiday periods for the Parisian too, and some of the restaurants and shops may be closed. Above all, remember to book your hotel early — Paris has ceased to be an easy city to visit on the spur of the moment and at the height of the season it can become almost impossible to find a room anywhere. The chic eateries, such as Alain Senderens and Lucas-Carton (where I tried — and failed — for over a week to get a dinner reservation) are booked up weeks in advance. So if you have a special hotel or restaurant in mind, book the minute you can.

SHOPPING HOURS

Most of the large boutiques and *grands magasins* are open from 9 or 9.30am until 7pm (with a late night once a week, sometimes, as with La Samaritaine and Bazar de l'Hôtel de Ville, as late as 10pm). The smaller shops and, in particular, the smaller food shops usually open earlier (some as early as 7 or 7.30am) and stay open until 8pm — however, they close for a hefty break between noon or 12.30pm until 4 or 4.30pm. Suss out the hours in your district on arrival so you don't get caught out. In Les Halles and the Marais, for instance, opening hours of the chic boutiques are distinctly on the late side, some not opening until 10.30am. Antique shops are often a law unto themselves (it's all part of their charm) and official opening hours seem to offer a vague guideline rather than a precise indication. Whilst the larger stores are open from Monday to Saturday inclusive, neighbourhood shops usually still close on Mondays.

OUVERTURE
LUNDI 11h A 19h
MARDI AU SAMEDI
10h A 19h

CREDIT CARDS

Most of the large shops, hotels and restaurants take credit cards these days but there are considerable variations in which cards will be accepted at which establishments. I know of no single card which is accepted everywhere. In addition some of the smaller shops, restaurants and even hotels sometimes won't take them at all (for small shops with small turnover the extra cost it would impose on sales prices would mean even fewer sales). My advice is not to depend on them too heavily for your daily purchases and to make sure you have

plenty of traveller's cheques. Remember that whilst credit cards offer some interest-free credit it's hard to keep check of spending when the exchange rate you will be charged will depend on the rates on the day you are billed.

TAX REFUNDS

You will notice many shops purporting to sell tax-free and duty-free goods, usually perfumes. Few, however, seem to offer proper tax refunds. They mainly give a small discount on some (very) highly-priced luxury things like perfumes, designer scarves and ties, watches and other small accessories. The price often seems to have been hoiked up to take account of the so-called discount. Such shops are usually best left alone — you will be better off buying at normal outlets which do at least tend to have a higher charm factor and anyway, you'll probably end up paying much the same in the end.

Officially, those who live outside France are entitled to a refund of the French VAT on certain purchases. Operating the system however requires persistence and a real commitment to saving money. Shops are not obliged to give you this refund and you are most likely to find it operating in the larger stores (Galeries Lafayette, BHV, Au Printemps all have excellent services for foreigners and will guide you through the system). The French initials for VAT are TVA and you should ask for the *détaxe* forms. The total value of your purchases has to add up to at least 1200 francs for those living outside the Common Market and to at least 2200 francs for those inside it (usually only the larger stores will let you add up smaller purchases to reach the required sum).

If you are interested, ask the store for help. The discount you may eventually get will vary between 13% and 23%. Some stores give you the discount there and then (and trust you to do your bit by handing in the forms to the customs official on leaving the country); others charge you the full price and forward the discount to you later. You will need your passport, much stamina and a relaxed attitude to time. Do not forget the additional catch, that you may be charged duty on purchases over and above your allowances when whatever it is you've bought comes into the country.

SIZES

Before you set out on your spending spree, it's wise to be armed not only with the measurements of your nearest and dearest but also with the equivalent in continental sizings. Here is a chart of the most common French, British and American measurements.

WOMEN

Dresses, blouses, knitwear (*robes, chemisiers et tricots*)

F	36N	38N	40N	42N	44N	46N	48N
GB	10	12	14	16	18	20	22
USA	8	10	12	14	16	18	20

Stockings (*bas et collants*)

F	1	2	3	4	5
GB/USA	8½	9	9½	10	10½

Shoes (*chaussures*)

F	35½	36	36½	37	37½	38	39
GB	3	3½	4	4½	5	5½	6
USA	4	4½	5	5½	6	6½	7

MEN

Suits (*costumes*)

F	36	38	40	42	44	46	48
GB/USA	35	36	37	38	39	40	42

Shirts (*chemises*)

F	36	37	38	39	40	41	42
GB/USA	14	14½	15	15½	16	16½	17

Shoes (*chaussures*)

F	39	40	41	42	43	44	45
GB	5½	6½	7	8	8½	9½	10½
USA	6	7	7½	8½	9	10	11

Sweaters (*tricots*)

F	36	38	40	42	44	46
GB/USA	46	48	51	54	56	59

GETTING AROUND

METRO This is generally agreed to be one of the best underground systems in the world. Anybody who has tried to grapple with the inexplicable irrationalities of the New York system will find the Paris version a model of clear, rational planning. Once you have spent about five minutes studying how it works you would need to try hard to get lost. Quite apart from its ease and speed it is also fun — here you see Parisians going about their daily business and you get a much better idea of how the city works than by travelling in insulated taxis (which are, in any event, almost impossible to find when you want them). The métro runs every day from 5.30am to 1.15am although on Sundays and holidays you will find services much reduced. You can buy tickets for single journeys but it makes much more sense to buy a block (*carnet*) of ten tickets which works out at half the price. There is first and second class travel which usually takes new arrivals by surprise: second class is perfectly adequate, merely much more crowded. But watch your handbags and wallets — Paris is currently plagued by a wave of serious pickpocketing and thefts.

L'AUTOBUS I have never managed to suss out the bus systems properly myself but quicker learners tell me it is an enjoyable way to travel. Buses usually run from 7am to 7pm. Bus and métro tickets are interchangeable which makes the *carnet* an even better buy. Although you *can* buy a ticket aboard a bus, because the ticket is sold singly this works out much more expensive than buying a *carnet* before you board. *Carnets* are available from bus or métro stations, *tabacs* and some slot machines.

Also at most bus stops nowadays, there is a small ticket machine. You should take a ticket as soon as you arrive at the stop. As Parisians don't know how to queue *à l'anglais* this system tries to ensure that you move onto the bus in ticket order number. It doesn't always work! Newcomers don't always realise that all stops are request stops — if you don't indicate when you want to get on or off, the bus won't stop.

RER (Reseau Express Regional) Very smart, very new, very fast. The RER is a very slick train, which travels underground and overground. It is really designed for getting quickly to and from the suburbs (it is, for instance, the most sensible way to head for the airport). It also links with several métro stations at *correspondances* (changing) points so it can be useful for travelling quickly within Paris. You can use a métro ticket on the RER system as long as you stay within Paris but if you want to use RER to go to the suburbs you will need to buy a special ticket. You could ask for a combined ticket (*billet combiné*) or you can buy a *billet de Tourisme* for two, four or seven days which is excellent value and allows you to travel on bus, métro and RER. If you are staying in Paris for a minimum of a week and intend to use the bus and métro a lot, a weekly *Carte Orange* (it also comes in a monthly version) is probably your best bet. It runs from Monday to Monday and allows you to travel by métro, bus and RER. Remember to take a photograph along.

SITU If you should spot a strange-looking box beside métro stations and wonder what it could be, joke not, for you have just spotted the pride and joy of the Paris transport system — SITU (*systeme d'information de trajets urbains*). In other words, a dispenser of computerised information. What this means to you and me is that if in doubt about how to get from A to B, SITU, in its flashy computerised way, will tell you in an instant. You tap into the computer the name of the street you're heading for (because it's so clever it, of course, already knows where you are) and SITU gives you a print-out of the quickest way to get there, whether by RER, métro or bus, as well as a rough estimate of the time it will take.

So far SITU computers are at ten major stations including Châtelet, Luxembourg and Saint-Germain-des-Prés, but in the next two years RATP hopes to have some 100 operating in the city. In the meantime at other métro stations you will have to make do with the large maps with illuminated buttons to show you which direction to follow.

TIPPING

Almost all hotels, restaurants, bars and cafés automatically add 15% to the bill and though it is customary to leave the small change behind, you don't have to add anything extra. If you notice the words *service non compris*, that means no tip has been included in the bill and you should add somewhere between 12% and 15% to the bill. Cloakroom attendants, tour guides, doormen and even cinema usherettes all expect small tips, whilst at airports and stations the porters have a fixed charge. Taxi drivers expect somewhere between 10% and 15%.

LA POLITESSE

France is a much more formal country than Britain and certainly more formal than the United States. A *Bonjour Madame* or *Monsieur* does a great deal to smooth the path. The best defence against the rudeness you will undoubtedly meet on occasion is to don an impregnable air of considerable dignity and remember not to take it personally. Parisians are busy people, life in their city demands quite an aptitude for survival and in any event none of the rudeness is intended to be personal.

The more you grow to love the city and the more of the language you learn, the more you will understand the Parisian temperament. The day will come when you will be able to forgive the times you are elbowed out of the way, the door that is allowed to fall back in your face and the haughty looks of the sales girls who seem to have an uncanny knack of pricing every item you are wearing. Personally, I find it helps to wear

my best clothes, don my newest haircut, my very best accessories and then saunter out with confidence. Parisians respect confidence and if you learn to treat them with immaculate politeness but no hint of uncertainty you will find they respond in kind. Put away your British diffidence, your American chumminess and don a little Parisian *hauteur*. When you know the rules you'll learn to love the game.

PART I

THE RIGHT BANK
(POSH PARIS)

The Right Bank is posh Paris at its poshest. Nowhere else in the world is it so easy to feel insecure. It can take but a certain look, a smile that is a trifle less than whole-hearted, a lifting of the eyebrow a shade more than is natural and most Anglo-Saxons are reduced to quivering jellies of insecurity.

All this is entirely unnecessary. The crucial thing to remember is that its very unchic to worry about being posh. Be yourself. If you act resolutely as the person you are and insist (without being aggressive) on being yourself, the Parisians will crumble. Look at the way the secretary walks down the street, observe the *vendeuses* in the smart boutiques, study your hostess at the next dinner party — outwardly there seems little to distinguish between you and them and yet they saunter down the boulevard as if they own it. Take your cue. Do a little sauntering yourself. True allure, which many Parisian women seem to imbibe at birth, is nine-tenths inner confidence, one-tenth packaging.

The other thing to remember is that anything English (even, unlikely as it may seem, *you*) is currently all the rage. Don your Burberry, your cashmere, your Jaeger, your ladylike Bally shoes; or if you're a man, emerge in your Turnbull & Asser shirt, your simple grey flannels, your Lobb shoes, and you'll be off to a flying start.

The current obsession with all things *Anglais* has gone to lengths that seem almost absurd but there is one important distinction to be made — the French interpretation will look so much newer, so much better thought out, so very much more self-conscious. It is all done a little too perfectly ever to be confused with the real thing.

Remember that Paris, too, has its equivalent of the Sloane Ranger — called the BCBG (the initials stand for *Bon Chic, Bon Genre*). Anybody who is interested in such things and can read French should get the bible on the subject — *Le Guide du BCBG* by Thierry Mantoux. Just like the Sloane Ranger, the BCBG cannot be made, they must be born. *On devient riche mais on est BCBG.*

The BCBG are as easily recognisable as their British counterparts. Spot them wandering down the rue Saint-Honoré with their clean, well-cut hair, their beautifully made skirts and simple navy *pulls*, the pearls at the throat, a child in either hand. On one side will be little Marie-Chantal in her hand-smocked Liberty print dress with the Peter Pan collar; on the other little Olivier in his smart Bermudas, his miniature button-down 'Oxford' shirts and his blazer — they couldn't be anything but French. No Sloane Ranger would have got her act quite so together as this.

See Monsieur BCBG in his grey flannels, his Argyle socks, his navy-blue blazer with the pocket crest, his Charvet ties, his Weston shoes and, if it's winter, note the Loden — you'll soon begin to recognise the plumage. This is authentic BCBG kit. Essential armoury in the style wars.

Poshest and grandest of all are the fine old establishments gathered round those grand-sounding streets on the Right Bank — the heart of stylish Paris is the rue Saint-Honoré, the rue du Faubourg Saint-Honoré, the avenue Montaigne, the avenue George V and the place Vendôme, though, just lately, some of the international nouveau riche brigade have been seen to invade these once impeccable addresses.

This is where the women whose daughters today probably shop in Les Halles or the trendier boutiques of Saint-Germain-des-Prés still do their own shopping. This is where they come to buy their couture outfits, to have their hair done, to replace the broken Lalique glass, to stock up on Porthault linen, to buy a string of pearls or the essential scarf. Turn to the section on fashion for some more names of both couture and prêt-à-porter houses in the Right Bank.

Few of us may actually do our own shopping in these splendid avenues but all of us may browse. A morning spent window-shopping is a feast for the eye. Parisians know better than anybody how to seduce the eye and tempt the hesitant to throw caution to the wind. If it's Christmas-time, in particular, no matter how small your budget you should make a point of wandering in that very, very *luxe* little triangle bordered by the avenue Montaigne and the avenue George V. There'll you see the great couture houses and the grand hotels. Take a drink, or even breakfast, in one of them and you'll get a real whiff of what luxury Paris is all about.

The rue Saint-Honoré is narrow and wanders through the district in its own idiosyncratic way. It lends itself to personal discovery more than most — there you can still find the small greengrocers, the fine *epiceries* and the wine merchants in

amongst the imposing purveyors of luggage and jewellery, silk dresses, and smart ties.

In the rue du Faubourg Saint-Honoré you are most likely to see that quintessential Parisian sight — the grand limousine inching its way down the street, keeping pace with its elegantly clad owner. Spot her emerging from one discreet and highly-priced establishment after another, flinging yet another parcel into the boot and heading off again on yet another foray.

The Champs-Elysées is still a great sight from afar and shouldn't be missed, although today it is notoriously easy to buy an over-priced cup of coffee and a stale sandwich or a tatty souvenir there. Some of the new shopping arcades may be to your taste. They are clean, bright and shining but also somewhat anonymous — you could be almost anywhere in the world. It would certainly be hard to know it was Paris.

Guerlain, of course, is an honourable exception and it is well worth braving the crowds to visit this, one of the best and finest *parfumeurs* in the world.

Some may consider the Right Bank a little old-fashioned, perhaps a little too establishment for their tastes, but remember that in those fine avenues, down even some of the smallest side-streets, you can find some of the finest workmanship and the most discreet service in the world. It won't come cheap but you will scarcely be able to find better.

A suitcase from Vuitton (you needn't have all those initials) or from Goyard Aîné, some finely-wrought crystal from Lalique, a soft cotton shirt from Charvet, a dress in rustling silk from St-Laurent, a ruffled romper for a pampered baby from Baby-Dior, some Shalimar from Guerlain, handkerchief — soft linen from Porthault — where else in the world could you find it better done? Nowhere that I know of.

CONTENTS

* Strictly speaking not all shops but also places to rest the feet, restore the spirits and engage the mind.

ART GALLERIES

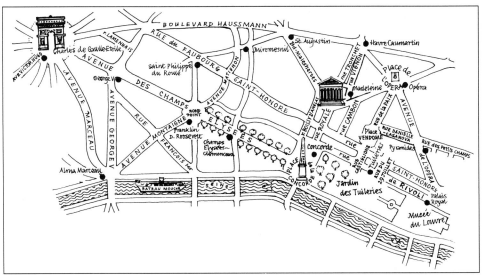

BOOKS

FASHION: WOMEN

HOUSEHOLD

ART GALLERIES

ARTCURIAL

9 avenue Matignon, 8e.
METRO: F. D. Roosevelt.

One of the most important galleries in Paris and a must for anybody interested in contemporary, or recent, art. It's simultaneously a gallery with regularly changing exhibitions of painting and sculpture (lots of interesting *retrospectives*), a bookshop specialising in art books, and a producer of limited lithograph editions of its own. Paris has always been an important centre for art and continues to be so — its posters, lithographs, and graphic design are alive and well and often worth buying. Look out for lively, modern prints by people like Sonia Delanay, Bonnard and others.

MATHIAS FELS

138 boulevard Haussmann, 8e.
METRO: Miromesnil.

A gallery specialising in the work of lively, young artists, particularly painters. Nothing here will be cheap but anybody interested in modern art will be able to see what the young are up to. For my money more interesting than many of the larger galleries.

GALERIE HUIT 10

25 rue du 29-Juillet, 1er.
METRO: Tuileries.

A gallery specialising in commercial art of all sorts, from illustrations and original drawings to paintings and photographs, all by artists working in the world of the media.

BOOKS

W.H. SMITH

248 rue de Rivoli, 1er.
METRO: Concorde.

You may one day just get a little nostalgic for a proper British newspaper or want a particular English book to read, in which case it is worth knowing where to find an outpost of that reassuring British chain, W.H. Smith. Besides being able to browse for free amongst those reminders of British life, upstairs is a tea-room which really will remind you of home. French guides tend to wax somewhat lyrical over the 'beans on toast', the '*thé* Darjeeling', the toasts, muffins, buns and crumpets, and to dismiss somewhat peremptorily the pastries (Gault–Millau says haughtily *d'un intérêt assez mince*) — you may think otherwise. All are agreed that the thing to ask for is *le sirop fantaisiste Anglais* (golden syrup to you).

GALIGNANI

224 rue de Rivoli, 1er.
METRO: Concorde.

Said to be the oldest bookshop in Europe, its history is wrapped around with romantic customers. Lord Byron passed through its portal on his European escapades, whilst Thackeray was once a sub-editor on Galignani's *Messenger*, in the days when Galignani published the continent's only English-language newspaper. Today, it is a place well worth browsing round and, if you are in Paris long enough to need to order a book, no matter in what language or where published, Galignani ought to be able to get it for you. They will certainly try.

FASHION: WOMEN

LA MAISON DU LODEN

146 rue de Rivoli, 1er.
METRO: Louvre.

If you fancy looking like a French Sloane Ranger, you could hardly do better than buy yourself a dark green, simple Loden — the choice here is wider than anything you'll find back home. And apart from what it stands for (which may or may not be to your taste) a Loden, I am reliably informed, is infinitely practical: it goes with most things, is nearly as warm as a fur and nearly as waterproof as a Burberry.

RITZ-ESPADON 15 place Vendôme, 1er.

METRO: Opéra.

If the sun is shining and you're feeling like getting dressed up and lashing out on a summer treat, go to the Ritz-Espadon in the place Vendôme. There you'll be beautifully looked after as you enjoy the sort of food that goes with the outdoors: simple grills of sea bass or turbot, preceded by asparagus and topped up with *fraises-des-bois*.

CHANEL

31 rue Cambon, 1er.
METRO: Opéra.

Coco Chanel, it will be remembered, was the first truly modern couturier. She it was who took to men's trousers because they were so comfortable; who liked to see women in jersey because it, too, was so easy to wear; who bobbed her hair when all around were sporting flowing locks; who took to making and wearing costume jewellery because it saved worrying about taking care of the real thing; who created the immortal Chanel No.5 which is still a bestseller today.

A visit to her rue Cambon boutique is a lesson in enduring chic. The hallmarks of the essential *mademoiselle* are all still there, but subtly adjusted and re-aligned to suit the modern eye. Karl Lagerfeld is the man responsible for reviving the slightly faded image, for reworking her classic designs, updating their proportions and turning the Coco look into a current fashion classic. The chain-handled bags, the ropes of pearls, the braid-edged cardigan suits with the gilt buttons and the soft cashmere separates are all eminently in tune with today's way of life and all to be found in the boutique. If you can't afford the whole look go for a pair of classic Chanel earrings, for a pearl necklace or a chain-handled bag. All in all, it is a look of charm, elegance and ease, perfectly expressed by the model Inès de la Fressange who, for unimaginable sums, has been chosen to convey to the modern world what Mme. Chanel was all about.

JEAN BERTHET
13 rue Tronchet, 8e.
METRO: Madeleine.

Classic hatter to what remains of the aristocracy. If to you a French *chapeau* is all wit and froth and delicacy, Jean Berthet will not let you down.

POLO RALPH LAUREN
2 place de la Madeleine, 8e.
METRO: Madeleine.

In Ralph Lauren's sumptuous new store, one of only three owned by Ralph Lauren himself (the other stores are in New York and London), the French may indulge their penchant for quiet, understated, timeless good taste. Taste *à l'Anglaise*. Nobody does the genteel, well-bred timeless tweeds, discreet silks and linens, the gentle cashmeres, better than Ralph Lauren, the boy from the Bronx. Lauren himself has described his clothes as 'quiet clothes'. Above and beyond the fashionable, they exude an aura of rich, old-established money. Every BCBG will treasure them for their nostalgic values: exclusive, traditional, understated but of the highest quality. In his clothes M. and Mme. BCBG can play the roles they love to play: the elegant country lady and gentleman used to manor houses, horses, tennis parties, elegant drawing-rooms and dignified dining-rooms. Though the world the clothes convey is one of old-fashioned innocence, the prices seem a lot less innocent — it will be interesting to see if the French will succumb as readily to the Ralph Lauren charm as London and New York, where the shoppers go on shopping regardless of price.

HERMES
24 rue du Faubourg Saint-Honoré, 8e.
METRO: Concorde.

One of the great temples of classic chic, this is the spiritual home of the true BCBG. Once almost the sole province of women *d'un certain age* and *d'un* very certain substance, today it has become newly chic as a younger generation discovers for itself the charms of fine workmanship and quality. Sporting the famous hand-rolled pure silk twill Hermès scarf, once very *vieux chapeau*, is today a sign that you are *au fait* with the winds of fashion. French teenagers now borrow their mother's scarves, tie their trainers with Hermès ribbons and long to own a Kelly handbag (the bag that Grace Kelly took with her when she left New York to marry Prince Rainier — it has now passed into the annals of mythology and despite its exorbitant price, has become one of the bestsellers of all

time). Nearly as desirable is the H-buckled shoulder bag. Jacqueline Onassis did for this model what Grace Kelly did for the Kelly — turned it into an internationally recognised and desired status symbol.

For the BCBG's 18th birthday, it's a close-run thing whether she'd prefer that distinctive gold bracelet with the anchor and chain from Hermès or the Cartier three-gold ring.

Meanwhile Eric Bergère is busy revamping the clothes and accessories, finding new and witty ways to tie the distinctive scarves and breathing new life into the classic motifs.

CRILLON HOTEL 10 place de la Concorde, 8e.

METRO: Concorde.

If you don't have the means to stay in one of the grand hotels, that doesn't mean that you can't sample a little of their style. Have a drink in the bar of the Crillon, hang-out of many of the legendary figures of literary Paris in times gone by. It may no longer be quite the place it was but it still has something of an air of old-style *luxe*. Peek into the dining-room — the *Salon des Ambassadeurs* is one of the most sumptuous dining-rooms in town. Before you order a drink, look at the price list: the champagne or the freshly-squeezed orange juice are not cheap but they come with superb nuts and what taste like home-made crisps. Or, on a fine spring morning, have breakfast at the Plaza Athénée and then saunter down to the nearby Pont de l'Alma, take a *bateau-mouche* and see Paris from the Seine.

CARITA 11 rue du Faubourg Saint-Honoré, 8e.

METRO: Concorde.

If you want to acquire that Parisian finishing touch you could hardly do better than go to Carita. One of the old-established grand names of Parisian hairdressing, this is where Maman BCBG goes to have her hair cut and where, when the time comes, she introduces petite Isabelle to her own favourite stylist. For many he is Jean-Michel Henry (some say he is the best hairdresser in town) but you may have to wait while he attends to locks more illustrious than yours. You can while away the time by having any manner of beauty treatments (from a facial to a manicure) or perhaps you might contemplate a little gentle colouring of the hair (*à la* Deneuve, Vartan *et al?*).

If the prices make you reel, ask to visit the *ateliers* on the 5th and 6th floors. Here you can see just what goes into producing those soft leather bags, those impeccably worked suitcases, the finely-crafted jewellery. Every bag comes with a lifetime's guarantee and though they tend to look a little too bright and expensive when new, they mature and improve with time, acquiring that marvellous patina that so becomes leather of the highest quality. Visit, too, the museum on the 3rd floor and you'll see for yourself the horsey history that began it all; you'll understand too, why the Aga Khan and a host of Eastern potentates come here to order their racing silks and saddlery.

Though saddlery is where it all began, the age of the motor car brought an impeccable range of luggage and today you can buy any manner of elegant clothes, furs, accessories and *petits cadeaux* (though not, of course, at very *petits* prices). Nevertheless, a little gift-wrapped *quelque chose*, beautifully packaged and tied with that inimitable ribbon, has a cachet and a glamour that would melt the heart of even the most curmudgeonly radical. The least expensive *objets* in this temple of elegance would probably be a splendid silk tie or a tiny, double-view photograph frame. For these sort of prices you will not be surprised to learn that anything you can buy can be delivered to your hotel the very same day.

If you hanker for the Hermès style but can't afford the prices, aim for the sales, which are usually held in mid-March or mid-October. Remember, however, that they attract *du monde*.

TETE-A-TETE 183 rue du Faubourg Saint-Honoré, 8e.

METRO: George V.

One of the last of the old-style *modistes* to survive. *Modiste* to many a couturier, here *jolie* madame and her like come to be hatted in old-style grandeur. This is where the old guard come to find their little *chapeau* to grace a wedding, a day out at Longchamp or a seductive little lunch for two.

BABY-DIOR

28 avenue Montaigne, 8e.
METRO: F. D. Roosevelt.

If Maman shops at Dior she might well like to make sure that *petite* Sophie or Olivier are just as impeccably turned-out. Baby-Dior is where the very rich and very smart buy their baby-clothes. The quality, the chic, the label are all *sans-pareil* and even the not-so-rich have been known to patronise this

little boutique for the odd party-going outfit or one-off indulgence. From Baby-Dior, Maman can move onto Junior where Sophie or Olivier can be equally expensively and chicly clothed until somewhere around the 12-year-old mark. Then, presumably, there is an inter-regnum until they are old enough to move onto Dior proper.

HOUSEHOLD

LALIQUE

11 rue Royale, 8e.
METRO: Madeleine.

Probably the grandest name in crystal in the world — the kind of shop that one hopes will go on forever. Even if you don't think it's quite your style, Lalique is certainly worth a visit. Take in the marvellous chandelier with its crystal leaves, look at the carved door handles, then take a look at the sparkling wares. Rene Lalique was the genius who lifted the company out of the ranks of mere producers of glassware: beginning with glass jewellery, he moved onto a series of magical vases (if you can buy one today they are investment pieces) and after the First World War the company began to produce crystal for the table as well. Lalique's speciality has always been in combining clear and frosted glass, and several of the ranges still use this to stunning effect today. Though almost all the crystal is very expensive, most of it is in exquisite taste and has none of the over-indulgent decoration that disfigures the designs of less skilful designers. You have to look on Lalique glassware as investments but you could buy a little something (say a tiny salt dish or a little crystal flower) without risking your bank manager's health.

CHRISTOFLE

12 rue Royale, 8e.
METRO: Madeleine.

24 rue de la Paix, 2e.
METRO: Opéra.

93 rue de Seine, 6e.
METRO: Odéon.

95 rue de Passy, 16e.
METRO: Muette.

Another of the grand names, supplying some of the appurtenances the elegant table requires. Like most of the other big names it is no recent upstart — its wares have been gracing the tables of the *haute bourgeoisie* and anybody else who could afford and appreciate them since 1830. Cutlery is what Christofle sells, but what cutlery — everything from a single knife or lobster fork to a complete service. Whether you are looking for something rich and baroque or something much more *raffiné*, you will find it *chez* Christofle. There is cutlery to suit almost every conceivable taste, except perhaps those whose tastes lie firmly in the direction of minimalism. Many of the designs are classics that customers go back for time and time again. Once again you wouldn't expect such quality to be cheap — and it isn't — but a Christofle set of cutlery is as much an heirloom as a fine piece of antique furniture.

LA CAUDRIOLE, MUSCADE
Palais-Royal, 1er.

METRO: Palais-Royal.

Hidden away in the garden of the Palais-Royal are two restaurants where on a sunny day (usually from May to October) they bring out the parasols and you can enjoy being out of doors without the whiff of petrol fumes in your nose. Neither are grand or expensive but you get a wonderful view of the rose-pink garden for your money. La Caudriole offers a simple menu whilst higher up, Muscade offers a menu with specialities like *Brandade de Morue* or *Blanquette de Veau* for the main course. You don't, of course, have to eat the lot; you could always just order a *café au lait* and a favourite *pâtisserie*. It is a soothing place to stop, with some fine 18th-century façades to admire and usually a charming French child or two to smile at.

PETER
191 rue du Faubourg Saint-Honoré, 8e.
METRO: George V.

As you might expect in the capital of a country renowned for its devotion to the culinary arts, Paris is well served for shops catering to the elegant table. For elegant, rarified and truly exquisite cultery, Peter is the place to go. Most famous for its silver- and gold-plated cutlery with semi-precious stone handles, it also offers handles in jade, ebony, and ivory. Go there too for wonderfully idiosyncratic pieces such as caviar spatulas and orange serving spoons. It caters, as you will have gathered, for the *luxe* end of the market so if your tastes run to the hi-tech or the spartan, this is not the place for you.

LES DOMAINES 56 rue François-1er, 8e.
METRO: George V.

Another of Philippe Starck's havens for the fashionable set but this is a wine-bar (as opposed to Café Costes, which is, *bien sûr*, a café) with encouragingly light delicious food and a less frenetic air than some of its rivals. A good place to head for after a tiring morning admiring the windows of the avenue Montaigne.

PORTHAULT
18, avenue Montaigne, 8e.
METRO: Alma Marceau.

Even those not intending to buy should make a point of visiting Porthault. It is an education for those of us not brought up in the kind of mansions where linen, towelling and other table accessories of this quality are part of the daily scene. Not for nothing has Porthault been called the couturier of table linen. All the material is not only embroidered

specially to its own designs, but it is also woven, dyed and printed exclusively for it. Ask to see the fine white organdie cloths, the bedlinen exquisitely embroidered with the most delicate of flowers, the matching designs for bathrobes, breakfast trays, nightgowns, sheets and bedcovers. There are some of the most luxurious towelling bathrobes in the world (though expensive, they would make splendid presents) and there are towels, too, that wouldn't be too prohibitive to buy nor too difficult to pack.

ALEXANDRE DE PARIS 3 avenue Matignon, 8e.

METRO: Alma Marceau.

With Carita, one of the two really grand *coiffeurs* in Paris. Nothing like as stuffy as you might think from the grandness of the reputation. Still very much in form. Christopher, I'm told, is the name to ask for. Besides getting a brand-new haircut, you'll get a close-up view of the smartest women in Paris — always an enlightening sight. If you want the full works, everything from a facial to a pedicure, you can be soothed and pampered by the most skilled hands in Paris.

MOD'S HAIR 57 avenue Montaigne, 8e.

METRO: Alma Marceau.

For a real Parisian *coupe* but in a more with-it, younger vein than that offered by the grand *coiffeurs*, try Mod's Hair. In spite of its grand address it really does seem younger, less imposing, less redolent of *ancien* Paris, than Alexandre or Carita.

TROUSSELIER

73 boulevard Haussmann, 8e.
METRO: Miromesnil.

If the idea of artificial flowers doesn't appeal, pay a visit to Trousselier and I guarantee you'll change your mind. Here you will find roses in full bloom, delicate pieces of blossom on a fine branch, pale delphiniums, overblown peonies, soft yellow mimosa, so beautifully made you can scarcely tell them from the real thing. Artificial flowers *chez* Trousselier have been turned into an art form. Rich Parisians have for years used a selection of these exquisite blooms to eke out nature's less plentiful seasons. Skilful interior decorators use just a few splendid blooms to plump out a collection of real leaves and branches. They never die, they never wilt, they just go on looking beautiful for years. You can buy one red rose or a whole cherry tree in full blossom. None of it is cheap, for it is all handmade.

PUIFORCAT

131 boulevard Haussmann, 8e.
METRO: Miromesnil.

An old-fashioned, stately store which sells quite simply some of the most beautiful and expensive cutlery in the world. Ever since Louis-Victor Puiforcat started producing his sumptuous creations in silverplate in the last century, the name of Puiforcat has been one to conjure with in the world of tableware. Much of Louis-Victor's collection is now in the Louvre, but copies of his designs are still being made and many of the best-selling lines were first created in the 1920s and 1930s. A visit to the collection of silver, housed on the first floor, would interest anybody who loves old silver and would reveal just why the name of Puiforcat rides so high. You will have gathered that it isn't a place to look for a bargain — its offerings are really in the heirloom class.

PERRIER

255 rue Saint-Honoré, 1er.
METRO: Concorde.

In a charming little courtyard just off the rue Saint-Honoré (very easily missed unless you're looking out for it) is one of the most delightful places in Paris to find a present for the house, large or small. It seems to have a quintessentially French flavour and to stock merchandise that is different from the international names that you can buy the world over. There is an especially good collection of tablecloths of all sorts and in the kind of sizes you can't easily track down. There are enchanting sets of salt and pepper, butter dishes, water jugs, cutlery, hand-painted china and exquisite *re-editions* of fine old patterns and designs, all beautifully displayed.

GALERIE MAISON ET JARDIN

20 rue du Faubourg Saint-Honoré, 8e.
METRO: Concorde

A good place to know about if you're looking for something special to take home for the house. Got up to look more like a house than a shop, here you can see some of the most charming domestic *accoutrements* in Paris. I like its mixture of old and new: the fine pieces of traditional furniture mixed with modern glass and beautiful *objets d'art*.

JEWELLERY

Buying jewellery is a wonderfully frivolous occasion. Jewellery won't keep you warm or covered. It can never be used *for* anything — it just *is*. It is *par excellence, la folie*. It exists solely to make its owner look and feel loved and cared for, and though there are those vulgar beings who use jewellery as a weapon in the status war — as a way of showing the rest of the world that their bank account is not to be sniffed at — we prefer to think of it as the perfect present from a man to a woman, the ultimate sentimental, romantic gesture.

In Paris you will find jewels for all seasons: from the grand old establishment jewellers clustered round the place

Vendôme and the rue de la Paix to the whacky exuberance of Scooter in Les Halles; from the minimalist expressions of the avant-garde displayed in the chic galleries, to the frankly fake and baroque fantasies in the many boutiques flourishing in the side streets of the Left Bank.

For real sparkling gems of the sort that Marie Antoinette would have eyed with pleasure, for authentic gold and silver and classic designs, there is nothing to beat the big names. Those whose families have been accustomed to patronising such establishments have long since decided with which house their affections lie — if it's a world that is new to you but one you'd like to get to know, here are just a few of the proudest and the best.

Bear in mind that no matter how grand the name, most of them have had to come to terms with modern times, and behind even the most daunting exterior you will find some lines aimed at more modest purses. It's no good entering those elegant portals if you really are on your uppers, but if you have anything from 1000 francs upwards, you'd be surprised at how many of them will have something to catch your eye.

TECLA

2 rue de la Paix, 8e.
METRO: Opéra.

Here you will find the obligatory pearl necklace and probably a pair of pearl stud ear-rings to match. You can buy them absolutely plain and simple or artfully mixed with sapphires, diamonds or what you will. There are creamy pearls and rosy ones, black ones and grey ones, small ones and fat ones — it is, as you will have perceived, the place where *tout* Paris goes for pearls of any sort.

JEAN DINH VAN

7 rue de la Paix, 2e.
METRO: Opéra.

Matchless simplicity and purity of design has made Jean Dinh Van a name to conjure with. Probably most well-known for his immaculate gold chains (recognised instantly by those in the know), he also offers ideas for men (this is the place to buy *his* wedding-ring) and children (treat a favourite godchild).

CAFE DE LA PAIX place de l'Opéra, 2e.

METRO: Opéra.

There is scarcely a better place to watch the world go by than the Café de la Paix, in the place de l'Opéra. You don't have to have a full-scale meal — you can toy with a glass of Kir and admire this magnificent historic monument, dating from the time of Napoleon III and designed by Garnier, the man who built the Opera.

MELLERIO

9 rue de la Paix, 1er.
METRO: Opéra.

The house of Mellerio goes about its ancient business discreetly. Ever since Marie de Medici favoured it with her patronage, Mellerio has been one of the names to reckon with. Not so well-known outside France, it still offers its unique experience and skills to those who prefer quiet good taste to exotic fantasies.

CARTIER

7 place Vendôme, 1er.

13 rue de la Paix, 1er.
METRO: Opéra.

Once a genuinely innovative and highly creative jewellery house, Cartier seems to have lost ground in recent years in the image stakes. The old, genuine early Cartier designs are still highly sought after and its stones are usually impeccable but today it is the output from Les Must that seems more sought after: the three-gold ring, the watches, the ear-rings, the little presents that are more in vogue than the *haut joaillerie* itself.

CHAUMET

12 place Vendôme, 1er.
METRO: Opéra.

Many a tiara, a crown or a royal *bibelot* has been perfected, discreetly of course, at number 12 place Vendôme. Chaumet could be said to be one of the oldest and most distinguished of the distinguished band clustered round the place Vendôme. Stones set in exquisite simplicity, gold rings of infinite variety, and a style that is at once classical and modern, have made certain that Chaumet bridges the gap between old and new with elegant ease.

BOUCHERON

26 place Vendôme, 1er.
METRO: Opéra.

Famous for its rigorous and classical way with stones, as grand names come they seldom come more grand than Boucheron. If you've been left a windfall (not too little) and you want to blow it on a piece of jewellery you can rest assured that at Boucheron you will be getting some of the best that money can buy. It won't come cheap (how could it?) and you could, if you were enterprising, do a lot better at an auction, but here you can be sure of quality, of workmanship and of design in the best of the old tradition of *haut joaillerie*.

MAUBOUSSIN

20 place Vendôme, 1er.
METRO: Opéra.

Not so well-known outside the refined circles of the Parisian *haut monde*, Mauboussin is one of the clutch of top jewellers where those with thousands of spare francs are happy to spend them. A touch more exotic than some of its more classic neighbours, Mauboussin seems to have a special line in mother-of-pearl but also offers the usual gamut of sought-after stones — emeralds, diamonds, sapphires and rubies — in impeccable settings. Many of the young set hurry here for their engagement and wedding rings.

VAN CLEEF & ARPELS

22 place Vendôme, 1er.
METRO: Opéra.

One of the most innovative and yet distinguished of the jewellers in this grand old part of Paris. Technically brilliant, this house was one of the first to mount stones apparently invisibly, to invent magical evening bags of gold and precious stones (the famous Minaudière), to find new ways of setting stones and new fantasies to show off their brilliance. A house of great originality and soaring prices, it is now possible for those without an oil-well to buy some of the authentic Van Cleef & Arpels-style jewellery at the boutique just a few steps away; here the double rings, the colourful ear-rings and the butterfly pendants have all been runaway successes.

BVLGARI

27 avenue Montaigne, 8e.
METRO: F. D. Roosevelt.

One of the current front-runners in the world of top-class jewellery, Bvlgari seems to have managed that difficult task of providing jewellery that is at once expensive and grand and yet a touch original. This is not at all easy, for anybody spending a bank's ransom on diamonds doesn't want them to be so original that next year they'll look out of date nor yet so predictable that they could have come from anywhere. With Bvlgari you know exactly where they came from; the style is distinctive but the designs are discreet, distinguished and entirely appropriate to the world they will inhabit.

HARRY WINSTON

29 avenue Montaigne, 8e.
METRO: F. D. Roosevelt.

If rare and precious stones are what you're after, Harry Winston is your man. They comb the world for the biggest and the best but that doesn't mean that you can't find a small carat diamond, too, if that's what you had in mind. Impeccably mounted in the classic tradition.

LE GRAND VEFOUR 17 rue de Beaujolais, 1er.
(Tel: 42.96.56.27)

METRO: Palais-Royal.

If you've something splendid to celebrate or you are just feeling in that slightly heady mood that so often overtakes one in Paris, then make for Le Grand Vefour. Here you can sample some of the best classic food that Paris has to offer in one of the most beautiful restaurants in the world. (A short while ago it looked a bit sad and down-at-heel but now it seems restored to its former glorious, confident self.) One of the oldest restaurants in the city, it still has echoes of the literary luminaries that were once its faithful clientele. So make the most of it, put on your glad rags and sit looking out over the rose garden of the Palais-Royal. But bring your credit cards along.

ANCOLIE

233 rue Saint-Honoré, 1er.
METRO: Tuileries.

Witty, up-to-the-minute costume jewellery. Whether you are looking for the huge, dramatic ear-rings currently so much in vogue or a whacky plastic tie to enliven a sober shirt, an elegant bauble to put upon your wrist or something a little more discreet, Ancolie will probably come up trumps.

ANGELINA 226 rue de Rivoli, 1er.

METRO: Tuileries.
10am to 7pm. Closed the whole of August.

Almost a legend, Angelina's is one of the best tea-rooms in Paris, though more noted for its incomparable hot chocolate than its teas. Treat yourself to its delicious Mont Blanc (a ravishing concoction of meringue and purée of chestnut) if you've the appetite; otherwise order a less daunting *pâtisserie*.

LUGGAGE, BAGS AND PRESENTS

LOUIS VUITTON

78 bis, avenue Marceau, 8e.
METRO: Etoile.

Even those who are averse to luggage so indelibly embellished with initials would find a visit to the Vuitton headquarters an education. Vuitton, after all, is one of the grandest and oldest names in the business and Georges Vuitton only resorted to all those initials after his designs had become so copied by lesser luggage-makers that he despaired of preserving their identity. All those famous trunks, now so familiar, but then so original, can be seen here, including the first flat-topped versions brought out to cope with the newly fashionable fad for travelling by rail. Then there are all those special designs, brought out to cater for personal whims, such as the trunks fitted with drinks trays, food compartments and exquisitely made pull-out drawers.

If you're in the mood to buy, today you can find a range of Vuitton luggage free of any logos, a status symbol so subtle that only those really in the know will be able to recognise. Made from finest leather, they are no cheaper for being so admirably bereft of the stigmata. But if you don't feel like lashing out on something as large and expensive as a suitcase or a steamer trunk, Vuitton produces a host of smaller items, all of the same impeccable quality. Perhaps you might like a wallet or a key-ring, a tennis racquet cover or a dog-leash? All these, and much, much more, are here for the asking.

CELINE

24 rue François-1er, 8e.
METRO: Alma Marceau.

58 rue de Rennes, 6e.
METRO: Rennes.

3 avenue Victor-Hugo, 8e.
METRO: Etoile.

One of the grand classic names, renowned for its shoes and handbags. The leather is of the very best, the styles are classic and built to last — which is just as well given the prices they charge. Don't look to Céline for the latest and the most modish, just for the finest quality in impeccably restrained good taste.

CRAZY HORSE 12 avenue George V, 8e.
(Tel: 47.23.32.32.)

METRO: Alma Marceau.
Shows start at varying times depending upon the day: the earliest is 9.20pm; the latest 12.45am (on Thursdays and Saturdays). So check times and make sure to book.

The classiest of all the girly shows. Surprisingly elegant and sophisticated, here the so-called strip-tease has been transformed into an innocent art form: beautiful girls, beautifully displayed. The show isn't cheap but you'll have an evening to remember.

LANCEL

4 rond-point des Champs-Elysées, 8e.
METRO: Champs-Elysées.

43 rue de Rennes, 6e.
METRO: Rennes.

8 place de l'Opéra, 9e.
METRO: Opéra.

Palais des Congrès, 17e.
METRO: Porte Maillot.

At first sight this looks a rather boring shop. Dedicated to handbags and luggage, objects for the table and fashionable accessories, the goods on sale all appear conventionally expensive and not at all original. There is also the matter of logos and initials which seem to be used in an over-intrusive manner. However, peruse a little further and you may find some surprisingly attractive and well-priced presents. A charming set of tiny silver salt and pepper pots, some truly splendid vacuum flasks, some nice jugs and other items for the table, as well, of course, as all the leather objects.

CASSEGRAIN

422 rue Saint-Honoré, 8e.
METRO: Concorde.

One of the most seductive purveyors of fine writing-paper, visiting-cards, menus, notebooks, files, boxes, folders and all the other charming paraphernalia connected with the world of paper and writing materials. Some 200 different sorts of paper to choose from in colours ranging from white and cream to sober browns and delicious pinks. One of the smart places for the Parisian *beau monde* to get their visiting-cards and writing-paper engraved; for tourists it is of more interest as a sanctuary to that endangered species, fine stationery.

MORABITO

1 place Vendôme, 1er.
METRO: Opéra.

Not for those with a reptile phobia. At first sight the window seem to contain so much crocodile that the future of the species appears in doubt. And not only crocodiles: lizards, snakes, and ostriches all seem to have ended up supplying some of the lushest, most exquisitely-wrought luggage and handbags to the *haut monde*. If you don't mind carrying the skin of a reptile around, there is no doubt that Morabito supplies some of the most sumptuous luggage I have ever seen: cabin trunks redolent of the grand days of travel, when porters and chauffeurs were *de rigueur* and when the great steamers still plied their regular routes; beautifully soft and important-looking briefcases: shoeboxes for the very best shoes; handbags for the fattest wallets. If this is in your price bracket and to your taste (everything reeks of expense) you won't find anybody who does it better.

E. GOYARD AINE

233 rue Saint-Honoré, 1er.
METRO: Tuileries.

This lovely old shop was founded in 1792. Less intimidating than Morabito nearby, it specialises in *articles de voyage* and *tout pour le chien*. The quality is still as high, though possibly less overtly sumptuous than Morabito. There are soft, soft, briefcases which look more like satchels and less like the appurtenance of a businessman wishing to tell the world how important he is. There are marvellous little things for the traveller, such as leather-covered vacuum-flasks. This is *the* place for the pampered dog. Here the doting owner can find a soft flannel blanket with a picture of its breed (dachshund, poodle, spaniel *et al*) charmingly embroidered and appliquéd in one corner. Nice for off-beat presents for people, too.

PERFUME AND MAKE-UP

GUERLAIN

68 avenue des Champs-Elysées, 8e.
METRO: George V.

2 place Vendôme, 1er.
METRO: Opéra.

29 rue de Sèvres, 6e.
METRO: Sèvres-Babylone.

93 rue de Passy, 16e.
METRO: Muette.

For many people (and I am one) these are quite simply the best perfumes in the world. Devotees of Shalimar, of Jicky, of l'Heure Bleue can never be persuaded to change their allegiance to more modish *fragrances*. Guerlain is a grand, old, classic house and even if you have never succumbed to their fragrant delights, pay a visit to the Champs-Elysées shop. With its marble counters and marble walls it is a haven of all things pretty and nice. Only in Paris can you buy the full range of Guerlain treats so if, for instance, Jicky is your

---

TAILLEVENT 15 rue Lamennais, 8e.
(Tel: 45.63.39.94.)

METRO: George V.
Closed Saturday, Sunday, two weeks at Easter and from the last week in July to the last week in August.

Some day you will have something to celebrate and you will want to experience what a really grand French restaurant is all about. You couldn't do better than Taillevent. Everything from the gentle but attentive service to the comfortable and *raffiné* surroundings helps to provide an experience that is about more than just eating, though the food, it goes without saying, is reliably some of the best in the whole of France. The experience will not be cheap but is well worth it for a memory that will last for many a long month.

favourite perfume, here you can spoil yourself by stocking up on the bath salts, the body lotion, the full selection. Remember that in Paris the Guerlain products are only available at one of the four Guerlain shops.

PHARMACIE LECLERC

10 rue Vignon, 8e.
METRO: Madeleine.

Many an international model makes straight for this little pharmacy the minute she steps off her plane. It is one of Paris' old-established pharmacies and its reputation is still largely spread by word of mouth. Models and those in the know head there for one of the lightest, most finely formulated face-powders in the world (in many tones, beautifully packaged in *belle époque* style), for the alcohol-free toning water, the fine shampoos and face-creams.

CARRE DES FEUILLANTS 14 rue de Castiglione, 1er. (Tel: 42.86.82.82.)

METRO: Tuileries.
Closed Saturdays and Sundays.

Alain Dutournier, one of the idols of Parisian *gastronomes*, has left Au Trou Gascon (the little restaurant in the 12th *arrondissement* to which foodies trooped in their legions) in the capable hands of his wife and opened a new temple to food in these elegant premises lying between the place Vendôme and the Tuilleries. From the moment you sit down, the air of simple *luxe* and the quiet sumptuousness of the place gives notice that here food is much, much more than just something to keep the wolf from the door — here it is art on the grand scale. So go in the right frame of mind, with plenty of money in your wallet or a good array of credit cards, and prepare to have the experience of a lifetime. Be prepared to be guided by the waiters. The best value of all is probably one of the special fixed-price menus: you will be served a succession of exquisite courses, which will linger in the memory for years to come. Don't forget to allow for the wine on top.

THE UNUSUAL GIFT

COUNTER SPY SHOP

35 rue Danielle-Casanova, 1er.
METRO: Opéra.

Paris is no longer the city it once was. With one of the biggest petty crime problems in the world it had to happen — Counter Spy Shop sells the kind of kit that once upon a time was only needed by James Bond. Today bullet-proof vests and mugger-proof purses, bugging devices and secret tape recorders — all these and more are available to make you and your loved ones feel more secure. And if you don't know where to begin you could always start with one of the essential guides to the problems of personal safety that are on sale, too.

EMERICH MEERSON

11 rue Tronchet, 8e.
METRO: Madeleine.

If you belong to the school of thought which believes that everything you wear says something about you, then look at the people who wear an Emerich Meerson watch. For some years now these beautifully made and timelessly classic-looking watches have been a discreet sign to those in the know. Less obvious than some of their swankier rivals, they speak of understated style; of people with the confidence to sport a watch that doesn't shriek loudly of expense, a wish to belong to the jet set or a clone-like following of fads. Emerich Meerson watches are realistically priced (you need taste, not money to appreciate them), simple in design and nearly all sport the distinctive white enamel dial and pigskin strap (the flashier plaited metal straps are much less authentic and much less agreeable).

JEAN LAFONT

11 rue Vignon, 8e.
METRO: Madeleine.

The place for the myopics of the world, Jean Lafont is famous throughout Paris for spectacles old and new, for glasses so sober they would suit a judge and so whacky Dame Edna would feel at home. Jean Lafont will make glasses to measure in any colour or shape you ask for and the prices are reasonable for the service on offer.

COLLECTION ORIENT EXPRESS

15 rue Boissy-d'Anglas, 8e.
METRO: Madeleine.

The Orient Express may no longer be quite the exotic and mysterious train it was in its heyday but it is certainly supplied with some exceedingly fine appurtenances. Here, in this wood-panelled, oval-windowed boutique, you can buy replicas of all those luxuries that make the Orient Express what it is: the towels, crystal, china, linen and silver and a host of other memorabilia.

JEUX D'AIGUILLES

269 rue Saint-Honoré, 1er.
METRO: Madeleine.

Probably the smartest needlework shop in town. Cheap it isn't but if you're into needles and thread, canvas and wool, then this is the place for you. Lots of original canvases to work, cushions to cover and linen to embroider. The small needlework accessories, such as travelling needle-and-thread cases, emergency kit repairs and tapestry-worked purses, make splendid presents. If you're in Paris for more than just a holiday and much of the intricacy seems above you, then you might like to know that Mme. Marechal, who manages the shop, also runs classes in tapestry work and embroidery every Saturday afternoon.

THE LEFT BANK
(RIVE GAUCHE)

The Left Bank (Rive Gauche) or Latin Quarter is more a state of mind than a precise geographical location. It's not just chance that in most people's minds it is inextricably linked with intellectual chat, with student life, with cosmopolitan comings and goings, with challenging views and colourful people. For here on the Left Bank you find the Sorbonne, the Beaux Arts and the famous *grandes écoles*, gateway in France to many a glittering career. It really is the intellectual heart of the city and not just a notion Puccini got hold of one happy day. The very name, Latin Quarter, arose because in the Middle Ages Latin was the *lingua franca* of the students, and so it stayed until the Revolution ushered in less elitist ways.

Though today Sartre is no longer writing at his table in the Aux Deux Magots, Aux Deux Magots lives on and a new generation of students will be whiling away some happy hours toying with a cup of *café au lait* or one of the 24 brands of whisky on offer and bandying their thoughts on structuralism or the other issues of the day. Over in the Brasserie Lipp and in the Café de Flore next door there'll be lots more chat and you, too, if you want to catch something of the atmosphere of the *quartier* could do a lot worse than spend an hour or two in one of these establishments gazing at the passing scene.

Don't miss a chance to go into La Hune, one of the best bookshops in Paris and just next door to the Café de Flore. Besides the books it's a marvellous place for people-watching. There are always some interesting prints or etchings in the La Hune art gallery in the rue de l'Abbaye as well.

Some of the *quartier*'s tourist virtues have been oversold and areas like those surrounding the place St-Michel are what my French friends now call *minable* — full of jostling, touting tourists with precious little room to rest your feet and enjoy a quiet moment. But that still leaves a maze of tiny streets for you to explore, for, besides its intellectual life, it is one of the most rewarding areas in Paris for the more worldly pleasures of *le shopping*. It is perhaps the most likely district to make a happy discovery of your own.

Whether it's antiques you're after (go to the rue Jacob, one of my favourite streets in the whole of Paris and then search through all those little alleyways leading off the streets running from the Seine) or art books, witty jewellery or way-out clothes, you'll find almost everything you're hoping for and more tucked away somewhere here. Many of the big Right Bank names have opened outposts of their empires on the Left Bank, so it isn't surprising that many a Left Bank *habitué* scarcely feels any need ever to cross to the other side.

The Left Bank's reputation for being avant-garde may have been somewhat upstaged by the goings-on at Les Halles but the Left Bank beats Les Halles hollow for charm. In its small streets you'll find jazz cellars and discos, art galleries and antique shops, some of the most exciting bookshops and some of the most wearable (if not the most avant-garde) of clothes. For the avid clothes-hunter there's a further selection of shops in the Left Bank listed in the Fashion and Bargain sections.

When hunger strikes, you'll never need to walk far, for restaurants, cafés and winebars abound. If you're feeling the need for a little food on the hoof, the market in the rue Buci is a must (and if eating is not on your mind, the rue Buci still gives you more of a feel for the true character of Paris than many a more obvious tourist spot).

Don't miss out on the charming little place de Fürstemberg (this is close to Aux Deux Magots and a stone's throw from the rue Jacob); Delacroix had his studio at no.6 and in the rue de l'Abbaye is one of the most charming hatshops in Paris, Venus et Neptune. Go, too, into the beautiful church of Saint-Germain-des-Prés, one of the oldest in Paris, and don't miss the Musée Cluny in the place Paul-Painlevé (an exceptionally interesting collection of tapestries all housed on the site of the old residence of the abbots of Cluny).

When you want a break from shopping, why not take a walk in the beautiful Luxembourg gardens? In the rue de l'Ancienne-Comédie is the oldest café in Paris, Le Procope, where Diderot, they say, played chess and Voltaire aired his views. Other streets not to miss out on are the rue du Dragon, with its Auvergnat restaurants; the rue Bonaparte with its art galleries, many selling good, modern prints; and the rue Mouffetard (tourist-ridden though it is, it is one of the oldest streets in Paris and its food market and its old food shops are well worth a visit).

Stroll down the 'Boul' Mich' and see the student life all around. Many a boutique lining the boulevard caters to their needs and it seems, in particular, one of the best places to pick up a witty sweater, a pair of up-to-the-minute shoes at inexpensive prices, or a whacky accessory.

There are Left Bank people and Right Bank people but even if the Right Bank is more your style, you'd be missing out on an essential piece of true Paris if you didn't take some time off to feel the heartbeat of this, one of the most charming, most vital parts of the city.

CONTENTS

* Strictly speaking not all shops but also places to rest the feet, restore the spirits and engage the mind.

ART AND ART GALLERIES

BOOKS

FASHION: WOMEN

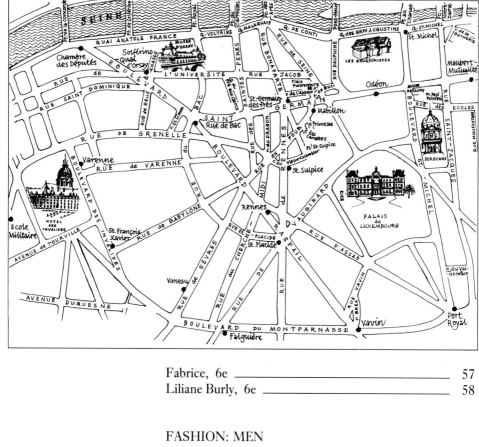

FASHION: MEN

FURNITURE, HOUSEHOLD AND KITCHENWARE

ART AND ART GALLERIES

M. BENEZIT
29 rue de Seine, 6e.
METRO: Saint-Germain-des-Prés.

Less serious art here; the emphasis is more on the charming and the decorative. A mixture of collages, prints and paintings.

LA NOUVELLE GRAVURE
42 rue de Seine, 6e.
METRO: Saint-Germain-des-Prés.

Particularly interesting because this is a centre for the work of extremely young artists — a chance to spot an up-and-coming Picasso for yourself.

GALERIE SOURCES
49 rue de Seine, 6e.
METRO: Saint-Germain-des-Prés.

Another good place for those interested in 20th-century prints to browse in. Here you'll find old, familiar names as well as ones new to you. Just one of the many galleries in this little road which is famous for its shops specialising in the visual arts, so, if these are your interests, wander up and down seeing what catches your eye. There are lots of shops, too, given over to books on the subject.

ANTOINETTE
7 rue Jacob, 6e.
METRO: Saint-Germain-des-Prés.

A specialist in naive art. All those interested in art of every kind will find the rue Jacob well worth wandering down.

LES MARRONIERS 21 rue Jacob, 6e.
METRO: Saint-Germain-des-Prés.

A little two-star hotel in the heart of the Left Bank just a few minutes walk from the boulevard Saint-Germain, Les Marroniers is well worth remembering, for it is one of the calmest, quietest hotels in Paris. It faces away from the rue Jacob towards its own little garden with the chestnut trees that give the hotel its name. Charming, peaceful, and reasonably priced — a little gem.

BIRON
31 rue Jacob, 6e.
METRO: Saint-Germain-des-Prés.

A good place to buy contemporary prints of all sorts.

LA HUNE
14 rue de l'Abbaye, 6e.
METRO: Saint-Germain-des-Prés.

Here La Hune does for lithographs what its boulevard Saint-Germain branch does for books: it displays them well, lets its customers browse and develop tastes of their own, and gives advice if and when it is asked for it. Lithographs are the chief speciality and there is many a young student whose first piece of art was bought at La Hune. Almost all the work is contemporary and much of it by youngish artists.

ADRIEN MAEGHT

42–46 rue du Bac, 7e.
METRO: rue du Bac.

The son of the famous Maeghts of the Galerie Maeght on the Right Bank has opened a marvellous gallery of his own. This is clearly the gallery of someone who loves art in all its forms, but particularly contemporary art. Besides regular exhibitions of the work of the great names of the 20th-century there is more affordable art at no.46 — here you can find lithographs, aquatints, engravings and signed reproductions, as well as some enchanting books, both for children and for adults.

SENNELIER

3 quai Voltaire, 7e.
METRO: rue du Bac.

Follow in the steps of Cézanne, Kadinsky and other luminaries of Paris' artistic past and buy your oils, your canvases, your turps and your brushes here. Everything and more that the aspiring artist needs.

GALERIE ALEPH

38 rue de l'Université, 7e.
METRO: Solférino.

Looking for undiscovered artists is always a lot more fun (and a lot cheaper) than going for established names. Go along to Galerie Aleph and do a little talent-spotting of your own — here you will find the works of contemporary artists who, on the whole, have yet to be discovered.

BOOKS

LA HUNE

17 boulevard Saint-Germain-des-Prés, 6e.
METRO: Saint-Germain-des-Prés.

Possibly the most famous of all the art bookshops in Paris. Always full of art and design students browsing, it has an incomparable atmosphere and, if there's something you particularly want, La Hune is almost bound to have it.

THE VILLAGE VOICE

6 rue Princesse, 6e.
METRO: Mabillon.

Open 11am to 10pm. Closed Sunday, Monday and the whole of August.

A cross between a café and a bookshop, The Village Voice has a uniquely sympathetic air. Though the brainchild of a young French woman, Odile Hellier, the atmosphere is resolutely American. The selection of books on sale isn't everybody's cup of tea — strong on women and the arts and the publications of small, often avant-garde houses — but the air of genuine literary vitality is invigorating. Lots of American influence, too, in things like the carrot cake and health juices on offer, but a lovely place to keep in touch with literary happenings. Join in the literary discussions, go to the art exhibitions, and keep an eye on the poetry readings. A unique and charming venture.

SHAKESPEARE AND COMPANY

37 rue de la Bûcherie, 5e.
METRO: Maubert-Mutualité.

Open 12pm to midnight.

Anglo-Saxon in spirit, but nonetheless no book-lover should miss out on this unique bookshop on the Left Bank, opposite Notre Dame. It has a wonderfully rambling interior with the books (mainly in English, many secondhand), piled hap-

LE PALANQUIN 12 rue Princesse, 6e.
(Tel: 43.29.77.66.)

METRO: Mabillon.

The Vietnamese presence is as vital a part of Paris as, say, Chinatown is of New York and just as no visitor to New York would give Chinatown a miss, so the visitor to Paris should try a little Vietnamese cooking. Le Palanquin is a good place to start. Run by the Tran sisters from, of course, Vietnam, you should broach the food in typical Oriental spirit and not try to order a standard three-course meal. Ask for help and choose a host of little spicy dishes, and you can hardly go wrong. But whatever you do, don't miss the crab claws.

hazardly wherever there is space. There are armchairs for browsers to browse in comfort and a pervasive air of quiet bookishness. Ever since George Whitman took it over some 34 years ago, it has been known as a friend of writers everywhere, and the signed copies of many such famous 'friends' bears impressive witness to this. From time to time there are poetry readings and seminars on a literary theme. Home from home for the literati.

LA BUCHERIE 41 rue de la Bûcherie, 5e.
(Tel: 43.54.75.06.)

METRO: Maubert-Mutualité.

If you're in the mood for one of those small, intimate restaurants serving delicious and original food that you're sure Paris is full of but haven't been able to locate, then La Bûcherie is the answer. Gault-Millau gives it two of its red *toques*, thus putting it into a fairly rarified little group from the strictly culinary point of view. More important for those in search of some elusive ambience, La Bûcherie is one of the most charming and seductive of restaurants around. On a cold winter's night there can hardly be a better place to dine than at the table next to La Bûcherie's famous open fire (make sure you ask for it when booking).

LE VERRE ET L'ASSIETTE

1 rue du Val-de-Grâce, 5e.
METRO: Port-Royal.

A foodie's haven — browse amongst the *recherché* collection of food and wine books (in French and English) and if you're looking for presents or mementoes, you'll find plenty amongst the assorted collection of vinous accessories: corkscrews, glasses, decanters, thermometers, the whole gamut.

FASHION: WOMEN

ANNICK GOUTAL

16 rue de Bellechasse, 7e.
METRO: Solférino.

Also in the boutique in the Crillon Hotel
10 place de la Concorde, 8e.
METRO: Concorde.

If ever I were to be weaned from my penchant for Guerlain perfume it might be Annick Goutal who would do it — she has the same deliciously delicate yet sensuous way with smelly delights and she uses them to create a whole range of lotions and potions to spoil the feminine form: creams, sun-milks, tonics and so on.

IRIE

8 rue du Pré-aux-Clercs, 7e.
METRO: rue du Bac.

This is a little boutique tucked away in the rue du Pré-aux-Clercs which chic Parisians make a point of keeping an eye on. It's the sort of place where you will find *the* blazer, classic enough to look good for many a year, but interesting enough to look as if it is *this* year's. It doesn't go in for the sort of slightly eccentric fashionability that the French are prone to criticise us British for but it offers good quality, well-made clothes with the little touches that lift them out of the boring or the banal. In short, it's where many a French woman buys this year's skirt, this year's jacket and knows that she can take them anywhere.

PEGGY ROCHE

7 rue du Pré-aux-Clercs, 7e.
METRO: rue du Bac.

Another little boutique for the fashionably-minded who want something a little less well known, a little less easily identifiable. Lots of seductive knits, including a marvellous deep grey jacket that would keep you warm all winter, a wonderfully Gallic knitted beret, and some witty jewellery to give it all a lift.

HOTEL SAINT-SIMON 14 rue Saint-Simon, 7e.

METRO: rue du Bac.

Another little gem of a hotel: three star, quiet and charming. All the rooms are different but all done in delightful country-house style. You can ask for a room with a view over the gardens.

MISSONI

43 rue du Bac, 7e.
METRO: rue du Bac.

A larger or, at any rate different, collection of the Missoni way with colour can be bought at this, the Paris branch of these distinguished Milanese designers. Feathery sweaters in magical colours, complete outfits of skirts and tops and jackets: all clothes which work together but look as if they had somehow just happened. Nothing too sharp, too strict or too obvious, ever.

DENISE BOURILION

101 rue du Bac, 7e.
METRO: rue du Bac.

Some marvellously original knits: in cotton and silk for summer or evening, in wools of every thickness for winter. Seductive, sensuous and easy-to-wear, Denise Bourilion's offerings may not have the rather restrained and severe air of high chic that is currently so popular, but they are charming and beguilingly feminine. Her little silk knitted tops could take you anywhere, from a posh evening dinner to a summer resort.

ISSEY MIYAKE

201 boulevard Saint-Germain, 7e.
METRO: rue du Bac.

One of the few of the Japanese designers to make their home on the Left Bank (most are gathered in friendly proximity in the rue Etienne-Marcel), Issey Miyake is, of course, one of the best-known, best established of them all. Styles are, it hardly needs saying, for those with real flair and panache — not for your average shy violet. Nonetheless one of the chicest French women I know, one who normally wears understated unflamboyant clothes which she invests with her own personal style, is frequently known to throw caution to the wind and indulge in an outfit from Issey Miyake, who, she says, has turned fashion into high art. If you've sussed out the British or American boutiques, don't worry, you will still probably find designs and ways with colour that are new to you: each Issey Miyake shop stocks its own selection and the French selection is, inevitably, very different from what is bought in London or New York.

SONIA RYKIEL

6 rue de Grenelle, 6e.
METRO: Sèvres-Babylone.

Fans of the Sonia Rykiel style, and there are many, will want to track her clothes down to source. Famous for her co-ordinating skinny knits, she has a way of providing authentic Parisian chic at bearable prices. The boutique is small, rather on the dark side, but it is where you will find Sonia Rykiel's latest ideas of how the busy, modern woman can dress easily, comfortably and elegantly. Her long, soft skirts and her comfortable jersey pants and culottes all have a cut that makes them eminently desirable. The look is always understated, the colours tending towards the dark and interesting section of the spectrum. She uses few fabrics, concentrating on wool, cotton-knits and velour (her least successful venture in my opinion). The latest designs include long, clinging V-fronted cardigans (very Chanel), simple kneelength Raj-type jackets, marvellously charming evening knits trimmed with bows and tie-backs, and the new-length skirt with bias-cut flounces.

Sonia Rykiel it was, you may remember, who put children into dark, chic colours, including some ineffably elegant black and grey stripes, and here you can find some of the smartest children's-wear in the world. Go next door for sweaters for men, for sheets and towels, and other Rykiel designs for *la maison*.

LA BOUTIQUE D'EMILIA

11 rue de Grenelle, 6e.
METRO: Sèvres-Babylone.

This is a marvellous shop if you want to equip yourself with some very Parisian accessories. Every Englishwoman is brought up to feel inferior to her French contemporaries in this vital matter of accessories — put this to rights and get yourself a little Gallic chic. Go for a soft, soft bag or a slim, chic clutch; for a belt that will give your sweaters a bit of dash; for some shoes that will add a jaunty air to this year's skirts.

QUELQU'UN

41 rue du Cherche-Midi, 6e.
METRO: Sèvres-Babylone.

Full of Gallic sprightliness, this is one of those little boutiques with a small collection of jaunty separates. Some very nice bathing costumes, long skirts and T-shirts, all in cotton jersey, all co-ordinating, simple and easy to wear.

SAMANTHA

60 rue de Rennes, 6e.
METRO: Saint-Germain-des Prés.

If you want just one small boutique where you can find the outfit that will make you look and feel as if you've caught a little of the Parisian spirit, I would recommend a trip to Samantha. It is tiny, crowded and crammed with easy-to-wear, relaxed but effortlessly elegant clothes. Wait until there is a lull in the constant press of customers and then enlist the help of one of the sales assistants. They all wear the Samantha clothes and you will be able to tell at once if it is your scene or not. If it is, my advice would be to buy an entire outfit here — miss out the bits and pieces and it will never look the same. You won't regret it and it isn't expensive.

Further down the rue de Rennes, at no. 66, is a younger, less expensive version concentrating more on leisure clothes, sweaters and trousers.

VENUS ET NEPTUNE

6 bis, rue de l'Abbaye, 6e.
METRO: Saint-Germain-des-Prés.

Once Paris was full of little *modistes* who would make you a hat to measure. Venus et Neptune, in this otherwise rather bleak street just off the place de Fürstemberg, is one of the few who will do it today. A young and modish clientele go there for ravishing hats, all made in any style, colour or fabric. They provide the finishing touches for many a haute couture show, which accounts for their gift for the dramatic and eye-catching. If you want a *petit chapeau* to create a sensation at Longchamp, to be the star turn at a wedding or to make an entrance at a cocktail party, you couldn't go to a better place. Materials are the very best: fine velvets, *crêpe-de-Chine*, fur and feathers, and the timid can test their nerve by trying on some of the many examples on show around the shop. Orders take from a week to 12 days so if you've only a short time in Paris you haven't a moment to lose. The waiting is well worth it.

CLEMENTINE

101 rue de Seine, 6e.
METRO: Mabillon, Odéon.

An elegant boutique, less hectic than those in the nearby rue de Rennes, with refined and well-bred clothes rather than sensationally up-to-the-minute ones. This is the boutique for those who would like couture clothes but can't afford the prices. Nothing here is cheap but the clothes are all of good quality, they have an *air* about them and are all Clementine's own original designs. You can also get clothes made to measure if you're prepared to pay the price.

LE PROCOPE 13 rue de l'Ancienne-Comédie, 6e.
(Tel: 43.26.99.20.)

METRO: Odéon.

Le Procope appears in every guidebook but no wonder, it is said to be the oldest restaurant in Paris and it looks like it. These days the food is no great shakes but there really is something about the atmosphere; about knowing that this was the place where Voltaire, Diderot, Danton, Marat, Robespierre *et al* revived their spirits.

CASTEL'S 15 rue Princesse, 6e.

METRO: Mabillon.

This is to Paris what Annabel's is to London, so if Annabel's is your scene you'll probably know lots of people in Paris who'll take you along to Castel's. Here you'll feel utterly at home, you'll understand the unspoken rules and enjoy the kind of nightlife you're accustomed to.

NOELLE ROUDINE

70 rue des Saints-Pères, 6e.
METRO: Saint-Germain-des-Prés.

Noëlle Roudine is a perfect example of the new breed of select little boutiques that are rapidly making this corner of the Left Bank an essential stopping-off point for the would-be chic. It has a suitably small but exceptionally elegant collection of own-label clothes: grey linen jackets to go with crisp short skirts or with long flowing ones (this gives a choice of the current looks). There are cropped trousers that work with the jackets and fine linen shirts that would be worn with skirts or trousers. If elegance is what you're after, you'll find it here.

SABBIA ROSA

71 rue des Saints-Pères, 6e.
METRO: Saint-Germain-des-Prés.

Open 10am to 7pm. Closed Sunday and the whole of August.

Forget your androgynous boxer shorts and your skinny vests; Mme. Rosa makes delectable underpinnings for women as they used to be before they'd ever heard of calories: voluptuous, feminine, all froth and frills. This is the underwear for the grand seduction, for playing at Carole Lombard waiting for Douglas Fairbanks, for taking along if you've been invited to a house so posh that somebody will have to unpack your things. The list of Mme. Rosa's fans is legion but rumour has it that Catherine Deneuve and other luminaries of the Paris thespian world are among them. For the rest of us, what Sabbia Rosa has to offer is nothing but the best: the finest silk or cotton (no synthetics here), beautifully wrought in palest apricot, primrose, soft grey, cream or white. Everything for the boudoir, whether a tiny bikini bottom or a luscious *peignoir*, can be found here. You may buy something from stock or have a design custom-made; choose from the fabrics on display and the vast collection of antique lace. Prices are high but then this is the world of *le grand luxe* and you must expect to pay accordingly. You can always come away with a lace hanky.

FABRICE

33, rue Bonaparte, 6e.
METRO: Saint-Germain-des-Prés.

This tiny boutique specialises in very Parisian *fantaisies* for the woman with sufficient personal style to carry it off. Much of what Fabrice sells is for evening: a shimmering headband adorned by wild plastic fruit or a wisp of chiffon topped by an Art Deco brooch. Everything is very individual, very sophisticated and needs a certain *élan* to get away with it. Not cheap but they do have that unmistakably Parisian air and could give any outfit you're bored with quite a lift.

LILIANE BURLY

76 rue des Saints-Pères, 6e.
METRO: Saint-Germain-des-Prés.

One of those quintessentially French boutiques full of understated female chic. If you're looking for an outfit that speaks of Paris, of elegance and of sophistication, you could hardly do better than start here. The current colours are the fashionable greys and blacks, creams and neutrals, and the line and the shapes add a dash of allure. The assistants, of course, are impeccably elegant and will give you a good idea of how to put the complete look together.

FASHION: MEN

LACOSTE

44 rue Saint-Placide, 6e.
METRO: Saint-Placide.

One of the best sporting shops in town. Nothing is very cheap but then what can you expect from the chicest sporting name in town? Beautiful tracksuits and running shoes, desirable polos and sweaters — even if your forehand isn't up to much you could at least impress off court.

WESTERN HOUSE

23 rue des Canettes, 6e.
METRO: Mabillon.

13 avenue de la Grande-Armée, 16e.
METRO: Argentine.

Relentlessly trendy so if that's what interests you, hurry along. Jeans by the trunkful, which still seem to draw the Americans, as if there were some kind of shortage back home! Co-respondent shoes, flying jackets, belts with buckles it would be impossible to miss, T-shirts ditto — you get the picture? If you're living out the American cinematic dream, kit yourself out here. To be fair, some of the sportswear is also very good and it *is* extremely fashionable.

FURNITURE, HOUSEHOLD AND KITCHENWARE

FORMES NOUVELLES

67 avenue de la Bourdonnais, 7e.
METRO: Ecole Militaire.

Some of the most dashing of contemporary lighting is displayed here in a setting that does it justice. Most of the big names are there: Emiliana, Ellio Martinelli and Gae Aulenti, as well as other names less big. A good place to catch up on the current lighting scene.

DESCAMPS

115 rue Saint Dominique, 7e.
METRO: Ecole Militaire.

Descamps is . . . well, Descamps. If you already know the name you will know that it sells some of the prettiest, most desirable bedlinen in the world. This little shop is clean, pretty and totally beguiling. Lots of lovely presents: a box of handtowels in pale blue and pink embellished with hearts, a great pot of bath-cream, or what about a sponge bag in one of their ineffably charming prints?

JULES VERNE Tour Eiffel, 2nd floor,
parc du Champ, 7e. (Tel: 45.55.20.04.)

METRO: Bir-Hakeim, Champ de Mars.

Open until 11.30pm, every night.

A trip up the Eiffel Tower at night is a must if you've never done it before — the view is incomparable. Avoid the crowds waiting for the main lifts by going up to the Jules Verne restaurant in its private lift where, for a price, you can sip a drink and look at the sights. If you want a full-scale meal the food is delectable, infinitely more delicious than you might suppose from its rather touristy surrounds. The restaurant itself is quiet, discreet and has one of the best views in town.

AEGINA 15 rue de Bourgogne, 7e.

METRO: Chambre des Députés.

When in Paris do as the Parisiennes do — have a little minor *crise*. Nothing too serious you understand, just a little *crise de foie*, a flutter of *les nerfs*. This will allow you to indulge yourself in a day at Aegina without guilt (we Anglo-Saxons seem to need excuses for such wallowings). There, in the tender hands of the staff, you can be cured of your nerves, your *dépressions*, your lassitude. Strictly speaking Aegina is an *institut de beauté* but the French have always recognised the intimate connection between health and beauty and this is one of those eminently respected organisations that bridges the two. Wallow in one of Aegina's baths filled with marine soothers (this, I'm reliably informed, leaves your skin soft as a baby's bottom), have a massage, a skin consultation or just a simple facial. Here you may be sure such eminently disturbing matters as the arrival of *la cellulite* will be given the attention they deserve (no bracing little sermons about how one's mind should be on higher things). So for a pampering day (or two if you really do want a proper *cure de détente*), book yourself into Aegina and enjoy the French way of beauty.

PERSONA

47 rue de l'Université, 7e.
METRO: rue du Bac,
Solférino.

Although this attractive shop devoted entirely to modern furniture and accessories has been open for some years now, it has recently been given a fresh lease of life with a brand new decor by Antonia Astori. Fashionable pale wood floors, pale blue marbling and lots of metal make it all look very *à la mode*.

Here you can buy your very own Philippe Starck (if you admired the chairs at Café Costes, well, here they are for sale), as well as the output of all those modish Italians like Castiglioni and Zanotta. A good place to remind yourself that there is more to Paris than croissants and *ooo-la-la*.

VENINI

93 rue du Bac, 7e.
METRO: rue du Bac.

A nice large bright airy shop with three floors full of modern furniture and housewares of all sorts. A good place to buy a present that smacks of today as opposed to yesterday. Some avant-garde glass, little slatted folding chairs, lovely pens and pencils, and some startlingly efficient torches.

ROCHE BOBOIS

197, 207, 213 and 213 bis, boulevard Saint-Germain, 7e.
METRO: rue du Bac.

Possibly the best known and certainly the largest source of contemporary furniture in Paris. From leather-covered sofas to chic little domestic accessories, Roche Bobois is always a good stopping-off place for those interested in the French domestic scene. There is usually a good selection by contemporary French designers as well as international pieces. All-in-all, an excellent shop for anybody wanting attractive furniture in a mood that is contemporary without being too avant-garde.

MOBILIER INTERNATIONAL

8 rue des Saints-Pères, 6e.
METRO: Saint-Germain-des-Prés.

Open 9.15am to 7pm. Closed Sundays and the whole of August.

Nothing whacky, nothing too self-indulgent, just the very best that modern design has to offer. Besides classics like the Charles Eames chair and the Corbusier chaise-longue, see the work of more up-to-date French and foreigner designers.

DINERS EN VILLE

27 rue de Varenne, 7e.
METRO: rue du Bac.

A good address to know if you want some dramatic additions to your dining-table. Besides some arresting *trompe-l'oeil* plates and dishes on fruit, vegetable and fish themes there is also a good selection of old dinner- and tea-services, some French, some English. It's the mixture of old and new which gives this shop its particular charm and, if you are by any chance looking for a complete new dinner-service you will find a large range of different patterns to choose from. The style is elegant and eclectic and ranges from Art Deco or even Empire to modern. You can find the glass and the cutlery to match your mood as well as an attractive selection of tablecloths, napkins and teacosies, many sporting the Paisley designs that are one of the themes of the shop.

BESSON

18 rue du Vieux-Colombier, 6e.
METRO: Saint-Sulpice.

46 avenue Marceau, 8e.
METRO: Alma Marceau.

This is where the well heeled and the not-so-young come to choose the papers, paints, the sofas and lampshades that will give their slightly worn homes a fresh, new look. A very pretty showroom, full of all the contemporary looks, it's lovely just to browse in but there are lots of small delights to clutch all the way home as well. It boasts one of the biggest selections of fabrics and wallpapers in Paris, featuring every mood from the wildly romantic to the avant-garde.

SOLEIADO

78 rue de Seine, 6e.
METRO: Mabillon, Odéon.

A large corner site provides ample room to display these enchanting fabrics, redolent of the sun and happiness of Provence, whence they come. Here the full range is shown in all its glory: made up into tablecloths and curtains, into quilted holdalls, napkins, washbags and cushions. These are the fabrics that defy time and fashion and just go on looking wonderful. More of everything, from fabrics to clothes, than can be found in its small London branch.

SIMRANE

23 rue Bonaparte, 6e.
METRO: Saint-Germain-des-Prés.

Simrane sells bright handmade Indian fabrics by the metre or made up (more carefully than is usual) into bedspreads, tablecloths of all shapes and sizes, napkins and other household items. The selection of colours and patterns is lovely and the prices are extremely good.

CAFE DE FLORE 172 boulevard Saint-Germain, 6e.

METRO: Saint-Germain-des-Prés.

Open 7.45am to 1.45am. Closed the whole of July.

It may be past its best — the days of Sartre, de Beauvoir *et al* are alas, long since gone — but it still has one of the prime positions on the whole of the boulevard for the battle-weary shopper to rest the feet and view the passing scene. And what a scene: along the boulevard pass some of the most colourful, interesting-looking people in all Paris. So, on a sunny day, sit at an outside table, forget about the past, *prend un verre* and celebrate today. Paris may change but at least the Café de Flore is still there.

ETAMINE

2 rue de Fürstemberg, 6e.
METRO: Saint-Germain-des-Prés.

An enchantingly pretty shop specialising in all the props of the world of *decor*, Etamine is full of papers and fabrics that seem refreshingly different and appealing. Besides giving the visitor a fine feel for what the chic inhabitants of the 6th and 7th *arrondissements* might like to use to update their houses, there is also a good selection of the best of British (Designers Guild, Osborne & Little *et al*).

MANUEL CANOVAS

7 place de Fürstemberg, 6e.
METRO: Saint-Germain-des-Prés.

Currently one of the most sought-after decorators in town, this is the showroom for Manuel Canovas' own range of fabrics and papers, many of them co-ordinating. The look is smartly pretty (lots of chintzes, silks and Jacquards) and though the fabrics aren't sold here you can always ask for samples. For those who aren't into monochrome chic and who want to take home a little of the smart Parisian domestic look, this is a good place to look.

SOPHIE CANOVAS

5 place de Fürstemberg, 6e.
METRO: Saint-German-des-Prés

Another charming shop in this enchanting little square off the boulevard Saint-Germain, where Sophie, wife of Manuel, has opened a boutique of her own to sell beguilingly pretty sheets and towels, as well as nightdresses, dressing-gowns and all the other pretty frillies that most women find so seductive. All fresh white paint and pretty colours, it's like going into a garden full of spring flowers.

PROSCIENCES

44 rue des Ecoles, 5e.
METRO: Maubert-Mutualité.

Simple, functional kitchen equipment that looks just right simply because it so clearly designed with the purpose in mind. Lots of plain white porcelain, clear glass, wood and other simple materials used to make the pitchers and jugs, the spoons, the mortars and pestles that every serious cook needs. A restful change from the over-decorated modern versions that are to be seen everywhere.

LA TUILE A LOUP

35 rue Daubenton, 5e.
METRO: Censier-Daubenton.

It isn't always easy in Paris to find a good selection of the charming regional ware that tourists come upon so happily when wandering around the highways and byways of provincial France. This little shop specialises in all those charming bowls and dishes that remind us of innumerable happy days in the summer sun — those inimitable deep green glazes, those artlessly hand-painted bowls, those capacious gratin dishes and the handsome wooden bowls. You can find all these here without making the detour out of town.

JEWELLERY

EXOTISSIMO

77 rue du Cherche-Midi, 6e.
METRO: Vaneau, Rennes.

A small shop, tumbling over with desirable jewellery: lapis lazuli, jet, turquoise, rings old and new, bracelets from India, necklaces from Mexico, lots of copies of old rings and brooches. Jewellery for all tastes except for those addicted to the avant-garde or the very precious. If you're looking for a wearable pin, a string of beads to give a friend or a brooch to put at the neck of this year's blouse, you could hardly do better than search out Exotissimo.

PETIT BACCHUS 13 rue du Cherche-Midi, 6e.

METRO: Sèvres-Babylone, Rennes.

Open 10am to 8pm. Closed Sunday.

Yet another example of the burgeoning popularity of winebars and with bars like this, it's no wonder the corner café is losing ground. The excellent Steven Spurrier is the new owner, Petit Bacchus is now serving wines by the glass of a much higher calibre than you would normally get in an ordinary café. With your glass of Bordeaux or sparkling Vouvray you may order as little as a plate of *charcuterie* or some of Poilâne's marvellous bread (Poilâne's famous shop is just across the road), or as much as three-course lunch. Those homesick for a proper English meal should call in on Wednesdays when one of the managers, who is Irish, makes a proper Irish stew. Lucky wine buffs who hit on the right Saturday morning can expand their knowledge of the grape with a little free wine-tasting.

OTHELLO

21 rue des Saints-Pères, 6e.
METRO: Saint-Germain-des-Prés.

All in among the enticing antique shops is Othello, a chic little boutique selling jewellery that would give a lift to many an outfit. Impeccably wrought ivory bracelets (you have to get used to the fact that the French are a little less squeamish than we are about which parts of which animals are used), turquoise, amber — whatever the mood of the moment happens to be. If you had to find a phrase to describe the style 'refined ethnic' is probably the one.

BIJOUTERIE FANTAISIE

79 rue des Saints-Pères, 6e.
METRO: Saint-Germain-des-Prés.

A little sliver of a shop selling smashing costume jewellery at not unreasonable prices. Really good 'pearl' and 'gold' ear-rings, looking almost exactly like some very famous versions; lots of turquoise and silver; and big, bold bracelets.

NEREIDES

23 rue du Four, 6e.
METRO: Mabillon, Saint-Germain-des-Prés.

Here, in a marvellously successful recreation of a 1930s setting, you can find what the French so charmingly call *bijoux fantaisies*: in other words, the sort of costume jewellery that makes no attempt to ape the real. It has great panache and makes the kind of statement it is hard to ignore. Lots of ear-rings, and necklaces worth making an entrance in.

SHOES

MAUD FRIZON

81–83 rue des Saints-Pères, 6e.
METRO: Sèvres-Babylone.

Fashionable women all over the world know the name of Maud Frizon and there's something special about making your way to her own shop in her own city. Maud Frizon got off to a flying start way back in the days of the midi-skirt when she launched a bright red, Russian-look boot which was just what the midi-skirt wearer needed to complement her outfit. Her shoes do not come cheap — how could they when they are to be found on the ritziest models, stepping out down the glossiest of walkways — but her style is unique. Her shoes are often a little on the whacky side but there are always more sober models to complement those whose tastes are less exotic. However, you need a reputation for chutzpah to get away with her kind of prices — Maud Frizon has.

CHARLES KAMMER

14 rue de Grenelle, 6e.
METRO: Sèvres-Babylone.

Another fashionable shoe shop in this increasingly fashionable area, Charles Kammer shoes are less noticeably distinctive than those of Maud Frizon, for example, but if you're looking for a well-made shoe to wear with this season's skirt, he is bound to have it. Nice colours, nice leathers, nice prices.

ROBERT CLERGERIE

5 rue du Cherche-Midi, 6e.
METRO: Sèvres-Babylone.

One of the most elegant Frenchwomen I know tells me that she buys most of her shoes at Robert Clergerie. He doesn't have quite the same high profile as Maud Frizon, Tokio Kumagai *et al* but any number of chic *Parisiennes* have been seen heading into his little shop, people from the smart magazines like *Elle* and the world of the cinema, like Isabelle Adjani. The shoes combine a classic good taste with fashionability and, as well as being stylish they are, I'm told, blissfully comfortable. The prices are good, too.

VALENTINE PALOMBA

23 rue du Dragon, 6e.
METRO: Saint-Sulpice, Saint-Germain-des-Prés.

Well heeled you will certainly need to be to emerge even moderately heeled from this luxurious new shoe shop in the

---

BRASSERIE LIPP 152 boulevard Saint-Germain, 6e.

METRO: Saint-Germain-des-Prés.

Open 8am to 2am. Closed Monday.

One of the most famous brasseries in the world (together with Café Flore and Aux Deux Magots, almost opposite) but do not go if you are under the illusion that you will be rubbing shoulders with distinguished writers and eminent politicians. The waiters who greet you at the door have the most immaculate nose for the visiting tourist and will usher you upstairs where you will scarcely hear a word of French, eat indifferent food and be served by bullying waiters. Downstairs, it is true, has an inimitable atmosphere, but it takes years of distinguished service and much exposure in the press and literary magazines before you can be sure of rating a table there.

AUX DEUX MAGOTS 170 boulevard
Saint-Germain, 6e.

METRO: Saint-Germain-des-Prés.

Open 8am to 2am. Closed the whole of August.

Another incomparable place to watch the life of the Left Bank go by. Made famous by Sartre, de Beauvoir and their intellectual cronies, it is still sought after by tourists from all over the world. Never mind, it presents as pretty a picture of Left Bank Paris as you could wish for and on a sunny day you could do a lot worse than order a *café au lait* and a croissant before setting out on yet another foray down the old back streets of the Left Bank.

heart of Saint-Germain-des-Prés. Not for the shy or introverted, more for those who glory in the opulent one-off and have the self-confidence to carry off this ultra modish look. Nonetheless, besides the more extravagant creations made from pythons, cobras, crocodiles and other nasties, there are some beautifully plain and ladylike pumps and ballet-shoes, and some quietly good-looking lines in less alarming skins. *Tout* Paris is hot-footing to see what Palomba has in store. A foot-fetishist's dream.

STEPHANE KELIAN

62 rue des Saints-Pères, 6e.
METRO: Saint-Germain-des-Prés.

6 place des Victoires, 1er.
METRO: Bourse.

13 rue de Grenelle, 6e.
METRO: Sèvres-Babylone.

42 avenue Victor-Hugo, 16e.
METRO: Etoile.

A big name in the world of shoes, Stéphane Kélian's growing success is reflected in the number of boutiques he now owns (seven at the last count of which the four principal ones are listed here). These are designer shoes at designer prices, so don't go looking for chain-store bargains. But for the money you certainly get a special *quelque chose* — they all have an air about them of sophistication, of chic, of being the very latest thing. So if your old flatties won't go with your new body-hugging dress, run along to Stéphane Kélian and you won't be disappointed.

FRANCE FAVER

78 rue des Saints-Pères, 6e.
METRO: Saint-Germain-des-Prés.

Some very, very chic London women of my acquaintance head straight for France Faver whenever they find themselves in Paris. Here they buy up the cheeky shoes with the little bow on the back in whatever colour happens to be that season's flavour of the month; France Faver always seems to have them in stock, the colour choice is immense and the shoe is the sort that looks at home in almost any city environment. She is less of a big name than, say Tokio Kumagai and Maud Frizon, and her designs are less outrageous but for quality and for variety she is a good name to go for.

SELF-INDULGENT SHOPS

LA BOUTIQUE A BOUTONS

110 rue de Rennes, 6e.
METRO: Rennes, Saint-Placide.

As you may well have guessed from the name, this is the place for buttons of every style, shape, colour and material. Something like 8000 different examples so there ought to be the button for you.

AU CHAT DORMANT

15 rue du Cherche-Midi, 6e.

Those who are dotty about moggies should head for this tiny but enchanting little shop. Spend a few francs on a delightful postcard or several hundreds on a feline painting. There are small replicas of cats in porcelain, marble and plastic as well

METRO: Sèvres-Babylone.
Rennes.

as a host of other little items all embellished with some emblem of one of the world's most popular pets.

LA MARLOTTE 55 rue du Cherche-Midi, 6e.
(Tel: 45.48.86.79.)

METRO: Rennes, Saint-Placide.

If you are in need of something more sustaining than winebar fare, this little restaurant could be the very place. Neither grand nor cheap, it is one of those increasingly hard to find *restaurants du quartier*, with a loyal local following, serving sound French food that is consistently good. Go for a comforting potée, a *pot-au-feu*, a traditional dish of lentils, properly turned salads, home-made noodles and (if you leave enough room) some sensational puddings.

MANDARINA DUCK

Espace Bonaparte, 64 rue Bonaparte, 6e.
METRO: Saint-Germain-des-Prés.

If you're looking for some new luggage or you've bought so much you can't get it all home, take a look at Mandarina Duck. Sometimes referred to as the Samsonite of the 1980s, Mandarina Duck produces bags and suitcases that owe everything to modern technology and absolutely nothing to nostalgia. There are four basic lines: Tank (made from corrugated rubber and nylon, very 1980s), Utility (rubberised cotton), Knock (from treated canvas) and System (nylon fabric with metal frames). Lots of sizes and shapes, from belt purses to huge suitcases as well as chic-looking document cases for the executive. Colours are the current vogue colours of black, grey, silver, khaki, red, gun-metal and dark green. These are the bags the design gurus like to be seen with.

POINT A LA LIGNE

177 boulevard Saint-Germain, 7e.
METRO: Saint-Germain-des-Prés.

A small but charming shop devoted almost entirely to candles. Some you will have seen elsewhere but nobody else offers such a large and complete range. There are candles in every colour and shape, from the simplest in plain white to candles masquerading as strawberry tarts, bunches of grapes or rainbow-coloured sundaes; there are candles that can be used on elegant tables and candles for more funky ones; candles to envelop the room in the most delicious of scents and candles to help keep away insects at night. To go with the candles there are napkins and tablecloths and a few other equally pretty table accessories.

RELIURE

55 rue des Saints-Pères, 6e.
METRO: Sèvres-Babylone.

Paper and all things connected with it are one of the great things to buy in Paris. Here you will find lovely paper by the metre. So desirable is it that you will be tempted to buy whether you can think of a use for it or not. Besides the reams of paper there are albums and notebooks, photograph frames and boxes — all the little seductive bits and pieces that make charming presents if you can bear to give them away.

LE MONDE EN MARCHE

34 rue Dauphine, 6e.
METRO: Odéon.

A small unglamorous looking exterior but inside it is full of charming wooden toys. Many are made by hand and are so beautifully wrought they seem almost too good to be given to children. Look for puppets on a string, model aeroplanes, a set of skittles and a marvellously rendered Noah's Ark.

DESPALLES

76 boulevard Saint-Germain, 6e.
METRO: Saint-Germain-des-Prés.

The ultimate garden shop. Pots from Provence, seeds of all kinds (grow your own sweet basil and genuine Provençale tomatoes), exotic plants and those lovely tin cats with the glittering marble eyes that scare the wits out of every marauding bird. If there's a seed or a plant that you're after and they don't have it, they'll do their best to track it down for you. For sheltering from storms, what could be better than a giant umbrella in pillar-box red or stormy blue as used by genuine Auvergnat shepherds?

THE UNUSUAL GIFT

CHAUMETTE

45 avenue Duquesne, 7e.
METRO: Saint-François-Xavier.

Men, it is well-known, are impossible to find presents for, so hurry to Chaumette where you may find inspiration. A restrained collection of beautiful, finely-wrought, wooden objects, ranging from lamps to vases, from pipes to ashtrays. Women should be happy with many of the things here, too.

LE PACIFICO 50 boulevard du Montparnasse, 15e.

METRO: Falguière.

One of the most *branché* cafés in Paris, this is where the trendy, fashionable, youngish crowd hang out. Not for those who like their comforts quiet, exclusive and luxurious but for those who want to take in all the latest looks, in clothes, hair-cuts, accessories and, yes, food.

AFFAIRE D'HOMME

15 rue Brea, Paris, 6e.
METRO: Vavin.

A nice little shop to know about if, like most of us, you're always on the lookout for something, anything, to give to the man in your life. It doesn't sell anything particularly original

LA COUPOLE 102 boulevard du Montparnasse, 6e.
(Tel: 43.20.14.20.)

METRO: Vavin

More of an institution than a restaurant, La Coupole has, in its time, served up some disgusting meals, but the word is that it is once again on the up. It has never failed to deliver on atmosphere and it is still one of the best places to twirl a glass late at night, to watch the comings and goings, the actors and actresses, the writers and the beau monde. If you also want something to eat, you can rest assured that there will always be some comforting *plats du jour* even if the delicacies you had hoped for fail to materialise.

but it is beautifully put together. Everything in the shop has been selected by a careful eye and presents one harmonious whole. The taste is modern, the value excellent. It's the place to go for the well thought-out, beautifully made object that also does all you expect of it: a pocket knife that is the best of its sort, a lighter that won't break down, a tennis racquet of the latest, lightest materials, a finely-wrought watch, a useful set of desk accessories or a gutsy towel for the athlete.

BEAUTE DIVINE

40 rue Saint-Sulpice, 6e.
METRO: Saint-Sulpice.

This elegant little boutique set in a charming square offers a seductive collection of anything and everything connected with the rituals of *la toilette*. If you're looking for a 'feminine' present you are likely to find it here. Beauté Divine sells a mixture of the old and new: Art Deco mirrors, scent bottles, linen handtowels, sponges and soap-boxes, little gadgets to trim the beard and elegant crystal bottles for dispensing bath oils. All are in tip-top condition and selected with an impeccable eye for the unusual and the distinguished. The brushes are all made by hand in the traditional way so that today they have an air of quality and old-fashioned charm. Lots of other *re-editions* of designs from times gone by, as well as one of the finest collections of antique *flaçons* around.

FRANCOISE THIBAULT

1 rue Jacob, 6e.
METRO: Saint-Germain-des-Prés.

1 et 2 rue Bourbon-le-Château, 6e.
METRO: Saint-Germain-des-Prés.

Closed Sundays, Mondays and the whole of August.

If I could only go to one shop to do my present shopping this would be it. Charm personified, it seems to be full of things that still retain something ineffably French about them. Free of all the familiar tat that we see in international shops around the world, Françoise Thibault has a gift for retaining an individuality that cannot fail to charm. Some of her things are old, some new, some serious, some just for fun. There are useful things like mirrors and lamps and photograph frames, but all will have something special about them. Then there is

the purely decorative, such as an antique porcelain hand (though you could turn it into a functional item by using it to house rings or necklaces in a most decorative way). The rue Jacob shop is mainly for the small, unusual present while the one in rue Bourbon-le-Château goes in for furniture of a gentle rustic sort as well as carpets and larger *objets*.

MADELEINE GELY

218 boulevard Saint-Germain, 7e.
METRO: Saint-Germain-des Prés.

Founded in 1834, this is one of the oldest shops in Paris still to be purveying its original wares. Here you will find umbrellas and walking sticks of every conceivable size, colour and originality. There are wooden hippo heads for children and rare collectors' pieces like the cat's head with a red tongue that comes out at the press of a button. There are sticks that conceal sharp-edged swords and pretty parasols for a day out at Longchamp. The most luxurious are made from purest silk, some double as shooting sticks, some have little clocks in the top. Scarcely bigger than a doll's house, this little shop manages to have umbrellas in more variety than you would ever have thought possible. You can order handles in wood, ivory, moulded resin, or bamboo and the fabric in almost any colour or material that is suitable.

METAMORPHOSES

44 rue Saint-Jacques, 6e.
METRO: Maubert-Mutualité.

If you like ferreting a bargain out from amongst a million little *trucs*, this shop could give you hours of enjoyment. Slightly eccentric, full of straw hats and old shoes, hat pins and silver boxes, you could be lucky and find the perfect present or the wittiest piece of jewellery. Bring your best pair of glasses though, as they seem to be having trouble with the electricity.

LES HALLES
(THE HEART OF PARIS)

Out of the ruins of what Zola once called 'the belly of Paris' has risen one of the most controversial, most visited districts of Paris. Whether you see it as a symbol of the city's ability to renew and modernise itself, or as a desecration of its old-world charm, this is a part of Paris you can't afford to miss.

Right in the heart of Les Halles, that area bounded by the churches of Saint-Eustache, Saint-Merri and the Reformed Oratory church, where for some 800 years the food merchants carried on their trade, is the Forum des Halles — a monument to modern consumerism, lacking as yet the charm of the old-style shops (and still undergoing further development) but hard to fault for sheer practicality. Beside it lies Paul Chemetov's subterranean sports and cultural complex, all avant-garde glass and chrome.

For those who remember the days when the market was alive with the sights and sounds of provisions from all over France being bargained for and fought over, the change is great.

Instead of rosy-cheeked women from Provence selling their flowers in the flower market, farmers from Normandy displaying their cheeses and fishermen struggling with their pots of lobsters, Les Halles is now a haven both for the jeans-clad youth of the world, clutching their trendy FNAC bags to the sound of raucous music pouring from the pop-shops, and for coachloads of camera-clicking Japanese tourists.

But gradually the area is acquiring a new sort of character. To be sure, the Forum itself is still a little soulless, full of bright, clean, shining emporia, many of them of distinguished lineage (Hechter, Charles Jourdan, Dorothée Bis *et al*) but all still in search of that elusive thing called charm. However, whether you want a big designer label, a brand new record, some suntan cream or a low-slung belt, one of the shops in the Forum will be able to provide it.

And on a rainy day the citizens of Les Halles could, without lifting an umbrella or being cast down by a leaden sky, spend all day in the Forum taking in shops, cinemas, art galleries, restaurants and cafés. It is worth remembering that Châtelet-Les Halles is one of the biggest métro stations in Paris — it stops right in the heart of the Forum itself and beside it stops the RER as well.

Wandering round Les Halles has become an essential Parisian pastime — you never know quite what you'll find, for new boutiques come and go. There are lots of charming pedestrian areas (in particular the place Sainte-Opportune and the rue de la Ferronnerie) which are bustling with energy and with enterprising boutiques.

If you wander away from the Forum itself you will find it still hedged in by some of the oldest streets in Paris. Take time off to wander through the pedestrian areas and down the sidestreets. Stop in at Saint-Eustache, after Notre-Dame the oldest church in Paris. It was here that Louis XIV celebrated his first communion and Molière was baptised — admire the stained glass windows and ribbed vaulting. Nestling right up against Saint-Eustache you will find some all-night restaurants and early morning food merchants, reminding us of Les Halles as it used to be.

For the flavour of the past go down the rues Montmartre and Montorgueil, take in the rue Berger, and wander into the places des Innocents where the Fontaine des Innocents should be admired — see it beautifully restored to its full Renaissance glory. Other streets not to be missed include the rue de Quincampoix, full of outlandish street art and home to

modern art galleries, as well as some brash and garish video bars. Take in the rue Saint-Denis if you have a taste for the lurid or if you want to see a little of the underside of Parisian life and can cope with the inevitable brushes with the ladies of the night — in the broad daylight! And don't miss the newly-restored Galerie Vivienne and the Galerie Vero-Dodat.

Don't miss a chance to see the Bourse de Commerce either — a monument to the French belief in their own ineffable superiority in things cultural and artistic. Gaze at its over-blown architecture, its huge Corinthian columns, its Greek pediments — the whole a hymn to the glories of money.

But make no mistake, though relics of by-gone days still abound, Les Halles is today one of the most innovative districts in Paris. It may be an architectural mess, it may lack the elegance of the more refined *quartiers*, but it is alive, always changing and a never-ending source of interest.

Today it is the place where you are most likely to stumble upon the new, the avant-garde and the imaginative. It is a mecca for those interested in the modern arts, whether furniture, fine art, fashion or pop. It's full of fashion designers whose tastes run more to the innovative than the *raffiné*, hairdressers with modish clients; cafés with customers so *branché* they have become *chébran*. Every street springs its own surprises. Though not everything you see will be to your taste (how could it be?) there will scarcely be a dull moment.

Make sure you visit the place des Victoires, which for some years now has been one of the places the chic Parisienne feels obliged to keep an eye on. Admire its circle of elegant façades and look in on those two pioneers: Kenzo and the little boutique Victoire, both still firmly in place, both still setting the pace. Off the place des Victoires runs the rue Etienne-Marcel, another street alive with new ideas and one that no fashion addict would wish to miss. Currently it looks like a little outpost of Japan, but see the Parisians lining up to buy.

Above all, you mustn't miss out on Beaubourg (or the Pompidou Centre). Though on the very edge of Les Halles, it seems to be the spiritual heart, a symbol of the renewal of the area, displaying to all the world one of the most cheerful intestinal systems ever invented.

Round its precincts you will find one of the cheapest entertainment shows in Paris. Watch the street shows, the acrobats, the strolling con-artists, the hucksters and hustlers, the down-and-outs, and the genuine eccentrics. Where else in the world can you have so much fun for so little money?

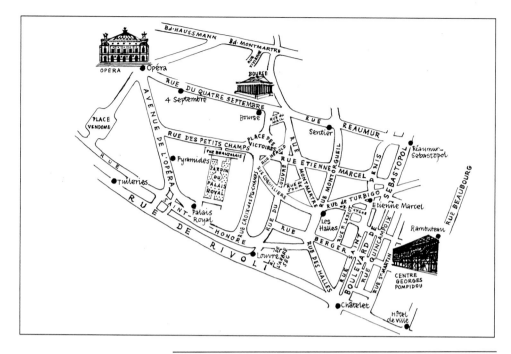

CONTENTS

* Strictly speaking not all shops but also places to rest the feet, restore the spirits and engage the mind.

FASHION: MEN

HOUSEHOLD

THE UNUSUAL GIFT

ART AND MUSIC

USA RECORDS

50 rue de l'Arbre-Sec, 1er.
METRO: Pont-Neuf, Louvre.

A feast for lovers of jazz and blues, soul and rock, a bigger selection than anywhere else in Paris.

LES MONDES DU JAZZ

2 rue de la Petite-Truanderie, 1er.
METRO: Etienne-Marcel, Les Halles.

Jazz fans might like to know of this address — a good source of real jazz records, many of them rare and special.

ROCK HAIR 9 rue de la Ferronerie, 1er.

METRO: Châtelet.

The name says it all — where the young and *branché* go to get their young and *branché* haircuts.

V.I.A.

place Sainte-Opportune, 1er.
METRO: Châtelet.

Anybody interested in the current state of French modern design should make a point of looking in on this exceedingly elegant and inviting shop which offers only the very best. Here grouped together so you can see them in one fell swoop are some of the finest desks and chairs, lights and tables, boxes and cupboards in modern France. They are quite simply superb — very fitting rivals to the otherwise beguiling charms of the antique shops.

CENTRAL UNION

28 rue de la Grande-Truanderie, 1e.
METRO: Etienne-Marcel, Les Halles.

A cult shop in the trendy Les Halles area, where kitsch and retro rule. Currently sought after are the limited edition signed lithographs by French cartoonist-cum-graphic illustrator, Floc'h. They take a cheeky look at America of the fifties when Hitchcock and Raymond Loewy were potent influences. They are neither cheap nor do they seem very French, but they are wonderfully strong images to hang up on a wall.

BOOKS

FNAC

(Fédération Nationale d'Achat des Cadres), Forum des Halles, level 2, 1er.
METRO: Les Halles.

A temple to the world of hi-tech and one of the most avant-garde of all book shops, this mega-sized store sells not only books (which are beautifully organised) but also records, electronic equipment ranging from calculators to computers, cameras and concert tickets. And its distinctive carrier-bags have even acquired a definite cachet of their own. The branch

136 rue de Rennes, 6e.
METRO: Saint-Sulpice.

26 avenue de Wagram, 8e.
METRO: Ternes.

in the Forum des Halles is the biggest of all FNAC shops, with the largest selection of its lines. There's a membership card on sale which gives the customer various discounts on cassettes, video and hi-fi equipment, cameras, and so on. It's also a good place to have your photographs developed — look out for FNAC service boutiques at métro or RER stations.

AU BAIN MARIE

2 rue du Mail, 2e.
METRO: Bourse.

Owned by Aude Clément who also owns the other Au Bain Marie at 20 rue Hérold nearby, this is a charming little shop specialising in books and magazines on the all-important subject of food. Browse to your heart's content among the selection of old and new books, in French and in English.

FASHION: WOMEN

OMOTE-SANDO

4 rue Pierre-Lescot, 1er.
METRO: Les Halles.

As if Paris wasn't already reeling from the influence of the land of the rising sun, six Japanese designers (not yet household names here though they are all well known back home) have banded together and are making a big impact in their brand new boutique. Fashionably hi-tech from top to bottom, there are two floors where each of the six — Ozone Community, Lu Coordinate, Iohshin Satho, Comme Ça du Mode, N. Masaki and Person's — have set out their avant-garde wares. It may be a little too avant-garde for your taste but it is certainly well worth a look — you won't be bored.

JEAN LOUIS DAVID 27 rue de la Ferronerie, 1er.

METRO: Châtelet.

If Carita and Alexandre aren't quite your style and Rock Hair sounds a little alarming, try this salon — I hear nothing but the highest praise for the small group of hair-dressing salons run by Jean Louis David. Standards are high, styles are fashionable without being frightening and you can safely put yourself in their hands.

SARA SHELBURNE

10 rue du Cygne, 1er.
METRO: Etienne Marcel.

Another designer with her own boutique who has built up a large and faithful clientèle over the years. There is many a frequent visitor who heads straight for Sara Shelbourne's boutique every time she arrives. You need to be a fairly well-heeled visitor, though, for her prices aren't low. She specialises in a seductive, feminine look and evening and cocktail wear is probably her greatest strength. These don't come cheap but you would get something special adapted to your own measurements.

ANA SALAZAR

2 rue de Turbigo, 1er.
METRO: Etienne-Marcel.

A smart little shop all got up in the current cult colours of black, grey and white; from top to toe it shimmers in elegant marble look-alike. Ana Salazar is a chic Portuguese lady who is adept at providing a sharp, contemporary look at not very high prices. You pay for it, though, with the fabrics which are not always as good as they ought to be. The colours, naturally, are mainly black and white. It's a pity about so much viscose but for not too high a price (by Parisians' standards, that is) you could cut quite a dash and if it doesn't last forever, well, next year you'll probably want something else anyway.

ELISABETH DE SENNEVILLE

3 rue de Turbigo, 1er.
METRO: Les Halles, Etienne-Marcel.

After the grand circle of haute couture names come a number of interesting and innovative designers who have a faithful following all their own. Elisabeth de Senneville is one of the most distinguished of their number. She is always worth looking at, an expert at providing a look that appears both adventurous and yet practical and easy to wear. She often experiments with new materials, although perhaps one of the most identifiable of all her characteristics is her continuing love affair with dear old dark-blue cotton, as used in Chinese workmen's clothes. Her prices are exceedingly reasonable — you could easily pay as much for a mass-produced affair. Take a look for yourself.

SCOOTER

10 rue de Turbigo, 1er.
METRO: Etienne-Marcel.

A very *branché* (or, to use the inverted language of the young, *chébran*) sort of place, Scooter was one of the first to launch giant ear-rings and the bracelets that look like motorcar parts. Still, in the forefront of fashion this is one of the favourite accessory shops of fashion editors. Nothing in this shop is understated — with ear-rings like African masks, bracelets that do seem to have fallen off a motorbike and the kind of brooch that will make your grandmother wonder what the youth of today is coming to — it's strictly for those with panache. Scooter also sells a selection of clothes of their own design — some of it outrageous. There are the bright African prints worn with startling confidence by one of the African salesgirls, also slinky, strapless dresses *á la* fifties and some nice, cotton, ballooning Arabian-type trousers. If you're looking for a present for a confident teenager, she'd be thrilled with anything from Scooter.

DUTHILLEUL & MINART

14 rue de Turbigo, 1er.
METRO: Etienne-Marcel.

Not many of us have chefs or waiters of our own who require clothing, but the young and enterprising might like to know of this source of authentic working clothes for the catering classes. Now that working clothes have become newly chic, come here for your nice white chef's jacket instead of Joseph's

POMPIDOU CENTRE Plateau Beaubourg, 4e.

METRO: Rambuteau.

*Open 10am to 10pm Saturday and Sunday; 12pm to 10pm
Monday, Wednesday, Thursday and Friday.
Closed Tuesday.*

The Pompidou Centre (or the Beaubourg as it is more popularly called) should not be missed. You may not like it (and you'd be in very good company) but Richard Rogers and Renzo Piano's building, commissioned by President Pompidou, is challenging, exciting and, above all, a genuinely vital gathering place for many of the arts. One of the first buildings to have its innards exposed, in the belief that pipes and escalators, girders and service funnels were as intrinsically interesting as bricks and mortar, it has achieved what it set out to do — to become a truly popular centre for the arts. Here the arts are seen to be fun, accessible, even intoxicating, far removed from the aura of hushed worship that seems to hang around more formal establishments. Beaubourg is truly for the people, not just of Paris but of all the world. Outside in the piazza there is always a multitude of things going on: clusters of magicians, mime artists, dancers and actors gathering to go through their acts for the milling public. Though the building itself is beginning to look a little tatty, its sense of life, fun, of informality is as potent as ever. Inside there are collections of modern art, a library (primarily of the 20th-century), an industrial design centre and a branch of the Cinémathèque Française — personally I've always found the inside much less riveting than the outside but there is usually an exhibition or two worth looking at.

latest *dictat*. The not-so-young will go for the fun sturdy cotton and pure linen dish towels — no flowers or birds and bees here, just plain classic items that are difficult to find elsewhere.

OBLIQUE

19 rue du Jour, 1er.
METRO: Les Halles.

The rue du Jour seems to be lined with shops selling much the same brand of chic, so take a wander down (it is very small and won't take you long unless you get beguiled by the animated entertainment that the customers provide) and get your eye in. Oblique has a lot to offer: very chic knitwear with a wonderfully *décontracté* air, and not expensive by current standards. You could buy an up-to-the-minute outfit for a lot less than the going rate in London or New York.

AGNES B

3 rue du Jour, 1er.
METRO: Les Halles.

There's many a snappy dresser who makes sure that if she only has time to visit one shop in Paris, it is Agnès B. A quiet cult fashion figure, she has that very Parisian gift of making

13 rue Michelet, 6e.
METRO: Port-Royal.

17 avenue Pierre-ler-de-
Serbie, 16e.
METRO: Iéna.

simple clothes seem sophisticated, of using natural fabrics in elegant ways. Her soft cotton jerseys, her fashionably crumpled linens and her ruffled silks are comfortably and stylishly cut and what her simple black and white shop misses in grandeur her clothes more than make up for by their desirability. Don't go there for a thoroughly dressed-up look; go there for understated simple cut and style — that plain white T-shirt with the perfect neckline or the essential polo-neck. The prices may seem high at first sight but when you try the clothes on and look at them closely you'll see why it is one of the most highly thought of boutiques in Paris.

AGNES B

Here in the rue du Jour is a mini Agnès B empire — if you have children, teenagers or men to clothe, take in the rest of her boutiques in this little street. Now the whole family can dress the Agnès B way.

LA NACELLE

10 rue du Jour, 1er.
METRO: Les Halles.

One of the many shops which seem to be following in the mood of Agnès B, but it's well done for all that. Simple clothes with a little *élan* to lift them out of the ordinary. Prices seem on the high side but the taste is impeccable. When you're visiting Agnès B, as you surely will, make sure you stop off at La Nacelle as well.

UN APRES MIDI DE CHIEN

10 rue du Jour, 1er.
METRO: Les Halles.

Very *drôle*. Lots of sweatshirts and sweaters covered in embroidered dogs, mini-mini skirts and frilly long shirts. This, you will have gathered, is not the place to buy your sober city suit. It's the place to amuse your recalcitrant teenager who is beginning to wonder whether Paris offers anything apart from understated chic. Yes it does — here. Prices, though, are very unteenagerish, so have a good look round, take in the heavily embellished jeans, the sweaters embroidered with dogs and go home and do it yourself for half the price.

CLAUDE BARTHELEMY

10 rue Etienne-Marcel, 1er.
METRO: Etienne-Marcel.

Chichi, Claude Barthelemy's wife, does most of the designing here — everything is exclusive to the shop and there are some fine, relaxed, elegant clothes. Nothing is especially cheap or avant-garde but it is a good place for the not-so-adventurous to find a soft, easy-to-wear city look. There is a particularly good range of linen trousers and skirts, and some nice loose cotton sweaters.

JACQUELIN 9 rue Pierre-Lescot 1er.

METRO: Etienne-Marcel.

For *fripes* that are clean, washed and well-presented, pay a visit to Jacquelin, which sells clothing from mainly circa 1940: lots of American jackets, circular skirts *à la* Marilyn Monroe, elasticated belts and loud Hawaiian shirts.

COMME DES GARCONS

42 rue Etienne-Marcel, 1er.
METRO: Etienne-Marcel.

This is Rei Kawakubo's shop for women and here you should not allow yourself to be put off by the bleakness of the interior (keep reminding yourself that this is what being in the forefront of fashion is all about). The clothes may look a little daunting at first, but they are wonderfully interesting and beautifully cut, and should you find a little *quelque chose* that is just 'you', rest assured that its class will show. Prices are quite expensive but they do give value for money when you consider the care with which they are made, and the interest and pleasure which they should give you. You could easily spend just as much on much less interesting clothes.

JOSEPH TRICOT

44 rue Etienne-Marcel, 2e.
METRO: Etienne-Marcel.

Londoners will already be familiar with the Joseph style but it is interesting to see how he presents his collection to the French: in stark, minimalist style, letting the clothes speak for themselves. Besides his own collection he has brought to the French some of our more original designers. Here you may see the output of Culture Shock and John Galliano, as well as the more reassuring baubles of Butler & Wilson.

YOHJI YAMAMOTO

47 rue Etienne-Marcel, 1er.
METRO: Etienne-Marcel.

Here side by side are the two boutiques marking the Yohji Yamamoto presence in Paris. Do not be put off by first impressions, by the air of minimalist desolation that hangs about the place (all this, you understand, has been carefully thought out — the bare decoration has been designed to focus attention on the clothes). If you want one really avant-garde piece of clothing and are prepared to pay what it costs, Yohji Yamamoto is your man. If you do decide to brave the store, choose carefully — don't buy anything so tame as a large T-shirt (you can do that without paying Yamamoto prices). Spend rather more; try on everything in sight and get the assistants to help you choose something that really works for you. Next door is the man's shop, and the same strictures apply. Don't dismiss it out of hand — difficult because the effect is initially off-putting. Even if you're usually into sober suits, buy just one beautiful, large, interesting and comfortable shirt: it won't be cheap but I guarantee you'll never throw it away.

CAPRICE DE SOPHIE

32 rue de la Vrillière, 1er.
METRO: Bourse.

If the full panoply of baby BCBG is a little too much for you, here are some alternatives that are neither cheap nor stuffy. Lots of delicious clothes for the small set which manage to have an air of French chic without looking too much like a uniform.

THIERRY MUGLER

10 place des Victoires, 2e.
METRO: Bourse.

One of the most original and inventive designers around. If you've read enough of the fashion press you'll know that you must not expect him to do anything so conventional as to make you look prettier. Thierry Mugler is into making statements, some of which it has to be said are very good statements. If all this makes you feel a little nervous, suss him out first in the excellent designer departments at the Galeries Lafayette, then, if he's your cup of *café au lait*, beard him in his shimmering cave of a boutique. If you have the *élan* to carry him off, the effects can be splendid — but you'll need a splendid bank account to match.

GISELE DELORME 2 rue des Petits-Champs, 2e.

METRO: Bourse.

One of those institutes devoted to the face and body beautiful that couldn't be anything but French. So clean and hygienic it almost might be a hospital, it specialises in assessing your problems on the spot and then putting together a collection of products designed specifically for you. A little *gout* of this, one of that, a few little additions and *voila* — just the thing to cure your acne/dryness/redness/wrinkles/cellulite. All based on plants and essential oils, the lotions and potions look delectably inviting — no wrinkle would dare to survive such concerted action.

JUNKO SHIMADA

54 rue Etienne-Marcel, 2e.
METRO: Etienne-Marcel.

One of the first of the wave of Japanese designers to make Paris their home, Junko Shimada is almost the most Parisian of them all, that is, although he is still a specialist in that peculiarly Japanese form of chic, all monochrome and fine, floppy materials, he also creates an elegance that not all his fellow countrymen can manage. The boutique boasts a typical new-wave minimalist interior. It is restrained to the point of extinction, leaving (this is the theory) the clothes themselves to stand out as decoration. Ignore the air of a slightly desolate warehouse and concentrate on the clothes which will need careful looking out and trying on for their potential to be understood. They are not for those who want to look pretty but are for confident, liberated strong women who are aiming, above all, for an elegant and individual look.

TOKIO KUMAGAI

52 rue Croix-des-Petits-
Champs, 2e.
METRO: Pyramides

The place where smart Parisians go for their whacky shoes at even whackier prices. The current darling of the fashionable set, Tokio Kumagai has turned the shoe from a functional object into a conversation stopper. Shoes topped by a terrier's muzzle or a cat's whiskers have become a recognisable status symbol, but for the less flamboyant there is footwear finished like a painting by Miró or Picasso, or leather painted to look like marble. The shoes are not cheap but those in the know save up for the sales, when everything goes for half price.

FASHION: MEN

MACDOUGLAS

20 rue Pierre-Lescot, 1er.
METRO: Les Halles.

9 rue de Sèvres, 6e.
METRO: Sèvres-Babylone.

155 rue du Faubourg Saint-
Honoré. 8e.
METRO: Saint-Philippe-du-
Roule, George V.

27 rue de Passy, 16e.
METRO: Passy.

As leather jackets go they don't come much classier than these. This is *the* place for beautifully-cut leather jackets: aviator style, motorcycle style or even rue du Faubourg Saint-Honoré style. They make them in the softest, finest leather and they won't be as expensive as you might think. Aficionados love the jackets above all, but there are skirts in the new season's lengths and strictly-cut trousers for men and women.

COMME DES GARCONS

40 rue Etienne-Marcel, 1er.
METRO: Les Halles,
Etienne-Marcel.

Rei Kawakubo is one of the grand names of Japanese designers and one of the cult figures of the Western fashion press. It is at first a little difficult to understand how she manages to sell a crumpled silk shirt or a crumpled cotton one for the prices she does. These are her clothes *pour les garçons* but as *garçons* go they will need to be very affluent, very open-minded and be prepared to dress almost exclusively in white, black or grey. Those who move in designer circles will, however, immediately prove that they have the right credentials if they invest in a single Comme des Garçons outfit. The rumpled silk shirts are recognised by those in the know the world over.

CHRISTOPHE LEBOURG

49 rue Etienne-Marcel, 1er.
METRO: Bourse, Etienne-Marcel.

Don't come to Christophe Lebourg if you want to see rows and rows of shirts, and racks of suits and jackets. Here we have yet another exercise in slimline collections — you'll either love everything on show, or like none of it. Immaculate linen shirts and fine heavy cottons for women. Another of those boutiques with an androgynous leaning: it's sometimes quite difficult to know who they're aiming at. If in doubt, the answer is usually both.

CACHAREL POUR HOMMES

5 place des Victoires, 1er.
METRO: Bourse.

This sells nice lines, particularly in casual wear, for men. Cacharel illustrates perfectly how much better the French designers cope with the problem of summer wear for men — the summer suits are entirely appropriate for office life and yet have an air of summer levity about them, separating them from the heavier, more sober navy-blue suits and the grey winter flannels. Good quality, good prices, good designs.

STRUCTURE

52 rue Croix-des-Petits-Champs, 1er.
METRO: Pyramides.

Any man in search of a little light relief in his wardrobe should head straight for Structure. Interesting, without being avant-garde, the shop is light, bright, clean and beautifully organised. Shelf upon shelf of wonderfully coloured sweaters, soft cotton shirts, socks, rainbow-coloured and patterned. It couldn't be called classic and yet even the most conservatively-minded could find something here to please. Don't come here for your city suits — look to it for the garments that will bring cheer and colour to your leisure hours.

HOUSEHOLD

LOIN DE CHEZ SWANN

1 rue du Cygne, 1er.
METRO: Etienne-Marcel.

Lots of lovely knick-knacks for the home — all with a little Gallic twist. So, when you've had your fill of clothes, drop into Loin de Chez Swann and buy a little *quelque chose* for the house.

A. SIMON

36 rue Etienne-Marcel, 1er.
METRO: Etienne-Marcel, Les Halles.

The Marais used to be one of the great wholesale districts of Paris and now that it is becoming increasingly gentrified, some of the wholesale houses are becoming less reluctant to sell to individual customers. At A. Simon, Depôt Ceramique-Porcelaines, you will find lots of very French-looking glass and china, knives and casseroles, copper pans and giant aluminium saucepans. Here much of the hotel trade buys its wares and here, too, you may wander and buy whatever takes your fancy. The staff aren't noted for their charm but if you persevere you could come away with some authentically Gallic presents.

QUATRE SAISONS

2–6 rue du Jour, 1er.
METRO: Les Halles.

Bright, attractive shop specialising in a mass of baskets and all sorts of appurtenances for the kitchen or dining-room: lots of bright aprons and bread baskets, as well as larger items such as sturdy pine tables. All is eminently agreeable.

LA DROGUERIE

9 rue du Jour, 1er.
METRO: Les Halles.

If you idea of a sewing and knitting shop is a little old lady presiding over some faded pastel wools and buttons, take a peek at La Droguerie, the most intriguing knitting and needlework shop in the world. The entrance catches your eye with its colourful strands of cotton, wools and yarns: bright reds, turquoises, yellows, creams and beiges all jostle together. Further inside are rows of bottles and jars filled with buttons, bows, beads and spangles, in glass and gold, silver and coloured metal and looking for all the world like a *bonbon* shop. Even those who never pick up a needle will want to look.

MARIE-CLAIRE

2 rue Berger, 1er.
METRO: Les Halles,
Châtelet.

The name says it all — everything for the house in the Marie-Claire style. Glossy, French and very much *à la mode*.

DEHILLERIN

20 rue Coquillière, 1er.
METRO: Les Halles.

Don't expect perfect service or much personal attention here — Dehillerin is far too busy supplying the chefs of Paris, whether grand or still up-and-coming, with everything that might be required for the business in hand. It could be as simple as a wooden spoon, as vital as the absolutely perfect knife or as large as a pan in which to poach a whole turbot. Dehillerin has been a mecca for chefs for well over 150 years and it shows. Nothing new or decorated about the goods on sale, just rows and rows of everything the true cook could desire: copper pans and *bain-maries*, wooden spoons and excellent knives, skewers and sieves, all the old-fashioned and proper equipment simply arranged. Marvellous presents for foodie friends. There's also a catalogue available — with an English version.

AU BAIN MARIE

20 rue Hérold, 1er.
METRO: Bourse, Les Halles.

One of the prettiest, most enchanting shops in Paris. A marvellous *mélange* of things old and new, all selected by the discerning eye of the owner, Aude Clément. It deals mainly in everything to do with the table, from wild ceramic dishes specially created for asparagus or strawberries, to great jugs full of knives with brightly coloured Galalithe (an early plastic) handles. There are decanters and claret jugs, serving spoons and cocktail jugs; some old, some new, all infinitely desirable. There are pieces rescued from the old Paquebots

Normandies, linen for the table and bed and, if somebody you know is getting married, there couldn't be a better place to find the perfect present. The style is elegant in a totally unpretentious way. Aude Clément, whose immaculate taste draws together the whole eclectic selection, has just started selling her own impeccably crafted objects for the house. Many are careful reproductions (the French word *re-editions* sounds so much nicer) that capture all the glamour of times gone by. I don't know another shop like it.

VAUDEVILLE 29 rue Vivienne, 2e.
(Tel: 42.33.39.31.)

METRO: Bourse.

Open until 2am.

A lovely, lively brasserie full of authentic Parisian bustle. Delicious food. On the fishy side, with the *plateau des fruits de mer* being a speciality. Book if you have a mind to it; otherwise join the queue and soak up the atmosphere.

TIPI
9 rue Rameau, 2e
METRO: 4 Septembre.

A new boutique, founded by interior decorator Yves Taralon and currently sparkling with his Mexican-inspired collection of fabrics. Look out, too, for lamps, cushions and the small accessories that would bring some Gallic *joie de vivre* to a dark corner of the house.

PIERRE FREY
47 rue des Petits-Champs, 1er.
METRO: Pyramides

Pierre Frey is a most Parisian decorator and designer, and if you visit his main showrooms in the rue des Petits-Champs, or the smaller ones in the rue Jacob, this will give you a good idea of how the better-off Parisian either decorates, or would

5 rue Jacob, 6e.
METRO: Saint-Germain-
des-Prés.

like to decorate, his house. Lovely papers and fabrics, carpets and rugs and if you don't feel like embarking on such a large purchase away from home you can drop into the boutique next door (in rue des Petits-Champs) and come away with some of his charming designs in tablecloths, cushions, bedspreads and quilts.

HARRY'S BAR 5 rue Daunou, 2e.

METRO: Opéra.

Night-birds, loath to while away the hours in sleep, should make for Harry's Bar. Haunt of many famous bar-proppers over the years, from Scott Fitzgerald to Gershwin and Hemingway, it serves an impressive range of famous cocktails, whilst in the basement there's a pianist providing soothing background music until 2am. The bar itself is open from 10.30pm to 4am.

THE UNUSUAL GIFT

INDIGENE

14 rue des Halles, 1er.
METRO: Châtelet.

A lovely *folie* of a shop where you can buy all those little witty inessentials that the French are so famous for. Blow some francs on a seductive velvet hat, on some naughty knickers, some whacky jewellery or some elegant gauntlet gloves.

CORVINUS (MAISON DE POUPEE)

16 rue des Halles, 1er.
METRO: Châtelet.

One of those small shops that attracts collectors from all over the world. Here is everything for the lover of dolls and their miniature, enchanted world: dolls with china faces; dolls decked out in the finest velvet; musical boxes; and the whole tiny panoply of houses, china, furniture and accessories the world of dolls requires.

L'HOMME CET INCONNU

1 rue du Mail, 2e.
METRO: Bourse.

Here the female in search of a present for the man in her life (or the man in search of something for the man in his life) may be sure of finding something original, beguiling and altogether irresistible. The shop itself is small but the selection impeccable, ranging from chic black minimalist numbers in exquisite taste for the designer brigade to slightly funky retro things for those who like things old and fine. Some marvellous old Bakelite pens and wirelesses left over from the days when a radio really was a wireless. In other words, toys for the boys.

CAFE COSTES 4 place des Innocents, 1er.

METRO: Châtelet.

Open 8am to 2am every day.

Mecca of the matt black design brigade, where chic Parisians will brave designer Philippe Starck's Prat Fall chairs and post-modernist decor for the sake of being seen in the right place at the right time. Last year's *rendezvous du moment* has perhaps become this year's overcrowded, overpriced meeting-place, but the mirrored loos are the most chic in Paris. Remember as you sip your Pernod that Philippe Starck set out to design a café that would last for a hundred years. He wanted it to be 'as beautiful and sad as the main station in Prague'.

So, order a coffee or an *aperitif*, gaze at the passing scene and admire the splendid Renaissance-style fountain in the place des Innocents. Fountain-fetishists should go on to compare it with Nicky de Saint-Phalle's surrealist fountain in the nearby place Igor Stravinsky.

PACIFIC PALISADES 51 rue Quincampoix, 3e.

METRO: Châtelet.

Open noon to 3pm, 4pm to 2am Monday to Saturday, noon to 3pm Sunday.

This was once a haunt of the fickle *branché* set, who have now rather abandoned it for newer pastures. Nonetheless it goes on trying hard and its food and service have improved. If you spend a lot of time soaking up the atmosphere in Les Halles and you can't take the crowds at Café Costes, come along here. Lots of delicious salads and light, reviving *plats*.

LE MONDE DU BAGAGE

4 rue des Petit-Champs, 1er.
METRO: Bourse, Pyramides.

A good selection of middle-of-the-road luggage and handbags — if this makes it sound dull, it isn't. It may not be very avant-garde, nor does it make too many loud statements, but it offers a selection of very attractive pieces at equally attractive prices. More a source of baggage at affordable prices than investment pieces.

THE MARAIS
(BROWSER'S PARIS)

For many who know Paris well, the Marais is the most attractive *quartier* of all. It has a grave and lovely beauty of its own, a peculiarly happy outcome of the quirks of fate that came its way. Through the centuries its fortunes have waxed and waned. Once the favoured residential preserve of aristocrats and those who served them, today their fine and gracious mansions, the *hôtels particuliers*, with their courtyards in the front and the more formal gardens at the back, have left an indelible mark upon the district.

Once the tumbrils began to roll the craftsmen, shopkeepers and traders began to move in, bringing with them life and vital skills. Today, ever since Malraux's statute of 1962 put an end to the piecemeal destruction of the area, they have been joined by some of Paris' more affluent citizens, giving the Marais a rich and varied population spanning every walk of life. The old and beautiful buildings are being restored to their former glory and the district throbs with new vitality.

There are those who complain that it is becoming overly trendy and that the poor artisans can no longer afford to live there. This is not altogether true. The *hôtels particuliers* may still exist but today they will be occupied by shopkeepers or artisans who fill the courtyards with their wares and bring an air of bustling real life to these relics of the past.

The Marais was singularly lucky to escape the revisionary zeal of the Baron Haussmann, so that to this day it still has what Leon Daudet (who lived in the rue Pavée) called 'that indestructible something that cannot age or wear.' Here you feel that at any moment you might stumble upon one of Mme. de Sévigné's elegant salons or run into Victor Hugo on his way to plot another drama. The *Grand Siècle* seems alive and well.

Its immense charm, of course, arises from the fact that past and present seem so happily intermingled here. The old arcades are still there but nowadays you can go to buy an old *armoire* or a fine engraving. The mansions secreted behind their high walls and deep gardens often house the services which make it such a popular *quartier* to live in — there you may find the furniture-restorers, the leather-repairers, the framers, seamstresses, plumbers, dyers and tanners. Sit in the sun in one of the courtyards and drink a glass of fine Sancerre or go round the corner where you may still find a *bistro de quartier* serving a fine dish of pig's trotters.

The Marais festival, held every year from mid-June to mid-July, has also helped bring new life to the district. Concerts, plays, operas, craft and art exhibitions are held in the churches, hotels and gardens of the *quartier*. All this underlines the unique combination it has to offer of magnificent museums, often in quiet secluded places, and packed clusters of tiny shops, each with a character of its own.

The heart of the Marais is the place des Vosges, once the place Royale. Henry IV, who designed it, decreed that the adjoining manors should all have identical façades of pink brick with white corner-stones, and he it is we have to thank for the dignified elegance that so pervades the district.

The Marais is a district perfectly suited to exploring on foot. You can get a detailed inventory map of the area from the *Association pour la sauvegarde et la mise en valeur du Paris historique* (the local preservation society) at nos 44–46 rue François-Miron, or from the Centre Culturel du Marais, 28 rue des Francs-Bourgeois.

The Marais lends itself to personal discovery. Set out on your expedition with curiosity but be prepared to be led by whim. The pleasure is as much in stumbling upon a shop as into it. But even the happiest discoveries can do with a little help. The area is so densely packed with an ever changing variety of small shops and workshops among the grand *hôtels* that it's as well to have a destination or two in mind to shape your visit. Fear not, this will not destroy the illusion of personal discovery.

Aim to take in the Musée Carnavalet, or the Hôtel Salé, a 16th-century *hôtel particulier*, now the new Picasso museum. Visit Victor Hugo's old house at 6 place des Vosges. See what is said to be the oldest house in Paris (no.3 rue Volta) and don't miss the old Jewish quarter centred on the rue des Rosiers. Waves of 19th-century immigrants brought a richness and variety to the district that it still benefits from today. There you will see long-bearded dark-hatted men with side curls on their way to synagogue; you will see the menus written in Hebrew, and you will be able to try some of the specialities for yourself — cheesecake, or enjoy a bagel, some Polish sausages or a Hungarian pickled cabbage.

Between the rue des Rosiers and the rue du Roi-de-Sicile lies a dense cluster of synagogues, Jewish bakeries and delicatessens, and Turkish, Greek and Algerian cafés. Here you can buy the cheapest couscous in central Paris, but also the most self-indulgent French home-baked puddings.

Remember to take in the lovely collection of old buildings

that starts on the corner of the rue Saint-Paul and the Quai des Célestins — these have been turned into an enchanting collection of shops selling anything from *fripes* to fine old antiques. When the feet get weary you'll always find a café to restore the spirits — sit outdoors under a parasol in summer, or take shelter in a darkened bistro in winter.

Wander across the Seine and enjoy the Ile-de-la-Cité and the Ile Saint-Louis — these, too, seem to have the same air of 'grave harmony' that Gerard de Nerval found so remarkable about the place des Vosges. Remember to visit the place Dauphine, just off the Pont Neuf: quiet and secluded, it is a perfect place to rest.

The flower market in the place Louis-Lépine is a joy to visit and on Sundays it is transformed into a bird market. Anglo-Saxon birdlovers sometimes find it distressing but it has become a traditional part of the Sunday scene. On a sunny day browse amongst the *bouquinistes* (they are mainly gathered along the Left Bank of the Seine), buy an icecream at Berthillon, and if you become so thirsty that you think longingly of a proper pint of beer you could always rest your feet in the Brasserie de l'Ile Saint-Louis, just beside the Pont Saint-Louis, and drink to the day with a few millilitres of good Alsatian beer.

CONTENTS

* Strictly speaking not all shops but also places to rest the feet, restore the spirits and engage the mind.

ART, MUSIC AND ANTIQUES

FASHION

FOOD

HOUSEHOLD

SELF-INDULGENT SHOPS

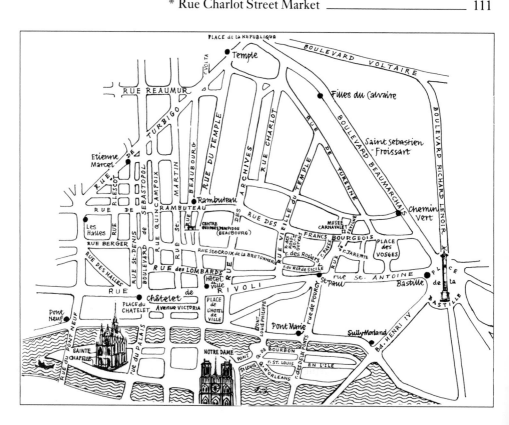

ART, MUSIC AND ANTIQUES

BLONDEL

4 rue Aubry-le-Boucher, 4e.
METRO: Châtelet.

An art gallery that all those interested in the contemporary scene should try to take in. It specialises in up-to-the-minute work by 20th-century artists.

OLDIES BUT GOODIES

16 rue du Bourg-Tribourg, 4e.
METRO: Hôtel de Ville.

If you're nostalgic for the music of the 50s, as well as a fan of rhythm, soul or blues, then hurry along to Oldies But Goodies, where you'll hardly be able to contain your excitement at the choice before you. Lots to be nostalgic over.

CASTA-DIVA

58 rue Vieille-du-Temple, 3e.
METRO: Saint-Paul.

If you're suddenly struck with a longing for music, Claude Vacherot will oblige, at most hours of the week. Open every day, Saturdays and Sundays included, from 10.30am until 8.30pm, here you can buy records of almost every opera ever recorded, and books and magazines on an operatic or balletic note to whet the appetite even further.

ARTIS FLORA

75 rue Vieille-du-Temple, 3e.
METRO: Saint-Paul.

39 rue du Paradis, 10e.
METRO: Château d'Eau, Poissonnière.

This is the shop for those interested in reproduction tapestries and tiles. The tapestries are made individually by hand from a selection of about thirty designs taken from famous medieval and renaissance French tapestries, by a sophisticated method of silkscreen printing. The chosen design is transferred in colours which are guaranteed against fading, onto a fabric woven from a mixture of wool, flax and cotton, thus achieving quite an authentic colouring and texture. The tiles can be bought singly, or mounted to form a picture. Again, many of the workshop's standard designs are taken from old French tilework. These are then transferred to the tiles themselves by a method of screen printing. You can also commission an exclusive design to be hand-painted directly onto the tiles themelves. The beautifully produced catalogue carries full details of prices, ordering, and manufacture, and you can inspect samples of their work in their display room here.

ARTS CATALOGUES LIBRAIRIE

76 rue Vieille-du-Temple, 3e.
METRO: Saint Sébastien-Froissart, Saint-Paul.

A specialist in lavishly produced art books, scholarly monographs, and exhibition catalogues.

SORTILEGES

9 rue des Francs-Bourgeois, 4e.

Sortilèges is presided over by a rather fierce woman who isn't too keen on you touching any of her small antiques. Since the space is crammed with tempting objects, from jewellery and

METRO: Saint-Paul,
Chemin Vert.

small picture frames to good quality clothes of the twenties and later, this is a pity. However, a sharp eye could pick up something to take home.

CARNAVALETTE

21 rue des Francs-
Bourgeois, 4e.
METRO: Saint-Paul.

Just on the edge of the place des Vosges, Carnavalette has a large selection of old original and reproduction prints and engravings; old books, some of antiquarian quality; old magazines, posters, and even some antique toys.

CENTRE CULTUREL DU MARAIS 28 rue des Francs-Bourgeois, 4e.

METRO: Saint-Paul.

Not only can you find out about the area here, but you can also buy old exhibition catalogues, a selection of good art books, and some excellent postcards. They also sell individual illustrations from old catalogues; these come in many different sizes and offer a higher quality of reproduction than the average postcard — some are large enough to frame. At the back there is a *salon de thé* serving interesting *salades*, savoury tarts, and blinis.

A L'IMAGE DU GRENIER SUR L'EAU

45 rue des Francs-
Bourgeois, 4e.
METRO: Saint-Paul.

This shop deals in turn-of-the-century designs on paper. Among the postcards, prints, and posters can be found 1900s scent-bottle labels, sweet-box images, and a few antiquarian books, particularly of local interest.

ECART INTERNATIONAL

6 rue Pavée, 4e.
METRO: Saint-Paul.

Andrée Putman is France's most famous interior designer. Renowned for her exquisite taste and for dressing in nothing but black and white, she has become a cult figure, synonymous with chic. Ecart International is her own shop, selling modern originals by people like Sacha Ketoff, Eileen Gray (the British designer who lived most of her life in France), and Mariano Fortuny, as well as 1930s *re-editions*. A must for those anxious to know whether Paris really has a modern design movement.

GLORIA D'HIER

15 rue Saint-Paul, 4e.
METRO: Saint-Paul.

Just one of the many enchanting little antique shops that form part of the Village Saint-Paul complex, Gloria specialises in attractive objects of the 19th century. Look to her for a mirror that will brighten up a sitting-room, voluptuous pewter (looking exceedingly unlike its British relations) shaped into sumptuous jugs which would give a lift to any dining-table,

chandeliers, candlesticks, pictures — all the quirky, one-off delights that give character and atmosphere to a room.

LES BAINS 7 rue du Bourg-l'Abbe, 3e.
METRO: Etienne Marcel.

One of the hottest nightspots in Paris. It's a club, so you need to make friends with a member, but angle an invitation if you can. Here, where there used to be a public bathing house, is now the meeting-place of the young and *branché*, the chic and the successful. Good place for celebrity-spotting. Watch out for theme nights.

FASHION

AS-ECO 11 rue Brantome, 3e.

METRO: Rambuteau.

Insomniacs or others with insatiable nocturnal urges for chocolates, records, books, peaches, new furniture *et al* might like to know that there is a store that caters for their needs — the AS-ECO. This is hidden away beneath a housing complex and unless you'd heard of it you'd never know it existed. It's open continuously from 9am on Monday to 11pm on Saturday night. This, of course, means that from late Saturday night to Monday morning, you'll have to rely on the drugstores for any urgent needs.

MADEMOISELLE-SANS-GENE

79 rue Vieille-du-Temple, 3e.
METRO: Saint-Sébastien Froissart; Saint-Paul.

The pillared and painted façade proclaims what the proprietor is proud to repeat: that this is a listed building in the style of the directory. As if to outface the aristocratic buildings, the window displays an unblushing array of delicate negligées and fine corsetry.

AZZEDINE ALAIA

17 rue de Parc Royal, 3e.
METRO: Chemin Vert.

The hottest new name in the fashion business for years. This small, slim son of a Tunisian farm labourer can scarcely put a foot wrong as far as the fashion press and his eminent clients are concerned (said to include such luminaries as Andrée Putman, Paloma Picasso, Grace Jones and Tina Turner). Ever since six British fashion editors were spotted at a Paris party during Collection time wearing the identical Alaia dress, it has been hard to avoid evidence of the Alaia influence. What really inspires him, he is reported as saying, is a good body, so it is no surprise to find that he is currently going for the body-clinging, slinky, distinctly seductive look. Whilst his clothes certainly aren't meant for the overweight, they are more flattering than they sound — he has a way with scissors and fabric that ensures a steady stream of customers. Hallmarks to look out for are raised seams, structured knits and lots of sculpted leather. His new premises may seem a little intimidating — you have to ring the doorbell to be let in — but the people who work for him are charming. It is just that his many famous clients need to be able to try on and undress in private, hence the new address. If you'd rather check out if he is your style in less daunting surroundings, go to the Galeries Lafayette which always has a good selection of his latest look.

LOLITA LEMPICKA

3 bis rue des Rosiers, 4e.
METRO: Saint-Paul.

A rising star in the world of ready-to-wear. If you have a figure worth showing off, Lolita Lempicka's soft, sexy, shapely knits well help you do it wonderfully. She goes in for invigorating colours: lots of bright pink, orange and yellow.

POPY MORENI

13 place des Vosges, 4e.
METRO: Chemin Vert.

Here, in one of the most beautiful and historic sites in Paris, Popy Moreni sells her far from classical styles. She is a bright new star in the fashion firmament producing original designs with an intensely alluring sophistication. They can be simple, almost minimalist, or extravagant and electrically coloured. A designer to watch.

LE GRAIN DE SABLE

79 rue Saint-Louis-en-l'Ile, 4e.
METRO: Pont-Marie.

Can't find the necklace of your choice in the shops? Then make your own. At Le Grain de Sable you'll find beads of almost every conceivable sort: metal, glass, pearlised, brilliant coloured plastic, wooden, ceramic — you name it, they have it. Having chosen your beads, you then pick some cord and a clasp, and off you go with a little occupational therapy in store and a necklace (or bracelet, why not?) for a fraction of the price of a store-bought version.

FOOD

PILCHI POI

7 rue Caron, 4e.
METRO: Saint-Paul.

This is, quite simply, one of the best Jewish food shops and delicatessens in Paris. In the rue des Rosiers itself at number 4, you can enjoy the best Turkish baths at the Hammam Saint-Paul, while at number 20, Jacques Coutellerie sells a wonderful variety of gleaming knives.

ALAIN COLLET

63 rue Saint-Antoine, 4e.
METRO: Bastille, Saint-Paul.

This is one of those shops for which France, and particularly Paris, is known and loved, but that are increasingly difficult to find. Specialising in Lyonnaise products, its long counter spreads in profusion a fine choice of *charcuterie* and ready-made dishes. At Christmas this end of the *quartier* is particularly brilliant, with fruit and vegetables of all varieties glowing in the dark; windows bright with pâtés, cheeses, quiches and quails; and the wet-fish shops, their cold grey marble slabs setting off the jewelled skin and pink shells of the seafood.

DELHOMME PATISSERIE

30 rue du Roi-de-Sicile, 4e.
METRO: Saint-Paul.

Here you will find French country cooking at its most consoling: luxurious apple pies, rich fruit puddings, custardy flans, and creamy quiches.

SPEGAL KLAPISCH

1 rue des Hospitalières-
Saint-Gervais, 4e.
METRO: Saint-Paul.

BOUCHERIE CHABAT

2 rue des Hospitalières-
Saint-Gervais, 4e.
METRO: Saint-Paul.

Here, Monsieur Bobo sells smoked salmon at wholesale prices direct to the public. All the fish is line-fished, and very fresh. The sides of smoked salmon are especially good value.

In this exotic bakery-cum-delicatessen you can find almost every variety of nut, oil, dried fruit, spice, herb, condiment and alcohol: are all distinguished and displayed with Linnaean precision. They also sell Turkish and Greek sweetmeats, and various made-up hot savoury dishes. Out of the window at the side (at lunch time follow the queue) you can buy blinis, pirojkis, falafels, and pitta bread stuffed with hummous or tahini.

MUSEE CARNAVALET 23 rue de Sévigné, 3e.

METRO: Saint-Paul.

Open 10am to 5.40pm. Closed Monday.
Entry free on Sundays.

This fascinating museum is given over to the history of Paris. Charming old tradesmen's signs, paintings, sculpture, furniture and decoration are all on view. There's a fairly grisly section on the Revolution, where you can actually see how a guillotine really worked, and a host of other touching mementoes. The house itself was once lived in by Mme. de Sévigné, and an aura of her charm lingers on.

LES JOUBLINIERES

75 rue Vieille-du-Temple,
3e.
METRO: Saint-Paul, Hôtel de Ville.

This is a shop for the serious gourmet. Out of cardboard boxes from all over France come fine wines, spirits, liqueurs, and champagnes; thick green olive oils; walnut, hazelnut and almond oils; smooth and speckled mustards of different varieties. The character of the shop, however, is created by the beautiful tins lining the shelves, austerely designed in black or grey and gold. These contain such exotica from the Langue d'Oc as *cassoulet*, duck and goose liver *confits*, and quails *en gelée*.

L'AFRUITDISIQUE 3 Rue du Bourg Tibourg, 4e.

METRO: Hôtel de Ville.

After admiring the classical architectural beauties of the Marais, the body may need a little refreshment. Try L'Afruitdisique — its freshly-squeezed fruit juices are better than its puns.

HOUSEHOLD

ART DEPOT

3 rue du Pont Louise-
Philippe, 4e.
METRO: Pont-Marie.

A haven for the browser in search of the idiosyncratic one-off
to enliven house and garden, charming small items that make
lovely presents, ranging from old toys and gadgets to rare and
beautiful pieces of Art Deco furniture. No matter how much
or how little you have to spend, you needn't be shy of
wandering round — the owners are browsers themselves and
well understand the serendipity spirit. Eclectic at heart, but all
the more beguiling for that.

AU FRANC PINTO 1 quai de Bourbon, 4e.

METRO: Pont-Marie.

This marvellously old bar-cum-restaurant is well worth a visit.
Upstairs is the bar, quieter and much less of a sartorial parade
than its pushier, later rivals; downstairs is a proper restaurant
serving elegant, sophisticated food. Take your pick — sip a
fine wine at the *comptoir*, order a plate of *saucisson* or *charcuterie*
to provide a little ballast, or enjoy a proper meal and take in
the atmosphere of the bloody past (a plot against Robespierre
was said to have been concocted here).

BRASSERIE DE L'ILE-SAINT-LOUIS 5 quai
de Bourbon, 4e.

METRO: Pont-Marie.

There are few more tranquil and charming parts of Paris to
wander around than the Ile-Saint-Louis, and when the feet
begin to flag or the rain begins to fall make for this old-
fashioned brasserie. There's nothing startling or particularly
new about it — it's just a reassuring, familiar, truly French
brasserie, specialising in those comforting Alsatian dishes that
really do warm the parts that other foods can't reach.

CONCIERGERIE 1 quai de l'Horloge, 4e.

METRO: Pont-Neuf.

Open 10am to 5.25pm every day except Tuesday.

Here history really comes alive. The French Revolution and
its attendant terrors seem only too real. Here is the little cell
where Marie Antoinette awaited her death; there the cells of
Danton and Robespierre — you can almost hear the tumbrils
roll.

BERTHILLON 31 rue Saint-Louis-en-l'Ile, 4e.

METRO: Pont-Marie.

Don't be put off by the queues — you wouldn't want to eat icecream that nobody else wanted, would you? Queuing is part of the Berthillon mystique and even in the coldest weather there they are, patiently waiting in line as if, good heavens, they were British! British Berthillon is not: it serves the best icecream in Paris (some say in the world) and is decidedly French and unaccommodating in always closing down for the whole of August, and most of the school holidays. There are at least thirty different flavours on offer, from dark bitter chocolate to passion fruit; from Elysian concoctions of honey and nuts to sorbets redolent of summer days. If you can't face the queues, nip round the corner to Le Flore en l'Ile, 42 quai d'Orléans or to the Restaurant Cadmios, 17 rue des Deux-Ponts, both of which sell Berthillon icecream and sorbets.

CHACTEALOP 6 rue de Jarente, 4e.

METRO: Saint-Paul.

Neither a proper restaurant nor yet an art gallery, this charming and restful haven is a place to remember for those moments when your feet can take you no further. Be soothed by the classical piano music and restore your strength with any one of the delicious little snacks on offer all through the day from midday to 10pm. The menu is a marvellous cultural mish-mash, with bacon and eggs nestling side by side on the menu with smoked salmon and caviar. Should be something there for all palates. Whilst the body is being restored with tempting little dishes, solace for the spirit is provided by the ever changing pictures that hang upon the walls.

JEAN LA PIERRE

58 rue Vieille-du-Temple, 3e.
METRO: Saint-Paul.

Not for the average tourist, who can hardly take an ancient chimney piece home in his suitcase; however, if you should need a hundredweight of historic masonry to prop up your home, this is the place for you. Much of it comes from Macon, nearly all of it is authentically old and suitably *historique*, and if you did happen to need a surround for your fireplace you'd certainly find a wonderfully distinguished one here. The roomful of awkward stone structures certainly presents an interesting sight from the road.

L'ARLEQUIN

13 rue des Francs-Bourgeois, 4e.
METRO: Saint-Paul, Chemin Vert.

If a silver cakestand from Jean-Pierre de Castro nearby might overpower your patisseries, you could buy one here in delicate cut-glass. While specialising in old glasses and glassware from different styles and periods, the shop also has a good display of modern engraved and painted glass: a shop as much for the collector as the merely appreciative.

S.M.A.R.T.

22 rue des Francs-
Bourgeois, 4e.
METRO: Saint-Paul.

The window display startles you out of any prejudice that, once past the soap and towels, baths could be boring. Under the consciously witty banner S.M.A.R.T., the shop is an outlet for new designs in tiles and ceramics, catching the eye with a wild variety of basins, sinks, baths, showers, and tile displays.

AUX BAINS-PLUS

51 rue des Francs-
Bourgeois, 4e.
METRO: Rambuteau, Saint-
Paul.

The name Aux Bains-Plus catches the wit of the idea. Although the main theme of the shop is the bathroom, it is the *plus* that makes it such a delight. Here you can find soap and towels, flannels, spongebags and sponges, toothbrushes and bathrobes. Not only do they come in every shape, colour and size, but they are also all of *la qualité grand-mère*. Here you can find the most luxurious cotton bathtowels, the most outrageous boxer shorts, the subtlest-scented soaps and lotions. And there is more: a back room opens out to display soft brushed-cotton pyjamas, striped with gentlemanly discretion; dressing gowns of various weights and textures, from a winter envelopment to light silk; while for the day there is a range of traditional shirts designed by *coup de coeur*. A shop for the Adonis in your life.

LE DOMARAIS 53 bis, rue des Francs-Bourgeois, 4e.
METRO: Saint-Paul, Rambuteau.

This is the sort of restaurant it would be hard to discover on your own. Tucked away in a little courtyard (though to be sure there is a sign in the street outside) this used to be a jewellery auction house, which accounts for the circular gallery (to keep the buyers separated from the valuables). The great glass octagon dome lets in a lovely light and besides the attractive atmosphere the food is delicious, too. A good place to rest the feet after wandering around the Marais.

SELF-INDULGENT SHOPS

LEFAX

32 rue des Francs-
Bourgeois, 4e.
METRO: Saint-Paul,
Rambuteau.

A tiny, new boutique purveying one of those loose-leaf information systems: part diary, part address book and part organiser. New to the French, though already embraced by Yuppies from New York to London, Lefax will shortly be the first to offer information sheets and maps in French.

HOTEL DE LA PLACE DE VOSGES 12 rue de Birague, 4e.

METRO: Saint-Paul, Bastille.

If you've had your fill of big hotels or you're not in that financial league, try the Hôtel de la place des Vosges. Very small (just 16 rooms) so you can't be sure of getting a room unless you book early, it is just besides the beautiful place des Vosges and I can hardly think of a lovelier place in all Paris to be close to. It also puts you right in the heart of one of the most interesting of all the *quartiers*. As old as Richelieu, the Hôtel de la place des Vosges is one of those small gems you can still find in the heart of Paris.

CARAMBOL

20 rue des Francs-Bourgeois, 4e.
METRO: Saint-Paul, Chemin Vert.

Jeux curiosités et autres objets indispensables is how Carambol sees itself. It caters for those moments when, as a flight is delayed or the car breaks down, hand and mind scream imperiously for diversion. Squabbling children in the back seat can be soothed into silence by one of their ingenious puzzles in two and three dimensions, or buy a set of travel scrabble (in French) or pocket chess. Carambol doesn't just cater for emergencies: the hand-carved tops and chess and solitaire sets, the marbles and wooden jigsaw puzzles are quite simply beautiful as objects — dispensable but lasting pleasures.

A LA BOULE ROUGE

42 rue Saint-Croix-de-la-Bretonnerie, 4e.
METRO: Hôtel de Ville, Saint-Paul.

Emballage it says in large letters and *emballage* it offers. With your bags full of shopping, it is nice to know that here you can buy paper, ribbon, sellotape, boxes and packagings for the most awkward present.

GOURMET'S 26 place Dauphine, 1er.

METRO: Pont Neuf.

Noon to 12.30am every day except Monday.

A rather luxurious version of the winebar is beginning to sprout all over Paris. The selection of wines available by the glass is long and interesting, ranging from a fine, sweet Sauterne to go with the excellent desserts or a beautiful, white Burgundy to accompany the smoked salmon or Gravadlax. The food here is rather more exotic than that normally found in wine bars and includes caviar and blinis, and *foie gras*, but it makes a comforting rest after a wander around the Ile-de-la-Cité.

LE SORBIER

70 rue Vieille-du-Temple, 4e.
METRO: Saint-Paul.

A little white cave of a shop filled with dried flowers. They hang from the ceiling in great profusion, they sprout in vases and in baskets on the floor — wherever you look there are yet more desirable bunches. They'd make a lovely present for a Parisian hostess. You can buy something as modest as a packet of dried petals for pot pourri or perhaps a scented candle, or seek advice for something as grand as a complete display of dried flowers. The allure of scent is complemented by an adjoining room, linked by an open arch, which has an ever-changing exhibition linked to flowers and vegetables of hand-crafted and glazed bases, bowls and jars.

ANONYMAT

72 rue Vieille-du-Temple, 3e.
METRO: Saint-Paul.

Here, Guy Mouchet, who is happy to reminisce about his years spent running a shop in Walton Street, has just opened his own shop. The window as I passed was dominated by a duck-head coat-rack and inside was a bizarre collection of modern decorative items: bulb-lights, duck-shaped umbrellas, vivid lamp-shades and an eclectic mix of boldly coloured and fancifully designed objects.

LA CALINIERE

72 rue Vieille-du-Temple,
4e.
METRO: Saint-Paul.

This is delightfully chaotic. Among the larger pieces of antique furniture are cluttered piles of old bric à brac of deceptively high quality. This is a shop for the dedicated rummager. With a little patience you can find pieces of old lace; pen and cigarette holders; antique dolls; Art Deco lamps and lights; hats and gloves from the twenties; a variety of china, cutlery and old glasses; and on the day I was there, a beautiful silk-embroidered shawl. Possibly of most interest to the British is the selection of old pens: now collectors' items in Britain, the prices are going through the roof. Here you could still find a fine old Bakelite pen at a reasonable price.

RETROMANIE

81 rue Vieille-du-Temple,
3e.
METRO: Saint-Sébastien
Froissart, Saint-Paul.

This is a new specialist shop that could cater for the most *recherché* whim of the Art Deco fan. The window is crowded with gorgeous lamps of every shape and colour, but they also sell an intriguing variety of cuff-links, cigarette-holders and other period objects.

CAFE BRASSERIE LE SAINT-GERVAIS
96 rue Vieille-du-Temple, 3e.

METRO: Filles du Calvaire, Saint-Sébastien Froissart.

This is an excellent example of a typical brasserie. The gleaming bar with steel-legged stools and plateglass windows may put you off at first, but in the back room there are lots of small tables crowded at lunchtime with a mixture of regulars and passers-by. The chalked menu board offers a few regular standbys: a selection of *hors d'oeuvres*, a *potage*, a steak, large plates of *frites* or cold beef salad and a luxurious *salade composée*, into which you seem endlessly to dive without ever coming to an end. The main point of the café, however, is the daily selection of two main dishes, both a warming plateful of meat and vegetables, and the homemade *clafoutis* or special cheese to finish.

BICLOUNE

93 boulevard Beaumarchais, 3e.
METRO: Saint-Sébastien Froissart.

It has to be said that bicycles are hard to pack but such is the charm of this shop specialising in ancient bicycles of all sorts (Bicloune is argot for *bicyclette*) that anybody passing through the district should pay it a visit. There are bicycles from all ages, authentically restored: some painted, some newly returned after being lent to film or television studios. Ordinary mortals can look and buy as well.

GALERIE DES ILES

8 rue Charlot, 3e.
METRO: Saint-Sébastien Froissart.

Reluctant landlubbers who dream of happier days at sea can escape into a maritime reverie by browsing amongst the 101 artefacts all devoted to the sea at this charming shop. Choose from the beautiful, handmade wooden model boats of your dreams, scaled down in size and worthy of a place in a museum. The shop sells miniature copies of great historic boats as well as a whole gallery of sea pictures and maritime instruments as varied as an hour-glass and a sextant.

RUE CHARLOT STREET MARKET
METRO: Saint-Sébastien Froissart.

Don't miss the little market between rue Charlot and rue de Bretagne if you're shopping in the area. A true little *marché du quartier*, it is patronised by the people who live nearby — here they buy their flowers, their fish, their great big tomatoes from Provence, the tiny golden apricots and the fresh basil when it comes into season; here they haggle over the size and quality of the *gigot* and pay a fraction of the prices in the better-known markets.

THE SIXTEENTH ARRONDISSEMENT
(BON CHIC, BON GENRE)

The 16th *arrondissement* is unique among the shopping districts covered by this guide. Off the usual tourist beat, lacking in obvious guidebook charm, short on quaint alleyways and olde-worlde cobbled yards, this is a residential district *par excellence*. Here is where the prosperous and the well-heeled live out their lives, proud to exchange at cocktail parties and private dinners the cards that proclaim their membership of a fairly exclusive club. This is the *haut-lieu de bécébégisme*, the stamping ground of the Parisian equivalent of our own Sloane Rangers, the members of the clan known as BCBG (*bon chic, bon genre*). If ever you were in doubt as to what it really means to be BCBG, a couple of hours spent wandering round this tranquil, spacious, prosperous part of Paris will soon give you an authentic feel.

See the younger members of the clan sipping their *chocolat* mid-morning or late afternoon at Carette in the place du Trocadéro; see them in their beautifully-cut grey skirts (or maybe their kilts from Marks & Spencer, very BCBG), their navy *pulls*; see the young men in their flannels or their 501s, with their *chemises* Lacoste, their Oxfords, their Shetland *pulls*, the Weston shoes, the Hermès scarves, the Burberrys and the Lodens. There they gather to plan the week's amusements, to see and be seen.

Though there are few tourist spots to visit, the ardent shopper may well find that it is a rewarding and agreeable place to *faire les courses*. Free from jostling tourists, it offers the delights of true neighbourhood shopping though of a rarified and elevated kind. Instead of competing with your fellow tourists for attention and some kind of service, you will find yourself accompanied by the prosperous citizens of the 16th going about their daily business and this in itself makes the 16th an attractive place to shop. Gathered here in this prosperous *quartier* are some of the best, if not the most quirky, shops in the whole of Paris. Many of the big establishment names (like Céline and Weston, Daniel Hechter and Renoma, La Bagagerie and The Scotch House, Per Spook and Torrente) have boutiques to catch the eye of M. and Mme. BCBG as they go about their daily round.

Wander down the rue de Passy, the rue de la Pompe, the rue de la Tour and the avenue Victor-Hugo. Not strictly in the 16th but within a stone's throw is that current cult-shop, Hemisphères at 22 avenue de la Grande-Armée, so make sure to look in on it — the beguiling mixture of old and new, French, English and American, all guided by a sure taste and eye make it almost unique in Paris. There is a smaller version in the 16th itself, at 1 boulevard Emile-Augier to be precise, and there you can spend more than you probably care to on some of the most beautiful shoes in Paris.

Because it is such a prosperous *arrondissement* (the famous avenue Foch is within its catchment area) it is, of course, one of the most fruitful areas of all to comb the secondhand shops

— it's not for nothing that the mini empire of Reciproque, all based on secondhand clothing, flourishes here in the rue de la Pompe.

As you take in the air of quiet prosperity and the calm and graceful apartment blocks, there is little to see in the way of grand sights, but don't miss the rue Raynouard where Jean-Jacques Rousseau, Benjamin Franklin and Honoré de Balzac used to live. Take in the Balzac museum (at no. 47) and see the back entrance where he used to slip away when his creditors arrived.

Wander on to the Musée Marmottan — much enriched in recent times with a grand gift of some splendid Monets — and, if the sun is shining, head for the Bois de Boulogne and admire the foresight of Napoleon and the Baron Haussmann in making sure that Parisians for generations to come would have somewhere to breathe in good fresh country air.

CONTENTS

* Strictly speaking not all shops but also places to rest the feet, restore the spirits and engage the mind.

FASHION: WOMEN

FASHION: MEN

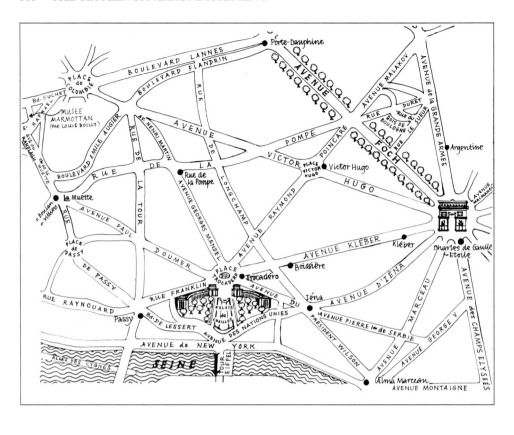

HOUSEHOLD

THE UNUSUAL GIFT

FASHION: WOMEN

LES NUITS D'ELODIE

1 bis, avenue Mac-Mahon, 17e.
METRO: Etoile.

Though you will find some delectable outfits for stepping out of an evening, the main reason for making your way to this elegant little Art Deco shop is for its voluptuous selection of nightwear. This is nightwear that most of us just dream about: langorous, sophisticated, made from the finest and the best. If you're a man and you want to take back to your nearest and dearest something a little special, look no further than Les Nuits d'Elodie — but not for skinflints.

HOTEL L'ETOILE MAILLOT 10 rue du Bois de Boulogne, 16e.

METRO: Argentine.

This not very well-known establishment, near to the Porte Maillot, offers some of the best hotel value in Paris. For the cost of a night in an average London hotel you can have a mini suite: bedroom, sitting-room and bathroom here. A wonderful bargain for those who need either to entertain in their hotel or to work. Also useful for those attending some of the many exhibitions held in the Porte Maillot. But if it's excitement and a sense of *vieux Paris* that you're after, go elsewhere.

RENOMA

129 bis, rue de la Pompe, 16e.
METRO: Victor-Hugo.

This is the sort of boutique that is perfectly adapted to serve the needs of the people living in its *quartier*, that is, it offers good quality clothes that are clearly up-to-the-minute but not so avant-garde as to cause a stir. They are well-behaved clothes — clothes for the business woman or for the wives of successful lawyers and doctors. Basic trousers and blazers, sweaters and blouses that look indisputably expensive but in a relaxed and unobtrusive way. Grown-up clothes for grown-up people. Renoma's men's clothes seem to me rather more exciting (see the section Something for Monsieur). The boutique has recently been completely revamped and now seems to glory in almost Egyptian splendour.

AGNES B

17 avenue Pierre-ler-de-Serbie, 16e.
METRO: Iéna; Alma Marceau.

The *très* chic inhabitants of this most desirable of Parisian *arrondissements* need not go all the way to Les Halles to find the understated elegance of Agnès B. Not the taste of every BCBG (after all, her clothes are so simple, their elegance so throw-away that not everybody will recognise quite what a sought-after label you are wearing) but those whose taste it is can now find this season's skirt, the essential jacket or the useful shirt on their very own doorstep.

BAR DU THEATRE 4 avenue Montaigne, 8e.

METRO: Alma Marceau.

If you don't mind a little trek to the 8e just close by, the Bar du Théâtre is a chic stopping-off place for a light meal, drink or snack at any time of day. Good to know about, too, either before or after a night at the theatre, as it stays open late. During the haute couture collections, this is the place where the fashion crowd rest their feet and catch up on the chat.

JAMIN 32 rue de Longchamp, 16e. (Tel. 47.27.12.27.)

METRO: Iéna, Trocadéro.

Closed Saturday, Sunday and the whole of July.

While Lucas-Carton, Taillevent and le Tour d'Argent grab most of the headlines, those in the know say that Joel Robuchon's Jamin is one of the best restaurants in the whole of France. His art, it seems, is to offer creative, inventive dishes that are never bizarre: to offer luxury without excess and to combine only the freshest of ingredients in new, inventive ways. Don't miss it. Patricia Wells, restaurant critic of the *International Herald Tribune* and author of *A Food-Lover's Guide to Paris*, describes his fixed-price menu (on offer at both lunch and dinner) as one of the city's gastronomic bargains.

LES FOLIES D'ELODIE

56 avenue Paul-Doumer, 16e.
METRO: Passy.

Just as Les Nuits d'Elodie concentrates on sumptuous wear for voluptuous nights, so Les Folies d'Elodie (the boutiques are run by two sisters) brings the same soft, caressing approach to daywear. Luxurious fabrics, beautifully cut, wrap the body in comfort and elegance. All highly sophisticated and much sought-after by stars of stage and screen — who may perhaps be the only ones who can afford the prices.

MEREDITH

14 rue de Passy, 16e.
METRO: Passy.

Not a cheap place to shop but a boutique where the salesgirls are adept saleswomen, that is, they can show you exactly how to make the best of everything on sale. If you display the slightest interest in a garment they will immediately go to the racks and pull out the very shirt, skirt or belt that will make it work. So if you are really out to buy, at Meredith you will come away with something classy, elegant and fashionable. Although it won't be cheap it won't come with the sort of price tag that the smart Japanese designers are currently charging. All in all a good address for those wanting a little something with an air of Paris about it.

GERARD MABE

37 rue de Passy, 16e.
METRO: Passy.

Gérard Mabe specialises almost exclusively in pullovers and shirts, all beautifully organised by colour. There are racks of T-shirts, polo-shirts and sweaters, almost all M. Mabe's own *marque*, though there is some Fred Perry as well. So if what you're looking for is a T-shirt or a polo in some obscure or even classic colour and you can't find it elsewhere, M. Mabe is almost certain to be able to help. And as if that weren't enough, he also has some exquisite hand-knitted sweaters — though at less exquisite prices.

NADINE SIMPSON

52 rue de Passy, 16e.
METRO: Passy.

If you're wandering in the area and don't fancy a trip to the main department stores, Nadine Simpson is stuffed with big designer names: look here for some of the most modish Italians such as Complice and Ginochietti, as well as some of the darlings of French ready-to-wear like Byblos, Claude Montana and Azzedine Alaïa. If you really want a new outfit you would be sure of finding something to your taste in this buzzing emporium.

BENETTON

75 rue de Passy, 16e.
METRO: Muette.

Here is one of the centres of the BCBG cult: *pulls* from Benetton are the mainstay of many an apprentice BCBG wardrobe and this branch is perhaps the most patronised of them all.

DEB'S

83 rue de Passy, 16e.
METRO: Muette.

Dresses, dresses, dresses — all with just the sort of look that *Maman* would love.

AGATHA

8 rue de la Pompe, 16e.
METRO: Muette.

If you've ever wanted the sort of jewellery that you see staring out from the fashion pages of *Elle*, you need look no further — Agatha will sell it to you. Agatha specialises in the very latest jewellery: whatever today's fad is for, you will find it here. Lots of *bijoux fantaisies*, lots of panache and *élan*. Dotty little numbers to put in your hair, silk flowers to put wherever you like, some very chic ivory bits and pieces and a big display of turquoise for those who want a little colour. Costume jewellery from the pages of *Elle* doesn't come cheap — and neither does it here.

ANASTASIA

65 rue de Boulainvilliers, 16e.
METRO: Muette

18 rue de l'Ancienne-Comédie, 6e.
METRO: Odéon.

These two little boutiques are highly successful, particularly with the young, and it's not difficult to see why. They have an air of happy, colourful, *joie-de-vivre* which contrasts quite strongly with the monochrome chic of most of the new arrivals in the rue Etienne-Marcel. Chic seems much less on the mind of Anastasia than charm and prettiness — bright floral dungarees (some enchanting mini versions for children) and soft crêpe-de-chine dresses in the colours that people used to wear for going out to tea (soft yellows, pinks and blues). If that sounds old-fashioned, it isn't meant to — the look is authentically 1980s, with its long-line skirts, its long, long cardigans and soft, silky *chemisiers*. But it is a colourful island in a sea of black, white and grey — no wonder it is usually thronged with young girls happily putting together a new outfit for their next big date.

CYRILLUS

8 rue Chanez, 16e.
METRO: Auteuil.

Another of the really establishment shops that flourish in the 16th. This one is for children, and at prices that will not give Papa too many headaches. Here are immaculate jackets and skirts, trousers and blouses; here petite Isabelle can rest assured that all is in perfect *goût*.

FASHION: MEN

AU PETIT MATELOT

27 avenue de la Grande-Armée, 16e.
METRO: Argentine, Etoile.

Another of those curiously trendy boutiques that somehow seem to have attracted the attentions of a fashionable crowd. But besides being fashionable Au Petit Matelot also sells immaculate gear for the yacht you may be about to visit or for simply ambling down *la plage*. Serious sailors will find much to please, as will those whose idea of marine pastimes is a good bowl of *bouillabaisse*.

VETEMENTS TROPICAUX

30 avenue de la Grande-Armée, 16e.
METRO: Argentine, Etoile.

This shop, and its sister one in the boulevard Saint-Germain, specialises in clothing for *les pays chauds, safaris et croisières* and very well it specialises, too. Besides some dramatically authentic topees and bush hats (exactly what you need for safaris and jolly hard to find they are, too) there is lots of other clothing, reminiscent of France's brush with tropical Africa. They sell good khaki-coloured clothing for the bush, for both men and women. Besides the safari shorts and jackets, dresses and skirts, there is a good selection of light and easy summer clothing, of which the collection for men seemed more desirable than that for women.

PARALLAX

39 rue de Passy, 16e.
METRO: Passy.

Another of those shops that reminds one of how much better the French know how to dress their men in summer, here you could buy some hot-weather gear that is neither too fancy or outlandish nor yet too dull. Go for a very wearable and elegant navy cotton jacket with a red lining or some beautifully-cut denims, or choose the pale pink sneakers for a nice insouciant touch.

HOUSEHOLD

PENELOPE

19 avenue Victor-Hugo, 16e.
METRO: Etoile, Victor-Hugo.

Those who love the Porthault quality but can't afford the prices should take a look at what Penelope has to offer. A tiny shop, tucked away at the back of a courtyard, Penelope produces some beautiful tablecloths and placemats, all made by a loyal co-operative of craftspeople working from home. There are relatively plain special cotton-blend cloths at reasonable prices or there are the special designs with hand-embroidered or hand-painted motifs that would cost a great deal more. A service to remember, however, is that Penelope will make up a cloth to match your own dinner service — take along a piece of china and Penelope will create something specially for you.

SORRENTE

49 avenue Raymond-Poincaré, 16e.
METRO:Victor-Hugo.

All the accessories to pander to the Parisian's urge to pretend he's *à la campagne* or *à la mer*, when in fact he is well ensconced in his oh-so-urban apartment. Here you will find the deckchairs, the parasols, the rustic plates and wicker baskets that the *vie en plein air* requires. All very pretty. There's lots for the tourist too — all the small accessories that would bring a touch of southern sunniness to your very own patio or poolside terrain.

CARETTE 4 place du Trocadéro, 16e.

METRO: Trocadéro.

One of the haunts of the *jeunesse d'orée* of this most BCBG of Paris *quartiers*. But never mind, it has a beautiful terrace open to the sun (should there be any) and some of the best *chocolat* and the most delicious patisseries in Paris. Sip a freshly-squeezed orange juice, order a *pain au chocolat*, or even a *plat du jour* if your appetite is on form, and see the privileged world of the 16th go by.

PLACE DE PASSY 16e

If you're shopping here, in the heart of the fashionable 16th *arrondissement*, you'll need to take a rest at some stage. When the weather is fine put your feet up in the little haven half-way up the rue de Passy — *prends un thé* or perhaps *un café crème* at the Coquelin Aîné and watch the world go by. The world here is a mixture of the smart BCBG and those who seem to have been here since time began. When you've rested, take a walk down the little passage at the back — the rue de l'Annonciation — and go green with envy at all the wonders the local inhabitants can buy on their doorstep. Rows and rows of gleaming, shimmering fish, so many sorts that most of us wouldn't know what to do with them all. Gape at the bundles of asparagus, at La Ferme de Passy with its vast selection of cheeses, at the pyramids of fruits and vegetables, and, if you have time, take in the little covered market opposite the place de Passy.

CARRE BLANC

5 rue Franklin, 16e.
METRO: Passy.

LA BOUTIQUE NAIVE

89 rue de la Pompe, 16e.
METRO: Pompe.

L'HOMME AU PRESENT

20 rue Franklin, 16e.
METRO: Passy.

POUPEE TENDRESSE

4 rue Poussin, 16e.
METRO: M. A. Auteuil.

One of the best buys in Paris is household linen of every description — not because they are any cheaper than at home (very often they are much more expensive) but because in Paris you can find finer materials, finer workmanship and, above all, a style that is quite different from what we find back home. If you have hankered for a little something for the house and haven't been able to afford it, you should run along to Carré Blanc, where high quality linens are sold at relatively low prices. It specialises in ends of lines, and in designer linens without the labels, giant bathtowels in subtle colours, beautiful dressing-gowns and sheets, pillowcases and hand-towels in beautiful materials and designs.

THE UNUSUAL GIFT

All those who love the style of Grandma Moses — those artless rustic figures, the strokable cats and informal flowers — will love this shop. Full of innocent charm, the same happy air of insouciance surrounds the toys, the furniture and the pictures here. There are papier-mâché puppets, clocks, musical-boxes, china, pictures and lithographs all celebrating the simple, domestic scenes that remind one of less violent times. For those who live in Paris, it is worth noting that the shop can arrange to have furniture painted to order.

This is the place to go to if you or your man are out-and-out supporters of the chic matt black design movement. Every object on display here has clearly passed a rigorous aesthetic test. From the watches (by Porsche), pens (by Mont Blanc) and cigars (by Davidoff) to the black and grey interior, everything forms an aesthetic whole. The taste is almost exclusively modern, verging on the hi-tech and futuristic, but everything is of very high quality. If you go in for executive toys and electronic gadgetry, here you will find one of the most interesting selections in town.

Some of the most beautiful dolls in the world are to be found here, so beautiful that they really are more collectors' items than children's playthings. And besides the dolls themselves there is everything the well set-up doll requires: houses to live in, from château-style to plush new bungalows, complete with curtains, pictures and lights that really work. And once your doll has a house, well, a house needs furnishings, so there are handcrafted miniatures — everything from sofas and chairs to china dishes, dressing-gowns and slippers. An enchanted Lilliputian world.

PART 2

ANTIQUES AND FLEA MARKETS

Antique shopping isn't what it was. The whole world seems to have got streetwise. It would be lovely to have been able to say that I had found just the very shop, the little place where you'll never be ripped off and where bargains abound. Alas, if it exists I haven't found it. By and large the dealers seem to get up earlier, be more knowledgeable and get sharper-witted by the hour, and you'd have to be a very early bird indeed to beat them at their own game. Which isn't to say that there aren't lovely things to buy — there are indeed, ineffably lovely things, but you are unlikely to get them for anything less than their full market value.

The markets (and the antique and secondhand shops) vary from day to day and season to season. Some are full of cheap and shoddy secondhand clothing, junk and bric-à-brac; others full of wonders at prices beyond imagining. Keep your eyes peeled and you may find a jug that will be just the thing to set upon your dresser, a pretty antique lace cloth for your table or even a picture that pleases.

You never know, and therein lies the infinite lure of rummaging around antique shops. It's the thrill of the chase that matters. Today just may be your day. Lurking in the corner may be the one grubby old painting that nobody's paid much attention to and it may, just may, turn out to give you infinite pleasure for the rest of your life.

So, put on your walking shoes, tuck your wallet out of sight, clutch your handbag firmly and set off to wander round the antique markets. It's some of the best free entertainment there is — you'll probably come across more strange characters lingering round the stalls than you'd find in a Dickens novel. Not all of them are entirely savoury so keep your wits about you. Remember that prices are rarely much more than an opening gambit, and be prepared to look cool and disinterested if you really want something: you may be surprised at what you'll get it for. If you can pay cash, so much the better and remember to use that as a bargaining point. Don't spend a lot of money on something purporting to be real without either knowing what you're about or bringing an expert along to check it out for you.

Before you set off, however, it is worth taking note that there are two words you will come across frequently and it's as well to get them straight. *Antiquaire* or *Antiquités* refer to shops or objects of some intrinsic worth, the finer end of the business. *Brocanteur* or *Brocantes* refers to the junkier end, to men selling secondhand, less expensive goods (which doesn't meant to say that they aren't often a lot more fun).

Finally, if you're a serious buyer and want to go in for more than just a jolly wander round to see what gives, you might like to get hold of a copy of the *Guide Emer* which lists most of the reputable dealers in Paris. Get it from 50 rue de l'Hôtel-de-Ville, 4e.

HOTEL DROUOT 9 rue Drouot, 9e.

METRO: Le Peletier, Richelieu Drouot.

This is the Parisian equivalent of Sotheby's or Christie's, that is, it is a national institution and probably not the place for the new visitor to go looking for a little something to take back home. However, if you have a serious interest in antiques, or maybe just a non-serious interest in auctions, you might like to go along. It is open every day except Sundays (and, in that maddeningly contrary French way it is closed on Saturdays during the peak summer months of July, August and September) from 11am to 6pm. There are three floors with many different salerooms selling anything and everything from a priceless Renoir to a load of (frankly) old junk. Ask at the door for a copy of what's going on that day and wander round. Remember that if you buy, you'll have to pay anything between 10% and 18% there and then (depending on the price of the object). Also remember the strict French laws governing the exportation of works of art (however, you'll need to be buying something of serious merit before this will affect you). Almost every dealer and auctioneer is, necessarily, absolutely *au fait* with these regulations and will advise you on a given piece. If you're likely to be tempted remember that just as in London and New York, the professionals are bound to be there in force and you are unlikely to beat them on their own territory. Caution is the name of the game.

CONTENTS

* Strictly speaking not all shops but also places to rest the feet, restore the spirits and engage the mind.

COVERED MARKETS

Just as in London where antique markets such as Antiquarius and Gray's Market have grouped together antique dealers and sellers in attractive, accessible covered areas, so in Paris there are now several places where you can be sure of seeing numbers of different shops and stalls together. They are attractively organised and it is perhaps the best way to start, for by taking in several shops you will begin to get your eye in and see something of what is on offer. You are unlikely to uncover any great bargains but most of the dealers are fair and honourable and you will come upon some exceedingly attractive, even beautiful, things at the going market price. Many of them offer guarantees as to the date and condition, and if something should go wrong you are much more likely to get some kind of restitution than you would in any of the flea markets. Most of these groups of dealers have the same sort of days and hours as ordinary shops, that is, most are closed on Sundays and Mondays.

LA COUR AUX ANTIQUAIRES

54 rue du Faubourg Saint-Honoré, 8e.
METRO: Concorde.

Closed Sunday and Monday.

One of the smallest collections of antique shops, this one is also one of the smartest. Its charming little boutiques sell a wide variety of things old and precious: from Greek icons to porcelain, elaborate gilt candelabra to 18th-century paintings, Chinese ceramics to stuffed chaise-longues.

LE LOUVRE DES ANTIQUAIRES

2 place du Palais-Royal, 1er.
METRO: Palais-Royal.

Closed on Mondays.

No visitor who has any interest at all in French furniture, pictures, jewellery and other antiques should give this a miss — it's more educational than many a museum. A grand and beautiful arcade, with comfortable armchairs (and excellent loos) to rest the feet between whiles, it has some 250 different shops to tempt you. It is, in short, an antique lover's delight. Each shop has its own speciality and the range takes in marine pictures and instruments, decorative provincial furniture and rustic cooking utensils. There is china (*faience*) and jewellery, pictures and exquisite lamps. All is beautifully displayed so that browsing is a delight, and the prices do not seem unduly high when compared with London. Visitors, however, must bear in mind that there are strict laws governing the exporting of antiques and works of art. Make sure to explain that you wish to export before you buy — it is then up to the dealer to get you the correct permit. He should also be able to organise the packing, crating and transport, though of course you will have to pay extra. So before you get carried away by the beauty of, say, a large and baroque *armoire*, check out the extra costs involved.

If you need to ponder on a purchase, remember that the arcade's restaurant, Le Jardin du Louvre, is so well thought-of that many a Parisian goes there just to eat without an idea of buying a single antique.

VILLAGE SAINT-PAUL

off the rue Saint-Paul and the rue Charlemagne, 4e.
METRO: Saint-Paul.

Closed Tuesdays and Wednesdays.

An enchanting collection of antique shops, grouped in a higgledy-piggledy way round the old streets and courtyards with a marvellous selection of the inexpensive *brocantes* and the fine *antiquaire*. I can hardly think of a more charming way of spending a sunny Sunday morning that poking around in this little bit of old Paris. As yet uncrowded, lacking entirely the sometimes very disreputable air of the flea markets, this is a true rummager's delight. Discover pieces of fine old furniture, a simple antique cloth for your table, a weird and wonderful piece of wrought-iron for your garden or a candlestick of stunning simplicity. Search for just the right decorative chandelier to 'make' your dining-room or hunt for a piece of jewellery for an anniversary present. When you get tired, on sunny days sit out in the courtyard where they serve a simple lunch under parasols, or seek out one of the ethnic restaurants in the nearby sidestreets.

VILLAGE SUISSE

approach it from the avenue de La Motte-Picquet or the avenue de Suffren, 15e.
METRO: La Motte-Picquet, Grenelle.

Closed Tuesday and Wednesday.

Antique dealers everywhere did not go into the business because they liked regular hours, so a little patience is sometimes required. Here a group of totally independent dealers trade in the Village Suisse location: some open at 10am, some at 10.30am, some come in on a Sunday, some don't. However, bear with it all, for there are some exceedingly charming pieces to be seen and some exceedingly charming dealers to talk to. The style, on a summer Sunday morning, is laidback but all the more pleasant for that — none of the hectic patter that accompanies a trip to the flea markets. The overwhelming impression is of a pretty, decorative collection of the sort of furniture and paintings that many of us would like to furnish our homes with, and none of it seems over-priced. One of the extra services Village Suisse offers is that, for no extra charge, they will supply an expert to verify a piece that you seriously intend to buy.

OPEN-AIR ANTIQUE MARKETS

Wandering round the open-air antique markets is a time-honoured Parisian pastime and one that any tourist would be unwise to miss. It is, of course, infinitely more agreeable during the languid days of summer but there are always sights worth seeing, people worth encountering and the ever-

present hope of the bargain to be uncovered. So here, then, are just a few of the best-known open-air antique markets that you might want to take in.

MARCHE D'ALIGRE

place d'Aligre, 12e.
METRO: Ledru Rollin,
Gare de Lyon.

Open 9.30am to 1pm. Closed Monday.

A circular market close to the Bastille — find it by looking for the market Marché Beauvau. Not a place to expect to buy any serious antiques; more a rummager's delight. There's lots of bric-à-brac and lots of junk, but if you browse seriously you might just find the odd piece of jewellery or a postcard with real charm. There are always some stands with clothes: some secondhand, some newish and cheapish.

Round by the bric-à-brac stalls is a food market and here you can buy all the ingredients you might need for a summer's day picnic: fruit and cheeses, olives and great red tomatoes, breads and terrines. Or buy some flowers for your hostess-to-be at tonight's dinner.

PORTE DE CLIGNANCOURT/ SAINT-OUEN

18e.
METRO: Porte de Clignancourt.

Open dawn to 7.30pm, Saturday, Sunday and Monday.

You've already been warned that your chances of uncovering a rare masterpiece beneath some grubby-looking paint, or some finely-worked silver masquerading as a battered-looking candlestick, are next to nothing. At Porte de Clignancourt your chances are smallest of all. Paris' best-known and largest flea market has been picked over by dealers, tourists and housewives in search of a bargain for years. This doesn't mean, however, that it isn't fun or that you won't find some truly attractive or even beautiful things — it's just that if you do, the dealer will be even more aware than you are of their attractiveness and beauty, and you'll be charged accordingly.

Like most antique markets these days the Porte de Clignancourt consists of various parts. It starts off particularly dispiritingly for the tourist who arrives from the métro Porte de Clignancourt: he is greeted by cheerless rows of cheap and usually nasty newish clothing. But persevere, penetrate into the inner areas and you'll find the true flea market atmosphere.

Remember that the market covers some four miles altogether so you can't hope to do it all on one visit. Remember, too, that the earlier you get there the better, though I don't think you'll ever get there earlier than the sharp-eyed dealers who will almost certainly have already cleaned up the only bargains before you even arrive.

There are five main parts to the market, all crammed with little stalls and shops, each with a discernible personality of its own and somewhere in the great bustling, lively mass you'll find a dealer specialising in almost anything you care to name,

from old buttons to postcards, from fine French provincial furniture to baroque candelabra.

MARCHE VERNAISON sells mainly small collectibles like jewellery, toys, old buttons, old pens, lamps and boxes. A magpie's delight. MARCHE MALIK has some good old clothes (fans of the army surplus look need look no further) but also old records, accessories, glass and china. MARCHE BIRON is where you are most likely to find the more substantial and the classier items. It is the finest end of the market with lots of stalls dealing in genuine antiques. MARCHE PAUL BERT is the place for crystal, gilt, mirrors, bric-à-brac and the junkier buys, including some furniture. MARCHE JULES VALLES is possibly the most fun — it sells some furniture, books and curios and is perhaps the most likely place for you to find a little *objet trouvé* to take home as a memento.

PORTE DE MONTREUIL

20e.
METRO: Porte de Montreuil.

*Open 7am to 7.30pm,
Saturdays, Sundays and
Mondays.*

Less frequented by tourists than Clignancourt, this is a charming market to wander round. It is probably one of the best places to find the newly fashionable clothing of the 1930s, 40s and 50s, and if you fancy a leather jacket or a pair of fine leather shoes, you'll have more chance of finding it here than anywhere. There are also stalls dealing with furniture, with African art (keep your antennae finely tuned and be prepared to bargain), with *objets* of all sorts.

PORTE DE VANVES

avenue Marc Sangnier, 14e.
METRO: Porte de Vanves.

*Open 7am to 1pm, Saturdays
and Sundays.*

A charming and not very crowded market close to the Porte de Vanves. There is, however, little to be found of real value — it is more a haven for the hunters of bric-à-brac. On a cold wintry day it might not be worth the journey, but in fine weather what could be nicer than a gentle amble browsing amongst the stands? Some nice old books, in particular there were some really charming, old, children's books (in French *bien sûr*), also old linen, postcards, glass decanters, the odd piece of silver (or more likely, silver-plate) and some quite nice china.

Round the corner, and very easy to miss, is the grandest end of this market. In the avenue Georges-Lefenestre you'll find some small pieces of quite attractive furniture, little pieces of silver that would look good on any sideboard, some nice old china and maybe the odd chandelier.

ANTIQUE SHOPS

Hunting for antiques often becomes a lifetime's hobby and those who are addicted won't wish to give it a miss on a trip to Paris. The main fun lies in the search, the gentle amble down the streets and round the *quartier*, the ever-present hope of coming upon exactly what you're looking for, or, even more exciting, finding what you didn't even know you wanted until you saw it and knew you had to have it.

Paris is an antique-lover's dream. Because Paris is a small and compact city, it isn't too tiring a business and it is fairly easy to pin-point the areas that the dedicated antique-lover should head for. Wander round the Left Bank in the area bounded by the Quai Voltaire, the rue des Saints-Pères, the rue de l'Université and the rue du Bac — here you will find anything and everything from a great garden statue to tiny pictures and *objets* for the house. Wander down the rue Jacob (possibly my favourite street), the rue Bonaparte and the rue de Seine

(mainly full of art galleries and art bookstores but some antique shops as well). Don't forget, if old books, postcards or prints are your passion, that wandering along the quais (in particular the Quais Voltaire, de Louvre, des Grands-Augustins, Conti and Malaquais) on a fine summer's day is a time-honoured Parisian occupation.

The Ile-Saint-Louis and Ile-de-la-Cité are both always worth a visit: apart from being beautiful to wander round for themselves, both of them have some good little antique shops. Then there is a goodly cluster in the rue du Faubourg Saint-Honoré in the 8th *arrondissement*, and the Marais, that enchanting, newly up-and-coming district just over the bridge from the Ile-Saint-Louis, also deserves many hours of happy hunting.

A L'EPREUVE DU TEMPS

88 rue du Bac, 7e.
METRO: rue du Bac.

Founded in 1826 this small but charming shop, full of dusty-looking pieces, has some enchanting old silver at prices that really don't seem bad. Some wonderfully ornate old pieces, from serving spoons to salt and pepper cellars, from knives with highly-decorated handles to some sleek-looking photograph frames. Everything from a complete canteen to a single teaspoon.

ANTIQUITES

35 rue Charlot, 3e.
METRO: Filles de Calviaire.

Not worth a grand detour but if you're in the area, drop in on this little shop full of bric-à-brac — you just have to take pot-luck and see what has come in on the day. You may be lucky and chance upon a charming antique patchwork quilt, or a sweetly pretty Art Nouveau lamp. On the other hand, if it's not your day, it may be filled with eminently discountable bits of junk.

ARCANA

83 rue Vieille-du-Temple, 3e.
METRO: Saint-Paul.

Find here anything to do with the scribbler's art: antique pens and desk sets, old ink bottles and blotters, relics of old printing-days, little boxes for keeping stamps or small (very small) notes. Good present hunting ground.

L'ARLEQUIN

13 rue des Francs-Bourgeois, 4e.
METRO: Saint-Paul.

Another shop for those who love browsing amongst things old and dusty; L'Arlequin offers a vast selection of antique glassware. Here you can find a complete set (if you're lucky), or else have more fun and put together a mixed collection of glasses that take your fancy. Everything from simple tumblers to elaborate cut-glass. A jewel of a shop.

AU TEMPS RETROUVE

6 rue Vauvilliers, 1er.
METRO: Les Halles.

If you like your dining-tables to be redolent of gracious times, then this is the shop for you. Here you will find antique collections of porcelain (Limoges, Gien, Vieux Paris, etc), as well as teasets, old glasses (either sets or single ones), antique linen and cutlery — the whole panoply.

BROCANTE STORE

31 rue Jacob, 6e.
METRO: Saint-Germain-des-Prés.

Look here for something small and charming to take home: maybe a lamp, a ravishing piece of china or a finely-crafted box. Another of those shops that it's hard to categorise but that always seems to have a collection that charms the eye.

BRUGIDOU

17 rue de Grenelle, 7e.
METRO: Sèvres-Babylone.

Hard to pin down but a shop worth a look. Everything catches the eye by virtue of its charm, and though the furniture is usually a little large to pack up (a pity, the owner has an impeccable eye for the decorative piece) there are usually lots of small delights as well.

LE CABINET DE CURIOSITE

23 rue de Beaune, 7e.
METRO: rue du Bac.

A charming shop to rummage round in. Everything is exquisite, if not necessarily rare. An eclectic collection of scientific instruments, old games and toys, old tools, pieces of treen — you never know what you'll find but it's nearly always worth a look.

LE CHEMIN DE TABLE

10 rue de Grenelle, 7e.
METRO: rue du Bac.

Anything and everything for the table: from fine old linen and glass, to china, silver and decanters; from the simplest glass to wonderfully rich and ornate candelabra. For the well-dressed table you need look no further.

GALERIE ANTIQUITES ET ART D'ASIE

4 avenue Bugeaud, 16e.
METRO: Porte Dauphine.

One of the most extraordinary and comprehensive collections of Asiatic art, ranging from relatively inexpensive Japanese Netsuke in ivory or wood to rare and almost priceless examples that could well end up in a museum. Lovers of Asiatic art should pay a visit — a rare and fascinating shop.

LA GALERIE MARIGNY

4 rue Miromesnil, 8e.
METRO: Miromesnil.

A good shop to seek out as it always has a fine selection of small and delightful *objets*, any of which might happily be packed and taken home: lots of little boxes, old pieces of crystal, little bits of this and that.

GALERIE MICHEL SONKIN

10 rue de Beaune, 7e.
METRO: rue du Bac.

This is almost a museum given over to reverent worship of the ancient culinary rituals that were part of our ancestors' daily lives. The emphasis is on the simple, the rustic and the truly practical and the whole effect is one of charm and authenticity. There are lots of simple heavy wooden bowls and boards, cheese and butter moulds, and the speciality is the collection of carved initialled bread stamps used in times gone by to stamp the loaves. Collectors of treen or ancient cooking implements will find this shop a treasure-trove.

GILLET

19 rue d'Arcole, 4e.
METRO: Cité.

Here, in this not very attractive, tourist-ridden part of Paris, is a good address for those wanting to buy antique jewellery: everything from rings to bracelets, from simple pairs of ear-rings to dramatic pendants and necklaces. A lovely selection for the jewellery lover.

JEAN-PIERRE DE CASTRO

17 rue des Francs-
Bourgeois, 4e.
METRO: Saint-Paul, Chemin
Vert.

Jean-Pierre collects and sells old silver, ranging in scale from baroque samovars to tiny thimbles. Some of the items conjure up a largely vanished way of life: exquisite decanter holders and chafing dishes; elaborate cakestands and teapots; and grand swollen roasting lids for the Christmas goose. Others are more modest: the simple platters, cups, dishes, toastracks and fishslicers, made in old silver, could bring daily pleasure to anyone. A particular speciality is old silver cutlery, whether bought in whole canteens, or piece by piece. On the day I was passing beautiful plain large silver spoons and forks were being sold by the kilo.

MADELEINE CASTAING

21 rue Bonaparte, 6e.
METRO: Saint-Sulpice.

The *grande dame* of things decorative and stylistic, Madeleine Castaign could be said to be to the Paris Salon what Syrie Maugham was to the London salon of the twenties. Room after room is filled with her idiosyncratic selection of things old and not so old. Much of it may be a bit kitsch for some tastes: elephants' feet may serve as ashtrays, tables may be supported by goats' feet, exotic foliage is to be seen everywhere. In Paris they find it all *très amusants* — you may be less amused by the prices.

LA MAISON DE POUPEE

40 rue de Vaugirard, 6e.
METRO: Saint-Placide.

A combination between a shop and a museum; that is, even if you're not thinking of buying, you'd probably think it worth visiting just to have a look. A large collection of dolls through the ages often available with the original clothes. You can see here some of the oldest porcelain dolls, some of the first to be made in celluloid and a big selection of theatrical dolls and puppets as well. Children would love it.

MICHEL PERINET

26 rue Danielle-Casanova,
2e.
METRO: Pyramides.

Like yachts, not really for those who need to ask the price, but a lovely selection of rare and precious old jewellery. If you've had an exceptional year and feel like treating somebody, here you'll be able to find anything from a great big stone from the time of Napoleon or a named piece of Art Deco.

PHILOMENE

15 rue Vavin, 6e.
METRO: Vavin.

A good little address for presents that are at once one-off, charming and old. Lots of little things: some turn of the century gold ear-rings, a bracelet embellished with crystal, little painted boxes, old frames, and a collection of fashion accessories such as silk scarves and old purses.

LA POUSSIERE D'OR

10 rue du Pont Louis-Philippe, 4e.
METRO: Pont-Marie.

If you love your linen old, fine and special, if you like your china fragile and antique, your glasses crystal and elegant, then search around amongst the treasures in this little shop. The eye that selects is immaculate, the quality high — none of the frequent tat that passes for antique — and the charm irresistible.

ROBERT GUIGUE

16 rue des Halles, 1er.
METRO: Les Halles, Châtelet.

A renowned specialist in painted furniture — irresistible, if that's your taste.

LA SALLE DES VENTES

117–123 rue d'Alésia, 14e.
METRO: Alésia.

Yet another reason to make a trip to this out-of-the-way part of Paris: a huge and airy *dépôt* full of secondhand treasures of every kind. Though furniture and pictures (of the rather gloomy, Victorian variety when I was there) are what they specialise in, it is a marvellous place in which to browse around — search for any number of smaller items such as secondhand glass, little pieces of jewellery or silver, photograph frames, ink-wells, old lamps and linen. Maybe you'll even like the pictures. It has the great advantage of seeming to be undiscovered by tourists and is full of earnest-looking dealers, and housewives on a limited income.

SORELLE

12 rue de l'Echaudé, 6e.
METRO: Mabillon, Saint-Gemain-des-Prés.

Here is another address for those looking for something old yet not in the museum category. Besides jewellery from the Art Deco period and onwards, there are lots of little *objets*, all or any of which would make splendid presents – vases and lamps, little purses and boxes.

STYLES

33 rue des Ecoles, 5e.
METRO: Maubert-Mutualité.

This is the address if you're looking for a piece of jewellery that isn't old enough to be fantastically expensive but is old enough to be of interest. Here you'll find pieces dating from the thirties onwards. Some of it wonderfully vulgar and therefore, of course, also wonderfully sought-after. Anything and everything from rings to the full regalia.

VICTORIA

6 rue des Francs-Bourgeois, 3e.
METRO: Chemin Vert, Saint-Paul.

This is a charming little shop in the old district of the Marais where you never quite know what you'll find — it could be anything from a beautiful old water-jug to a bureau. It's good hunting-ground for small, unusual presents as there is usually a large selection of things like glasses and jugs and old *objets* for the dressing-table or the bathroom.

BARGAIN PARIS

Though to be young and rich in Paris is indeed a wonderful thing, surprisingly, it is also not a bad city for those whose boat has not yet come in. Paris abounds in cheap treats. Its hotels, pound for francs, are infinitely better value than those in London or New York. There are still small family-run hotels where it is possible to stay in a clean room in a decent, though not grand, district at a very low price. A bargain compared with any other capital city.

Though it may at first seem hard to be in a city with some of the finest restaurants in the world and not be able to afford to sample them, console yourself. You are also in the city with the finest small food shops and corner *epiceries* in the world. Where else could you buy such a marvellous assembly of *charcuterie* and cheeses, of ready-made *pâtés* and *terrines*, such golden apricots, such aromatic tomatoes, such wonderful bread? Add a bottle of wine (not too cheap if you can help it — go for at least one marked VDQS) and all you need is some green space and a 'thou' to share it with.

Paris is a city where the careful shopper (and they scarcely come more careful than the French housewife on a budget) can eat like a King, dress like a Queen and never pay full retail price.

If you know where to go, you can buy couture dresses at knock-down prices and household necessities at well below what you'd normally expect.

Every Parisian has her *astuces* so if you have Parisian friends, quiz them ruthlessly, for the astute bargain-hunter who lives on the spot will be absolutely *au fait* with every latest ruse. This chapter will give you some ideas but as Paris is a living, changing city you will find that some of the best shops specialising in *soldes* and *dégriffés* come and go with remarkable rapidity. Your Parisian friend will know which of the stores has currently received a big intake of unsold couture, which has the best household bargains and where the best current pickings are at.

When it comes to bargain buys in end-of-line clothes, remember that most of the best buys are to be found far from the smart areas like the Madeleine and the rue du Faubourg Saint-Honoré (though the contrary, of course, is true when it comes to secondhand). The 'stock' or discount clothing shops which offer designer clothes at up to half price are to be found in the grimy 14th *arrondissement*, in particular in the rue d'Alésia and in the 9th *arrondissement* (Mendes Yves Saint-Laurent). The rue Saint-Placide in the 6th is lined with shops selling cut-price clothes (*dégriffés*, *soldes permanents* or *les prix dignes* are the words to look for), while the rue Saint-Dominique in the 7th (paradoxically in a very smart district) is always well worth taking a trip along.

If you're under 26 and if you're likely to be staying more than a few days and have some excursions and expenditure in mind, be sure to buy the special pass called a *Carte Jeune*, introduced in 1985 by the French Prime Minister, Laurent Fabius. Along with the pass you'll get a guide which lists the (literally) thousands of different services you become entitled to buy at reduced rates. You get the card from the Crédit Mutuel and CIC banks, from railway stations and travel agents. Remember to take your passport along. Besides reductions on the French railways (if you're going out of

Paris), the pass allows you to use university restaurants (often some of the best value in town), reduced entry fees to museums and galleries and reduced prices in some fast-food restaurants.

This section is divided into two parts: under 'Discount Stores' are listed the places to go for *new* goods at bargain prices, while 'Secondhand Shops' lists shops selling second-hand goods.

CONTENTS

* Strictly speaking not all shops but also places to rest the feet, restore the spirits and engage the mind.

DISCOUNT STORES

DESIGNER CLOTHES AT KNOCKDOWN PRICES

FABRICS

HOUSEHOLD

SECONDHAND SHOPS

FASHION: WOMEN

FASHION: MEN

FRIPES

JEWELLERY

DISCOUNT STORES

RUE SAINT-PLACIDE, 6e.

METRO: Saint-Placide.

This is the street, possibly above all others, that the poor but would-be well-dressed tourist should make a point of visiting. It is lined with shops on either side specialising in *soldes* and *dégriffés*. You won't expect, and certainly won't get, the kind of service you get in the expensive boutiques (you can't, after all, have everything), but if a certain lack of *gentillesse* doesn't bother you, and you're a born bargain-hunter, this is your street. Boutiques come and go. Stock comes and goes. It all depends on which factory has over-produced; which shop has over-bought. Some of the shops seem to purvey clothes so cheap and nasty, one wonders who could possibly want them; others really do have some astonishingly good buys. Here is a small selection of just some of the ones that caught my eye.

MOUTON CINQ PATTES The place for cotton jeans, T-shirts and jolly children's wear.

BOUTIQUE STOCK Good quality khaki gaberdine suits for women, nicely made and at excellent prices. Not too crowded, more of an edited collection of attractive clothes.

ANNEXE DES CREATEURS One of the best in the street, selling higher quality clothes, better displayed and with some of the better-known designers than the others.

MODA SOLDES Shoes, shoes and more shoes. From Bally to Zanu, lots of shoes by well-known manufacturers when I was there. Prices are not rock-bottom but you will find a good selection of all the currently fashionable lines for the feet.

DESIGNER CLOTHES AT KNOCKDOWN PRICES

If you thought designer clothes were only for those with designer incomes, think again. Paris is better served for clothing discount stores than almost any other big city. All those smartly dressed secretaries and harassed housewives don't look the way they do by paying full retail prices — they couldn't afford to. No, they know exactly where to go to find their droopy linens, their silky shirts, their classily-cut trousers, without ever having to pay full Paris prices. The secret is to keep regular tabs on what the *stocks* or discount stores are up to.

The first thing to remember is that they aren't to be found in the smart *arrondissements*. The second is that what is on offer varies from moment to moment. One day you may come away with armfuls of stunning bargains, the next you may be disappointed by a very poor selection. Pot luck, particularly for the visitor with little time, is the order of the day.

Here, then, is a list of some of the best-known of the discount houses.

BIDERMAN

114 rue de Turenne, 3e.
METRO: Filles du Calvaire.

This is probably the best known of all the *dégriffé* shops for men. Marcel Biderman, brother of the disco queen, Regine, has access to a wide range of well-known grand names that are end of line or end of season, and here the would-be man-about-town can buy a suit, a jacket, or just a pair of trousers. When you think that these have all come from the sharpest scissors in town, you'll see what bargains they are. Prices are often up to 40–50% less than you'd pay in the proper place at the proper time.

CACHAREL STOCK

114 rue d'Alésia, 14e.
METRO: Alésia.

A beautifully large and airy *dépôt* for last season's or leftover Cacharel designs. There are changing-rooms where you may try on in privacy and prices seem to range from between 30–50% of the full price. There usually seems to be a large selection to choose from, all neatly and helpfully organised. It's also a marvellous place to buy some mini-chic at less than full price: the clothes won't seem cheap by British standards, but they are much cheaper than the prices in the stores. Chic colours like navy and khaki, beautifully-made, would make handsome presents for children, whether one's own or other people's. Look out for the beautifully-cut navy corduroys or the enchanting dresses, smocked *à l'Anglaise*. Not cheap, but very charming.

CENTRE DE LA MODE

101 rue Réaumur, 2e.
METRO: Sentier, Bourse.

Open from 10am to 6.30pm every day except Sunday.

Officially, it seems, you need an invitation to be allowed in, for here you can buy high quality clothes at wholesale prices. However, you can always chance your arm and wander in, as I did, looking confident and as if you belong. It's well worth summoning up the chutzpah because here you will find 100% cashmere sweaters, for men as well as women; you'll find suits and shirts; ties and blouses; blazers and polos; T-shirts and skirts, all way below retail price. No haute couture but good prêt-à-porter names.

CHARTIER 7 rue Faubourg Montmartre, 9e.

METRO: Le Peletier, Montmartre.

Open 11am to 3pm and 6pm to 9.30pm, seven days a week.

This is the classic, tourist-guide restaurant for those whose boat has not yet come in and so you will probably find it filled with all the other tourists wanting a good, inexpensive meal. If you don't mind that, you will find it excellent value. Several hundred meals a day are served so don't expect personal attention but if you're worn out from shopping and want to save your francs for something more solid than food, this is the place for you.

CHAUSSURES YVES

71 rue de la Pompe, 16e.
METRO: Pompe.

Here men and women can find new shoes at a discount. They are neither absolutely the very latest thing nor are they astoundingly cheap but they are well-made, conventional styles and sold at prices which do seem a little lower than they would be in a normal retail outlet.

LA CLEF DES SOLDES

126 boulevard Raspail, 6e.
METRO: N-D des Champs, Vavin.

99 rue Saint-Dominique, 7e.
METRO: Latour Maubourg, Invalides.

This is the sort of place to stock up with your basics; you won't find very much high fashion here (though I bought a beautiful white cotton shirt by Equipment which I saw later in a smart boutique in Passy for three times the price) but you'll find lots of marvellous leisure clothes. Shirts by Facconable and New Man, cotton trousers and massed racks of children's clothes. It's all a bit haphazard, you don't get much help (unless, of course, you are one of the numerous regulars, who will be greeted with warmth and jokes) but scrummage around and you'll find lots that you'll be pleased with.

DOROTHEE BIS STOCK

74 rue d'Alésia, 14e.
METRO: Alésia.

If you've always loved the clothes of Dorothée Bis but always felt they were beyond your means then head for the rue d'Alésia out in the 14th *arrondissement.* Here you can find cotton sweaters and striking cotton jumpsuits reduced by about 30%. Besides the clothes for everyday, there were the season's fashionable flat sandals and a vast selection of Dorotennis gear. (Tennis is a very chic sport these days in France, and Dorotennis, along with Lacoste, is one of the smartest labels on court.)

EMMANUELLE KHANH

6 rue Pierre-Lescot, 1er.
METRO: Etienne-Marcel.

Here, on the edge of the Centre Pompidou, you must climb to the first floor where there are again no changing rooms and precious little proper sales help, to rummage amongst the rails in the hope of finding just the thing you're after. There are clothes for men and women (men are politely asked to wait whilst the women try things on in the open changing area) and usually it is the men who have much the larger choice. Most of the models are the previous season's leftovers, selling at prices that seem on average to be about 40% less than full retail. On the day I was there, I found wonderfully soft and pliable leather jackets and skirts.

GIANNI

104 rue du Bac, 7e.
METRO: Sèvres-Babylone, rue du Bac.

Shoes for men and women, not startlingly cheap but cheaper than in the smart shoe shops of the rue du Cherche-Midi and rue Etienne-Marcel *et al.* Without designer names, there were the current flat lace-ups for women and lots of good plain classic brogues and loafers for men, all in proper leather.

JEAN-LOUIS SCHERRER

29 avenue Ledru-Rollin, 12e.
METRO: Gare de Lyon.

Another very big name, one of the gilded members of the *Chambre Syndicale*, who sells his last season's leftovers in more salubrious surroundings than most. There are proper private changing-rooms and they will do alterations for you, at a price. The prices may seem still quite high but they are much, much less than you'd pay in the avenue Montaigne salon.

MENDES (St-Laurent)

65 rue Montmartre, 9e.
METRO: Montmartre, Richelieu-Drouot.

Possibly the most famous of them all and the one the ardent fashion pundit should take in first. Sometimes I've had marvellous luck and found the most wonderful up-to-the-minute warm winter suits; sometimes I've found precious little. Prices seem to be roughly half what they would be in the boutiques for leftover models from the haute couture collections as well as for the remains of the last season's collections from the boutiques. There are no private changing-rooms, no helpful sales assistants and you won't be able to exchange the item if you decide later you don't like it, but it is a chance to find an elegant label at a knock-down price.

MODUS, DEGRIFFE

31 rue Varenne, 7e.
METRO: Sèvres-Babylone, Varenne.

If you don't feel like trekking out to the rue d'Alésia or braving the scrums of the rue Saint-Placide, this little shop in the heart of the fashionable 7th *arrondissement* is a good place to start looking for a few bargains of the moment. Neither big nor crowded, you would hardly be aware that it specialised in *dégriffés* if you didn't see the sign. I found a pair of Ara trousers, fashionably cut rather like jodphurs, in a chic stone colour. There were also some very pretty Liberty fabric blouses. Stock, clearly, as in all such outlets, depends on what is cast off at the moment, so you just have to take pot luck.

LA SOLDERIE

85 rue de la Boetie, 8e.
METRO: Saint-Philippe-du-Roule.

A good address to know about because it's one of the few discount shops in a very smart district, so if this is where you've been getting your eye in, you won't have to travel far. It undercuts shops in the district by something like a third.

STOCK AUSTERLITZ (Hechter)

16 boulevard de l'Hôpital, 13e.
METRO: Gare d'Orléans-Austerlitz.

Right by the Gare d'Austerlitz is the discount house for the leftover models of Daniel Hechter. Like most of these houses, the penalty of lower prices is that you can't get your money back if you change your mind, and the surroundings aren't exactly up to Faubourg Saint-Honoré standards. But if you persevere make the journey out to the Gare d'Austerlitz, you will find the authentic Hechter look (all those impeccably causal blazers, trousers, raincoats, those sweaters and chic shirts) at prices between 30–50% less than full retail prices.

STOCK SACS

109 bis rue Saint-Dominique, 7e.
METRO: Latour Maubourg, Invalides.

This is the place to buy your cut-price handbag or purse. The shop doesn't go in for fancy window displays so it may look a bit dispiriting to begin with, but persevere and you may be lucky. Many of the designs are pedestrian but the prices are good and if your taste runs to conventional but smart lizard- and crocodile-skin they have quite a selection.

These then, are just some of the best-known and largest of the *stock* houses attached to the big names, but remember that most of the designers and couturiers have outlets for out-of-date and leftover items (Nina Ricci, for instance, has it in the basement of her boutique) so if you have a favourite designer and want to track down his leftovers you can always ask. Remember, too, that the rue d'Alésia is almost lined with *stock* houses and that in Paris the sales really are proper sales. If you can organise your visit round the January or July sales you will be able to find some remarkable bargains — there's many a smartly-dressed Parisian who never, ever, pays full price for anything.

FABRICS

CASA MIGUEL 48 rue Saint-Georges, 9e.
METRO: Saint-Georges, N-D de Lorette.

The cheapest meal in the Western world, says the *Guinness Book of Records*, is to be found in the heart of Paris at the Casa Miguel, where the price has hardly changed over the last five years. For less than a pound you get a simple but wholesome three-course meal, including wine and bread. Mme. Maria Codina who owns the restaurant and does all the cooking and serving is now 76 — so hurry whilst her strength lasts!

LA COUPONNERIE

252 boulevard Jean-Jaurès,
Boulogne-Billancourt.
METRO: Boulogne-Jean-
Jaurès.

Though way out, past the Porte de Billancourt, it really is well worth the journey if you're on the track of fine materials at low prices. Take the métro and find yourself in this airy boutique filled with the finest and the best. Lots of grand names, lots of silks and swiss cotton, pure wool tweeds and the softest jersey. There's also a good selection of dress patterns (most of the fabrics are dress fabrics) and an exceedingly useful list of that dying species, the dressmaker.

MADAME COUPON

125 rue Cambronne, 15e.
METRO: Vaugirard.

Leftovers from the fashionable couturiers find their way to Madame Coupon where you can buy pure wool and cottons as well as silks, satins, laces and linens.

MARCHE SAINT-PIERRE

2 rue Charles-Nodier, 18e.
METRO: Anvers.

This is where many a grand career was launched: designers as eminent as Kenzo and Jean-Paul Gaultier made their first samples with fabrics from here. It's worth making the journey out to this vast emporium of four floors filled with fabrics for every conceivable purpose, from the finest evening-dress to the heaviest-weight upholstery. Look also for sheets, towels and household linens of all sorts.

MENDES TISSUS

140 rue Montmartre, 2e.
METRO: Bourse,
Montmartre.

More fabrics from the world of haute couture, in particular, fabrics from St-Laurent, can be found here six months or so after the very same designs were seen strutting down the catwalks. Silks, cottons, tweeds, wools and cashmeres, all at reduced prices. If you're looking for a winter fabric they tend to turn up around September; summer ones start arriving in February.

LE PRINCE

17 rue de Cléry, 2e.
METRO: Sentier, Bourse.

Those who for one reason or another are looking for silk for painting on will find it here at very interesting prices — all 100%, mostly in white or cream.

LA REMISE AUX TISSUS

146 boulevard Voltaire, 11e.
METRO: Charonne.

The place to go for household fabrics — if you long to change your curtains or make up a tablecloth or two, here you will find every kind of suitable fabric at considerably reduced prices.

SEVILLA

43 rue de la Convention,
15e.
METRO: Javel.

Another of the many outlets for the same materials as those used by the big-name couturiers. Here they appear several months after the couture models have been sold but they are nonetheless beautiful and fine quality for all that. Come here for soft silks, sensuous satins, crisp cottons and luscious linens.

TEXAFFAIRES

5 rue Saint-Martin, 4e.

Here, just off the rue de Rivoli, you can buy sheets and towels, tablelinen and towelling wraps all at prices way below

METRO: Hôtel de Ville,
Châtelet.

TOTO SOLDES

70 boulevard de Clichy, 9e.
METRO: Blanche.

75 avenue d'Italie, 13e.
METRO: Tolbiac.

normal. It's the place to stock up on the Primrose Bordier designs you feel you can't normally afford or to indulge in a richly fluffy bathrobe.

Lots and lots of fabric, again of every conceivable type, all at permanent sale prices. Well worth the journey to track them down.

HOUSEHOLD

BLANC CASSE

60 rue de Boulainvilliers,
16e.
METRO: Muette.

13 rue du Bac, 7e.
METRO: rue du Bac.

This is one of the places to buy your household linens at less than full Paris prices — it is to the world of sheets and towels what the *stocks* and *dégriffés* are to the world of suits and dresses. Here you can buy lovely pastel-coloured towels of very good quality, blankets, duvet covers and towelling dressing-gowns, all at two-thirds the normal price. A complete selection of everything the linen cupboard might need can usually be found, though, as with all *dégriffés* outlets, the stock itself is very much a moveable feast.

PORCELAINE

93 rue Saint-Dominique, 7e.
METRO: Latour Maubourg, Invalides.

Here you can not only replenish any gaps in your own *batterie de cuisine* or china cupboard but find a host of inexpensive presents as well. Good-sized white soufflé dishes, sets of glasses of exceedingly good shape and size (though clearly not made of fine crystal), simple, white, porcelain gratin dishes and all the other appurtenances of the well-dressed table: candles and candlesticks, tablecloths and napkins, decanters and vases. The taste is not impeccable but the prices are hard to beat.

LA PORCELAINE BLANCHE

112 bis rue de Rennes, 6e.
METRO: Rennes.

108 rue Saint-Honoré, 1er.
METRO: Tuileries.

25 avenue de La Motte-Picquet, 7e.
METRO: La Motte-Picquet-Grenelle.

These are just the three most central branches of this chain of shops selling the sort of plain, white porcelain that cooks all over the world desire. This is the place for a simple, white soufflé dish; for a series of white serving dishes that double up as ovenware; for classic, tall, white mugs for steaming-hot morning coffee and for those giant bowls that are just right for *moules marinières.* Much of what is sold is officially *rejet* but the defects are almost invisible and it is all certainly sound enough to use. The prices, therefore, are exceedingly good. Besides the simple rustic ware there is now also a collection of linen and glass, cutlery and other kitchen and table accessories in similarly sympathetic mood.

SECONDHAND SHOPS

See them tripping out on a fine spring morning. There go the girls of Paris, setting out in the season's very latest look, carrying nothing but the most stylish of bags and luggage, feet shod in shoes that surely must have cost more than several weeks' dinners. Perhaps each has a little *patron* who likes to see her well turned out? No, nothing so *vieux chapeau.* These days shopping secondhand is nothing to be embarrassed about. *Crise oblige,* and now even the most fashionable of women who like to wear nothing but this season's garments, don't mind taking their cast-offs to a *dépôt-vente* where they can earn a little towards the next outfit. And those who have a taste for designer outfits and fine fabrics but not the purse to match are not too proud to step out in somebody else's little-worn Chanel.

Because Paris is Paris, you are more likely to find a really good name — a St-Laurent, Valentino or Chanel — lurking on the rails in a good *dépôt-vente* then you ever would in London. The good ones will never take anything that is out-of-date: it has to be currently in fashion, it must be in top-top condition and, above all, perfectly clean. Many of them have been going for years and have regular customers: rich, fashionable women (total discretion guaranteed *bien sûr*) who turn in their little-worn models and on the other hand the less rich but no less fashionable women who come here to buy.

Some also sell the used models from the couturiers' haute couture collections. These will only have been worn by the models but will, of course, be model-size. Anybody tall and thin enough should have a field day.

The cardinal rule when buying in these shops is to check every detail very carefully, for usually there is no question of bringing anything back. Finding some kind of fault can also be a useful tactic for bringing down the prices. So look for stains and spots (usually there are none; most demand almost impossible perfection from the vendors), check the seams, the hems, the buttons and the linings.

Prices are usually clearly marked and there is no bargaining but if you don't see a price-tag you can take it that Madame in charge may well ask for what she thinks you can pay. Here it pays to act tough. Adopt the French habit and never seem enthusiastic and they may (I repeat, may) come down considerably.

Though there are far more *dépôt-ventes* specialising in women's clothes, it is nowadays possible for men to dress chicly by buying secondhand. As men have become more interested in fashionable clothes, as the fad for nostalgia and retro have taken hold, more of these shops are catering for *Monsieur* as well.

The smartest of the secondhand shops are, not surprisingly, to be found in the smartest *quartiers* — it's no good searching for a once-worn St-Laurent in the grimier reaches of the 14th *arrondissement* where there would be no need for an inhabitant ever to own one.

Head for the *quartiers* where what you wear really matters. Not for nothing are the two mini-empires in the world of secondhand to be found in the 6th and the 16th respectively. On the Left Bank, Claude Bayonne is the entrepreneur behind the Chercheminippes empire, whilst over in the 16th we have Nicole Morel with her beautifully-run group of Reciproque shops.

So here are some of the best secondhand shops in Paris — good hunting.

FASHION: WOMEN

ANNA LOWE

35 avenue Matignon, 8e.
METRO: Saint-Philippe-du-Roule, F.D. Roosevelt.

Probably the grandmother of them all in one of the grandest *arrondissements* of Paris. Here chauffeur-driven cars often pull up and a chauffeur discreetly deposits his cargo of couture clothes for which Madame has no further use. Prices may at first sight seem high for something already worn, but remind yourself of the savings. If grand evening dresses aren't high on your list of priorities, there are usually day dresses, suits and silk shirts by the handful. You'll recognise all the names: Ungaro, Jean-Louis Scherrer, St-Laurent, Valentino, Chanel — this is the place to buy your investment clothes at less than full price.

AR'CHANGE

106 rue de la Tour, 16e.
METRO: Pompe.

One of the more inviting of the secondhand clothing shops with some exceedingly up-market merchandise. I found a marvellous Lanvin green linen jacket, beautifully cut and in such fine condition it could have been worn to the smartest of weddings. Going with it was a fine black linen shirt — together they would have made an outfit to be proud of. There were soft jersey skirts in the fashionable long lengths, a beautiful yellow pleated linen skirt and a St-Laurent navy and white dress. In the basement there's a men's department where you could buy a conventional worsted suit in excellent condition or a smart cotton shirt. Altogether well worth a visit by those with haute couture tastes but prêt-à-porter incomes.

BABY-TROC

16 rue de Magdebourg, 16e.
METRO: Trocadéro.

4 rue du Commandant-Pilot, Neuilly.
METRO: Pont de Neuilly.

This is the place to kit out your children in classic French clothes at very good prices. All the chic names in the world of children's wear are to be found here: look out for Bon-Point and Cyrillus, Osh-Kosh and Tartine. What Maman BCBG wants is refined smocked dresses, long-length Bermudas, mini-Shetlands and lambswool sweaters, soft cotton shirts and blouses, and adorable clothing of every sort. So this, needless to say, is what Baby-Troc sells.

BAMBIN-TROC

4 rue de l'Abbé-Groult, 15e.
METRO: Convention.

Here you may find more than just clothes for the mini-set; you can buy all the appurtenances for the mini-life. Prams and children's books, cots and toys, cast-off or outgrown playpens and climbing frames. The clothes on sale here seem to be less impeccable, and therefore, happily, a lot cheaper, than in most of the other *dépôts*.

CAMELEON

13 rue Gustave-Courbet, 16e.
METRO: Victor-Hugo, Pompe.

More 16th clothes for 16th lifestyles: all those reassuring, comforting names such as Ungaro and St-Laurent, Chanel and Sonia Rykiel can be found here. Look, too, for leather jackets and the odd fur come the winter. Mainly for women but a selection for children as well.

CATHERINE BARIL

14–16 rue de la Tour, 16e.
METRO: Passy.

A small but elegant resale shop serving the rich and not-so-rich women who live in this, the most sought-after of residential *quartiers*. Most of the clothes are top designer labels and many of the clothes come from famous names, for Catherine Baril has connections dating back to her days in the world of fashion. Her taste is impeccable; the clothes often a snitch.

CHERCHEMINIPPES

109–111 rue du Cherche-Midi, 6e.
METRO: Vaneau.

Another little empire wrought from the world of secondhand clothing. It is the place for those who don't want to make it over to the 16th *arrondissement*, which seems to be the spiritual home of high-quality secondhand. Here at Chercheminippes, there are truly bargains to be had. The windows do not at once reveal that the clothes they are selling are secondhand, so *à la mode* and impeccable are the offerings. For children, at number 110, there are charming little Liberty cotton smocks, cotton-check Bermudas with matching shirts, pink and white striped rompers for babies — the whole panoply of chic Gallic mini-clothing. At 109 there are women's clothes which, on the day I was there, seemed to veer more towards the high-quality and the conventional than the trendy. At number 111, Monsieur can kit himself out with immaculate 'Oxfords', fine sweaters, cotton trousers, the works. Nothing here is shabby; nothing obviously out of date. Amongst the secondhand clothing there is always a small selection of *dégriffés*, the designer-label clothing that is new but either end-of-season or end-of-line and so selling at reduced prices. Nothing is very cheap but it is all excellent value.

CHLOROPHYLLE

2 rue du Sabot, 6e.
METRO: Saint-Sulpice, Sèvres-Babylone.

If Rive Gauche is your style (the trademarks are a sense of adventure and informality), then this is the secondhand boutique for you. Close to the heart of the Rive Gauche headquarters (Saint-German-des-Prés), many a young and trendy fashion assistant or photographer deposits her week-old outfit here. Impeccable, up-to-the-minute with lots of bargains for the young-in-heart.

LE DEPOT D'ANGELIQUE

As you might expect from a shop right in the heart of BCBG country, here you will find big occasion clothes, almost new.

104 rue Boileau, 16e.
METRO: Michel-Ange
Molitor.

Been asked to the races at Longchamp? Have a fine wedding or reception to attend? Worry not, Le Dépôt d'Angelique will kit you out. Find here a smart Hermès scarf, a Vuitton bag, shoes by Maud Frizon or France Faver, and, if you really do only need something for one big occasion, well, you can always hire the clothes, instead of buying them. There is usually a large choice and a wide range of prices. This is for women only.

LES DEUX ORSONS

106 boulevard de Grenelle, 15e.
METRO: La Motte-Piquet.

If you've always wanted a fur but felt it was beyond your reach you may be lucky at Les Deux Orsons. Roland Pinault, who used to be a furrier himself, sells furs of all sorts, many of them sold to him by well-heeled ladies from the provinces who feel it is time to change their pelt. He knows exactly how to put the furs into excellent order: the linings are nearly always changed and the choice ranges from 50s models to the very latest couture fur that for some reason just didn't sell. Some of the furs are never worn, others are traded-in models from his regular clientele. If you already own a fur that you feel is less than fashionable, you can always try and trade it in.

LADY TROC FOURRURES

13 rue de l'Etoile, 17e.
METRO: Etoile.

Here you will find a mixture of secondhand and new furs all at extraordinarily reasonable prices. The secondhand ones are in beautiful condition, all cleaned and restored, and in almost every (legitimate) fur you care to name. Everything from sheepskins to mink. You can buy as little as a fur hat or as much as a full-length evening coat.

MAGUY-DEPOT

30 rue de la Pompe, 16e.
METRO: Pompe, Muette.

In theory the 16th *arrondissement* should be a good area to scout for secondhand cast-offs, in practice it often is, but much depends on the day and the season. One hears of those who have found many a bargain at Maguy-Dépôt but on the day I was there they seemed thin on the ground. Dusty-looking crocodile handbags, neither very smart nor very elegant; and though there were some exquisite couture shoes they were certainly not cheap, given that they were second-hand. However, if you're in the area and are a persistent rummager, you should give it a try.

MAMAN-TROC

6b rue de Fourcroy, 17e.
METRO: Ternes.

Almost everything here is about half the normal retail price, and besides the usual selection of children's clothes that Parisian mothers seem to go for, there are also secondhand clothes for the expectant mother and, from time to time, a selection of prams and nursery furniture.

MAXIPUCES

18 rue Cortambert, 16e.
METRO: Pompe, Trocadéro.

Another elegant little outlet for the cast-off (but impeccably cast-off) designer clothes of the fashionable 16th *arrondissement* set. Here there is usually a combination of big names, slightly worn; and some end-of-season, end-of-line clothes

straight from the factories. It's also a good place to hunt for the fashionable accessories that say so much and cost even more — look for Hermès scarves at knock-down prices, crocodile belts, jewellery and furs if and when they turn up.

MINOU-TROC

40 rue Saint-Ferdinand, 17e.
METRO: Argentine.

Besides charming secondhand children's clothing of the by now familiar BCBG genre, look out for a good selection of some of the grandest names in the children's wear business: Bon-Point and Cyrillus seem currently to be the hottest names. Mme. BCBG, it seems, would rather pay for a secondhand smocked dress than resort to Prisunic or Monoprix.

MONIKA

136 avenue Emile-Zola, 15e.
METRO: Emile-Zola.

Don't head for Monika if you're in Paris in the summer (she closes down for all of May, June, July, August and the first week of September) but if you're in need of a fur in the cooler months then she is well worth the detour. The range is small but very choice and Monika often has some remarkable bargains. She keeps in touch with some of the best furriers and buys from them as well as from private customers.

PARC DE BAGATELLE Bois de Boulogne, 16e.

METRO: Pont de Neuilly.

On a fine sunny day, make for the Parc de Bagatelle, near the Neuilly gate, in the Bois du Boulogne, which is open every day from 9am onwards. If you're feeling really poor, take your *baguette,* your *saucisson* and your cheese, and enjoy this lovely garden, created for that saddest of figures, Marie Antoinette. Try to go when the tulips or roses are out. If you're feeling only moderately short of funds visit the charming little restaurant, reminiscent of a country inn. Here you can eat a simple meal (no culinary pyrotechnics) at a price that is slightly over the odds but nothing like as high as most of the other restaurants in the Bois de Boulogne.

RECIPROQUE

95, 101 and 123 rue de la Pompe, 16e.
METRO: Pompe, Victor-Hugo.

This is possibly the first place the visitor in search of a secondhand bargain should head for. The first Reciproque was started some seven years ago by Nicole Morel, who, working in public relations as she did, quickly saw that there was many a woman who needed to be well dressed but couldn't afford top designer labels. The rich, well-heeled and fashionable like, and need, to change their clothes often, while the less well-heeled are happy to buy secondhand if that's the only way they can get to wear their favourite designers. Hence Reciproque.

It is beautifully organised. Clothes are put in racks and labelled clearly according to designer or manufacturing house. Size, price, materials and any other relevant details are clearly indicated. Number 95 is light and airy and concentrates on women's clothes. Almost every designer from St-Laurent to Agnès B, from the fashionable Japanese groups to Chanel and Valentino are to be found, as well as plenty of names amongst the better-known ready-to-wear labels.

At number 101 are men's and children's secondhand clothes (also some nursery equipment such as prams and nursing chairs) whilst at number 123 there is Boutique Cadeaux, specialising in gifts and accessories, where you could find a crocodile handbag, a porcelain lamp or a dashing piece of costume jewellery.

VICTOR-HUGO ECHANGERAIS

141 avenue Victor-Hugo, 16e.
METRO: Victor-Hugo, Pompe.

Very new this very trendy little secondhand shop. Here the more *branché* members of the BCBG set can find numbers that their mothers would never wear. They pop in daily to check whether there's a Yohji Yamamoto, a Jean-Paul Gaultier or Comme des Garçons cast-off. The word is that the turnover is fast, so fast that if you're really after something special you need to look in early in the day.

FASHION: MEN

FABIENNE

88 rue Chardon-Lagache, 16e.
METRO: Chardon-Lagache.

A tiny, hard-to-find agency but worth the effort, for you might hit upon an almost-new Cerruti suit, some handsome Weston shoes or a cast-off Burberry.

> ## RECIPROQUE 101 rue de la Pompe, 16e *and* CHERCHEMINIPPES 111 rue du Cherche-Midi, 6e.
>
> Both have branches devoted solely to men's secondhand clothing (see pages 153 and 156).

SECOND HAND

3 boulevard Pershing, 17e.
METRO: Porte Maillot.

The great bonus that Second Hand offers is that it is open on Sundays, as well as every other day of the week, from midday to 8pm. Here, too, you can search for Weston shoes (prices, *bien sûr*, depend upon condition and age); Burberrys, and suits from that master of the look *Anglais*, Arthur et Fox. Prices are good, so it's well worth a look.

FRIPES

There's a world of difference between the world of second-hand and the world of *fripes*. Secondhand shops or *dépôt-ventes* are, as you will have gathered, where you buy this or last year's fashion at very reduced prices. *Fripes* are where you rummage for a 20s couture dress in finest lace and *crêpe-de-Chine*. *Fripes* are also where you'll find a 60s Hawaiian shirt, or a 50s elasticated belt. *Fripes*, in another words, are where you never know what you'll find; where you can chance upon an amazing piece of authentic Art Deco jewellery or find a jokey, plastic duck. *Fripes* are fun, usually cheap and they certainly stand for individuality.

Here are some of the best sources of *fripes* in Paris.

BOUZOU

79 rue Rambuteau, 1er.
METRO: Les Halles,
Rambuteau.

As it has become more and more permissible for men to show a certain eccentricity in their dress, so *fripes* for men have begun to flourish. Here the male of the species can kit himself out 60s style and at prices that seem hardly to have moved on.

IL ETAIT UNE FOIS

10 rue Jean-Jacques-
Rousseau, 1er.
METRO: Les Halles, Palais-
Royal.

Possibly the most famous *fripes* in Paris; certainly, the highest quality. Look here for the matchless silks and satins, laces and velvets of the early years of this century. There are 'smokings' and velvet robes; beaded headbands and feather boas; handbags and costume jewellery; soft kid gloves and exquisite lace collars. It's an absolute treasure-house and even those who don't need anything will enjoy the browse. It seems to be slightly erratic about opening hours (something that seems to go with secondhand and antique shopkeeping) but in general is open from 11am to 7.30pm, Mondays to Saturdays.

KILLY WATCH

9 rue des Canettes, 6e.
METRO: Mabillon.

100 rue Saint-Denis, 1er.
METRO: Les Halles.

More crazy clothes in a mixture of styles — everything from punk to retro. If your teenagers are complaining of a surfeit of museums, send them here for a little change of scene.

MARCHE MALIK

stand 57, Puces
Clignancourt, 18e.
METRO: Porte de
Clignancourt.

One of the best of the many shops in the market specialising in *fripes*; if you ever fancied a bit part in *West Side Story*, here is the place to get your gear. Authentic 50s and 60s Hollywood gear: the swirling skirts, the elasticated belts, the loud shirts.

NEXT STOP

45 rue Saint-André-des-
Arts, 6e.
METRO: Odéon, Saint-
Michel.

For men and women, *fripes* of the more recent kind. Mainly dating from the 1960s, these are more likely to appeal to the younger set. Slick and cheap.

RAG TIME

23 rue du Roule, 1er.
METRO: Louvre, Les Halles.

This is probably more the sort of *fripes* that most people have in mind: the truly elegant creations of the old-style couturiers, everything from grand chiffon evening dresses to tailored tweeds. Buy just one beautiful silk blouse or even, if you hit a lucky day, a fur.

SURPLUS DE NEUILLY

2 rue Gustave-Courbet, 16e.
METRO: Victor-Hugo, Pompe.

Here the young can buy their Indian moccasins, their jeans, their Levis 501s, their sweatshirts from California and all the other totems of American culture. Lots of elasticated belts and wide skirts for girls. With a little care you too could look as if you lived in California.

SURPRISE PARTY

30 rue du Cherche-Midi, 6e.
METRO: Rennes, Sèvres-Babylone.

Not the place for your straight up-and-down businessman. Gaudy Hawaiian shirts, glittery jewellery, wideboy suits, dotty bow ties and some very flash spectacles are the things that first hit you in the eye. The spirit is mainly 50s and 60s with touches of the 1930s, but in fact some of it is specially made today as the supply of the authentic is threatening to run out. There are *cravates rocks* and *cravates psychodelic*, underpants so gaudy you can't imagine who would want to wear them. Look out, if it's the sort of thing you're after, for *robes style Marilyn* (geddit?) and for little flirty skirts. There are Harris tweed jackets from America and secondhand suits (dating from the 50s and 60s) from both England and America. It's clearly quite a cult shop but not for the stockbroker or legal set.

JEWELLERY

BIJOUX A TROQUER

20 rue Miromesnil, 8e.
METRO: Miromesnil.

Not the place to go to if you're seriously short of cash, but if what you're looking for is some lovely jewellery at less than full price, Bijoux à Troquer could well have the very piece for you. Because it deals only in high-quality *haut jouaillerie*, prices cannot be rock-bottom, but if you have a lot of money to spend on a piece you could probably spend it more wisely here than anywhere else.

TROC DE BIJOUX

3 rue Coëtlogon, 6e.
METRO: Rennes, Saint-Sulpice.

A real find this: here you can buy (and indeed sell), very big-name jewellery at less than full price. You may find pieces from the grand names clustered round the place Vendôme as well as work by much more avant-garde people like Jean Dinh Van and Paloma Picasso. Gold, diamonds, silver, old and not so old, all can be found here, depending upon the day and the stock. You may chance upon an old piece of Tiffany, a newish but secondhand piece by Cartier, or a simple gold chain by nobody in particular. It's well worth a hunt. Prices start low and go on up and up, for the finest of the finest. Look out for pictures, as well, if that's your scene.

CHILDREN'S PARIS

Paris is not the easiest of cities for those with the young in tow. It is an ordered city, with highly civilised pleasures. It lacks the exuberance and the extroversion of, say, Rome or New York. It yields its pleasures slowly and it yields them most fully to those with the taste, the wit and the know-how to discover them. But there can scarcely be a child who won't thrill to some aspects of Paris, who won't fail to be moved by its beauty. So be not afraid, take them with you and build into the trip some pleasures specially for them.

No doubt largely because life in Paris requires order and discipline, the authorities have gone to immense trouble to encourage endless (ordered) diversions for children, though they are mainly of a cerebral or indoor kind. They are nevertheless, on the whole, exceptionally well done.

Start off by giving them an overall idea of Paris by taking them on some of the excellent official tours of the city (see the introduction). Take them up to the top of the Tour Eiffel, to the Tour Montparnasse, to the top of Notre-Dame and Sacré-Coeur; there they will see the splendours of Paris laid out before them.

If the weather is fine, many of the parks have special sections for children and one of the best is the Jardin d'Acclimatation, a special children's area on the edge of the Bois de Boulogne. Here there are puppet shows, mini-golf, a miniature train and a host of other *divertissements*. The Musée des Arts et Traditions, also in the Bois, is one of those museums that believes in giving children plenty to do — lots of knobs and buttons to press. But don't let them wander alone into other parts of the Bois.

More puppets are to be found in the Jardin du Luxembourg, whilst the Bois de Vincennes has a boating lake and a zoo. We haven't met a child yet who didn't think that the Musée

Grevin (10 boulevard Montmartre) was the best way yet devised of passing a rainy afternoon: waxworks *à la* Mme. Tussaud and a conjuring show seem to keep them absorbed for hours.

If the circus is in town don't miss it. Unlike the theatre or the cinema you don't need to speak French, and French circuses are currently undergoing a revival, returning to traditional acts. You'll love it, too.

CONTENTS

* Strictly speaking not all shops but also places to rest the feet, restore the spirits and engage the mind.

CLOTHES

TOYS AND FURNITURE

CLOTHES

AGNES B

2 rue du Jour, 1er.
METRO: Les Halles.

17 avenue Pierre-1er-de-Serbie, 16e.
METRO: Iéna.

For that ineffably French, understated look that would make any child look chic, Agnès B is the place. Much the same formula that is used with the clothes that Maman wears is applied to *l'enfant*: simple, practical shirts and skirts, cardigans and trousers, all in cotton-knits or jersey. Easy to wear, comfortable and yet with that indefinable air of style. Makes Liberty prints look over-styled.

BABY TUILERIES

326 rue Saint-Honoré, 1er.
METRO: Tuileries.

Doting grandmothers should head for this small boutique where they may indulge themselves by buying the sort of clothes that nanny would have loved. Clothes made from the softest cottons and lawns with fine smocking are just the thing for promenading in the Jardin du Luxembourg and entirely in keeping with the very best makes of pram. Prices, you will

have gathered, are not low — how could they be when only the finest materials and workmanship are used?

BONPOINT

67 rue de l'Université, 7e.
METRO: Solférino.

64 avenue Raymond-Poincaré, 16e.
METRO: Victor-Hugo.

184 rue de Courcelles, 17e.
METRO: Péreire.

You could hardly find a shop that more perfectly encapsulates the world of baby BCBG. Here Maman can clothe *petite* Isabelle or Guillaume from birth to adolescence in all the exquisite raiments of the caste: the beautiful smocked dresses, dresses made from the finest silk and satin, all exuding an air of refinement and taste, symbols of that well-ordered world in which nanny knows best. For Guillaume there are the inevitable Bermudas, the fine cotton shirts and the navy-blue jackets. For Maman herself there are equally finely-made and exquisitely tasteful clothes to see her through her pregnancies. From head to toe, from early morning to late at night, Bonpoint can provide the props.

CYRILLUS

8 rue Chanez, 16e.
METRO: Porte d'Auteuil.

One of the best and most comprehensive sources of fine children's wear *à la style Anglais*. Go there for smocked Liberty cotton dresses, for Viyella shirts, for grey flannel trousers, for blazers and good quality sweaters, for well-made shoes and sportswear — in short, for the classic lines that are the backbone of the wardrobe of the well-dressed child *de bonne famille*. Once the staple of the English child's wardrobe, today it is easier to find these clothes in France, where Anglo-Saxon chic rules. If you are tempted by the idea but can't make it in person, Cyrillus runs one of the most efficient mail-order services in the business. Write to B.P. 25, 91160 Longjumeau for one of its biannual catalogues.

DANIEL HECHTER

50 Champs–Elysées, 8e.
METRO: F. D. Roosevelt.

12 rue du Faubourg Saint-Honoré, 8e.
METRO: Concorde.

If you want a really French look but one that isn't quite so redolent of the nostalgic prettiness of the *enfant* BCBG, Daniel Hechter is a good name to look out for. Thoroughly modern, hardly any smocking in sight, with lots of charm and bright colours, a Hechter outfit would make any child look convincingly Gallic in the most delightful way.

HIPPOPOTAMUS CHAIN

If your children don't take easily to French cuisine (don't worry, they'll come to their senses later) take them to one of the Hippopotamus chain (6 avenue Franklin-Roosevelt, 8e and 46 avenue de Wagram, 17e are just two amongst several in the Paris region). The menu is always the same: steak or hamburgers, a green salad and French fries. The price is fixed; dessert is extra; and for accompanying grownups who need a little soothing, a *pichet* of Bordeaux is on offer.

JACADI

38 place du Marché-Saint-Honoré, 1er.
METRO: Pyramides.

7 rue Gustave-Courbet, 16e.
METRO: Victor-Hugo.

Jacadi is one of the grand chains that most bourgeois parents visit at one time or another. Well known for offering value for money, the designs are nonetheless up-to-the-minute and well thought-out. Girls and boys can be kitted out here from head to toe, from birth up to their mid-teens. And if junior should need a haircut during your stay, it's worth noting that at the place du Marché-Saint-Honoré branch, there is a good hairdresser *in situ*.

LAINES ECOSSAISES

181 boulevard Saint-Germain, 7e.
METRO: Saint-Germain-des-Prés.

You can't be in Paris very long, particularly in the colder months, without realising that *le look Anglais* (or *Ecossais*) is rampant. Here you may buy the classic kilts and sweaters that Maman BCBG is so fond of, but even if you're English (or from the land of the kilt itself) you will find here that *le look* is put together with a little Gallic air.

MINI-MADD

20 rue Tronchet, 8e.
METRO: Madeleine.

If you're after a look that isn't too redolent of rampant Anglomania but is something a little more Gallic, Mini-Madd is the place for you. Daniel Hechter provides much of the gear here and very nice it is, too.

MUSEE DES ENFANTS 12 avenue de New York, 16e.

METRO: Alma Marceau.

Most children would love a trip to this section of the Musée d'Art Moderne de la Ville de Paris: lots of lively events are always being held here (see the weekly magazines for details of the goings-on) such as dance-shows and painting sessions. All in French, *bien sûr*, but perhaps a good way of making them realise that French is a living language which it could be fun to learn. Entrance is free on Sundays.

MUSEE–PALAIS DE LA DECOUVERTE
avenue Franklin-Roosevelt, 8e.

METRO: F. D. Roosevelt.

I can hardly think of a child who would not be captivated by a visit to this wonderful museum. Even the most unscientific are entranced by the live demonstrations of basic scientific principles (see the doves learn to tap in a certain order if they want their food); by the Planetarium; by the marvellously clear setting out of the thoughts of Newton, Galileo and the other illustrious names. Don't miss it.

NAHALA

8 rue des Saussaies, 8e.
METRO: Miromesnil,
Champs-Elysées,
Clemenceau.

Worth a look, even if you can't afford the prices, Nahala is *la folie* for children — couture clothes at couture prices. If you have some really grand occasion (a royal wedding perhaps?) where your child needs to shine, I suppose it could be worth it. For most of us, though, a place just to look at.

LE NID A L'ECUREUIL

25 rue Bonaparte, 6e.
METRO: Saint-Sulpice,
Saint-Germain-des-Prés.

Another impeccable address, but this time offering clothing that has a little more to do with the real world than the refined offerings of Bonpoint: here you may buy some Osh-Kosh dungarees and other more robust appurtenances of the infant world.

LA PETITE GAMINERIE

28 and 32 rue du Four, 6e.
METRO: Mabillon.

As you might expect from a shop in the heart of Saint-Germain-des-Prés here you can find a thoroughly modern look for the small set. Such impeccably up-to-date names as Cacharel, Hechter and New Man loom large, and no child will feel ill-at-ease with their offerings. The look may be modern, but the quality is high, so don't go expecting bargains. Number 28 specialises in clothes for children up to about six years of age and number 32 for the 6- to 15-year-olds, whilst in between (at number 30) you can see a range of furniture for the nursery set.

LE PETIT FAUNE

33 rue Jacob, 6e.
METRO: Saint-Germain-des-Prés.

Another of those exquisite shops providing the sort of children's clothes most people only dream of. From a beautiful christening robe to a complete layette for the new-born baby, Le Petit Faune provides only the finest and the best. Exquisite though it may all look, the shop is also noted for taking great care over the practicalities of life. Babies and children, it acknowledges, don't just look exquisite, they cry, they get sick, they scuff their knees, so almost everything is made with an eye to washability. Look out for the charming knits and, if you're in Paris when the sales are on, you might find the bargain of a lifetime.

SCAPA OF SCOTLAND

71 rue des Saints-Pères, 6e.
METRO: Saint-Germain-des-Prés.

This is where the well brought-up children of good family are kitted out with the uniform that at once declares their class and status. In spite of all that, the clothes are charming. This is where Mme. BCBG goes for those Liberty prints, the smocked dresses, the small-size Shetlands and long-line Bermudas that make up the look she is after. There are also little button-down collared shirts just like Papa's and beautifully plain sweaters of good quality, everything that the small person needs to convey that sought-after air of Anglo-Saxon chic.

SONIA RYKIEL

6 rue de Grenelle, 6e.
METRO: Sèvres-Babylone.

Sonia Rykiel was the first designer to think of dressing children in black and her high chic of sober stripes and plains is still very much in demand. Her soft knits and velours are turned into charming sweaters, trousers, skirts and all-in-ones. What makes them stand out from the crowd is the colours — so much more sophisticated than those usually allocated to the children's range. Very much for the out-and-out modern child, with nothing of the *nostalgie* that is so rampant elsewhere.

VIVIANE GUIRE

63 rue de Boulainvilliers, 16e.
METRO: Muette.

Here, right in the middle of the 16th *arrondissement*, it is no surprise to see a children's boutique providing the sort of adorable clothing that Mme. BCBG loves to see her children in. Here are the little blouses with hand-embroidered collars, the cable-knit sweaters, the chic Bermudas, the adorable little-girl dresses, all like something out of the most beautiful of nostalgic films. Prices will be a good deal less nostalgic, but if you have a child you really want to treat (or perhaps its mother would find it even more of a treat) then splash out on something of exceptional charm.

TOYS AND FURNITURE

FARANDOLE

48 avenue Victor-Hugo, 16e.
METRO: Victor-Hugo.

A large selection of toys both nostalgic and utterly modern. Not quite so magical or special as Le Nain Blue but it is nonetheless an address worth noting if the 16th *arrondissement* is where you're based. If you need a present in a hurry, you'll not come away empty-handed.

MARIA KRISTINA

59 rue de Boulainvillers, 16e.
METRO: Muette.

A charming shop specialising in dolls and marionettes, animals and mobiles. Everything is exceedingly pretty (no plastic tat here) and there's lots to delight a child besides just toys. Candles and decorations at Christmas, pretty plates and dishes — a good address for present-hunting.

LE MONDE EN MARCHE

34, rue Dauphine, 6e.
METRO: Odéon.

Tiny but enchanting. Come here for a hand-painted wooden puppet on a string, a wooden Noah's ark or an exquisitely hand-crafted aeroplane. A charming selection of children's books as well. Everything in the shop is exceptional.

LE NAIN BLEU

406–410 rue Saint-Honoré, 8e.
METRO: Concorde, Madeleine.

One of the most famous toyshops in the world and rightly so. The windows are always a treat but if you're in Paris at Christmas-time then you're in for a very special treat. Toy soldiers have always been a speciality and you may find some wondrously rare and special one-offs. However, if you don't come into the oil-baron class, there are still lots of toys that more ordinary bank accounts can afford. Especially good on puzzles of all sorts, with enchanting wooden ones so lovely any adult would be captivated, too. Beautifully presented dolls' teasets, made from the finest china and complete with miniature croissants and pots of jam. Some exceptionally soft and lovely stuffed animals as well as (of course) dolls of every size and nationality. If you have a small child with you in Paris it would be the cheapest treat in the world to take him or her round the store — a treat they would never forget.

PIXI & CIE

95 rue de Seine, 6e.
METRO: Odéon.

A little shop but full of fantasy; most children would love to visit it. Here are miniature figures from the world of the imagination: formally-clad nannies wheeling out their charges in highly-sprung prams; soldiers standing stiffly to attention; formally-dressed *grandes dames* on their way to a ball; policemen in their *képis*; old-fashioned photographers under their black cloaks about to pull the string; bakers with their baskets of loaves — it must be seen to be appreciated. All the figures are for sale and there is usually a special exhibition on related themes to admire as well.

POCKET MONEY

74 rue du Ranelagh, 16e.
METRO: Ranelagh.

Here you may send the mini-set to buy the innumerable little bits of this and that that their pocket money will run to: T-shirts and funny-faces, jokey toys and watches, balloons and knick-knacks. Not aimed at adults — Papa and Maman are unlikely to find much that appeals to them — and no pretty nostalgia here, but lots of jokey bits and pieces that the kids will love.

ROCHE BOBOIS YOUNG STORE

92 boulevard de Sébastopol, 3e.
METRO: Réaumur-Sébastopol.

10 rue de Lyon, 12e.
METRO: Gare de Lyon.

I'm not suggesting you lug home a complete nursery, but take a look at the French way with furniture for the young — sleek, comfortable and beautiful — and it should give you many ideas of your own. Lots of small accessories such as lights and storage boxes, which could certainly be taken home.

TORTUE ELECTRIQUE

To be truthful this is probably more a toyshop for grownups who remain enchanted with the world of childhood, than for the children themselves. It was George Bernard Shaw who

7 rue Frédéric-Sauton, 5e.
METRO: Maubert-Mutualité.

said that childhood was wasted on children; well, so are these toys. But children give you a good excuse, if you need one, (and you can always take them afterwards to see Notre-Dame, which is just *en face*) to drop in. Here you will find games and toys from times gone by, everything from an old chess-set to a mediaeval puzzle. There's also a selection of works on the theme of play through the ages — an eye-opener for children weaned on the avalanche of plastic and microchips that toy departments seem to consist of these days.

DEPARTMENT STORES

These may not have the immediate charm of the little boutiques and speciality shops tucked away in the side-streets but they do have their uses. If you have little time or if you don't want to wander round hoping to chance upon a happy discovery you should make for one of the big department stores, where you can shop quickly and efficiently. After all, you wouldn't dream of visiting London without stopping off at Harrods, or New York without taking in Bloomies. A trip to Galeries Lafayette or Au Printemps will give you another perspective on *la vie Parisienne.*

It is also probably the least intimidating way to shop for those who aren't exactly sure of what they want; who don't speak French; and who don't like coping with impeccably-turned out, haughtily-mannered salesgirls.

Most of the large stores have information desks and *hôtesses* who will speak some English and help divest you of your francs as painlessly as possible.

Visitors from abroad should remember that they can always ask for *le détaxe*, a refund of the French excise tax, to which they are entitled on purchases adding up to 2200 francs or more if they live within the EEC; 1200 francs if they live outside. *Le détaxe* is much easier to organise in the big department stores than in the small boutiques for they usually allow receipts for smaller amounts to be kept and collected until they add up to the necessary sums.

If you're buying presents, you probably won't even have to ask to have them gift-wrapped. The French are specialists when it comes to the art of presentation — it's all part of the service. They are also experts at packing and delivery.

Big stores are usually open from 9.30am to 6.30pm from Monday to Saturday and a few stay open late (until 8pm) on Wednesdays. Remember that the main branches in central Paris get very crowded so it is best to go early in the morning if you can. They also get very hot, particularly in winter, so even if you're tempted to wear your best new coat, dress as lightly as you dare.

By and large the major department stores are to be found in the area around the Opéra or near the Hôtel de Ville on the Right Bank, though Au Bon Marché is a distinguished elderly example on the Left Bank.

CONTENTS

AU BON MARCHE

38 rue de Sèvres, 7e.
METRO: Vaneau, Sèvres-Babylone.

One of the few department stores to be found on the Left Bank, this is a good solid family store, one of the oldest shops in Paris. Like Aux Trois Quartiers, it is much less crowded than its more fashionable relations, but it is a good place to look for less modish merchandise at more agreeable prices.

Au Bon Marché is particularly good for household linens of all sorts; for a fine selection of self-service food; for its do-it-yourself departments, its carpets (in particular it has an outstanding selection of antique Oriental rugs of all sorts) and those hard-to-track-down necessities that come under the name of haberdashery. There is also a surprisingly good selection of antiques, and some people say it has the best selection of underwear in Paris — not beautifully displayed, but it's all there and you can rifle through the stock without being intimidated by the staff who are, incidentally, reputed to be charming.

It's marvellous, too, for children's wear and much less pricey than Printemps or Galeries. Go for beautifully cut cotton Bermudas, chic blouson jackets and nice plain tracksuits.

AU PRINTEMPS

64 boulevard Haussmann, 9e.
METRO: Havre-Caumartin, Opéra.

There are those who prefer Galeries Lafayette and those who plump for Au Printemps. Some have detected service that is a little more polite at Printemps, a little less rushed, although the prices are a little higher. Some say Printemps is more upmarket; others give this accolade to Galeries Lafayette (I tend to think that these days Galeries Lafayette is the chicest). You will have to decide for yourself which you prefer. What is certain is that they both try hard to woo you.

When it comes to fashion, I would hand the honours to the Galeries. Though Printemps has its collection of designer clothes, grouped by name, the names are, on the whole, just a little less starry — if you really want your name in lights, you have to be at the Galeries. But wander down the rue de la Mode. Dip into Kenzo, Anne-Marie Beretta, Issey Miyake, Elisabeth de Senneville and Jean-Paul Gaultier.

Do as the Parisians do and keep your eye on Selection Printemps, the store's very own collection. Here you can find trendy clothes, the latest look at affordable prices. All very cleverly done. Printemps' answer to Galeries' Galfa Club is Au Brummel, and here you'll find some impeccable *pulls* and shirts: they'll even alter the sleeves to fit and add your initials.

Don't miss the Primavera boutique: everything you might need to give your house or garden that finishing touch. From a huge antique *armoire* to a few frankly fake flowers, it radiates charm, colour and fantasy.

Where Printemps really comes into its own, however, is in the field of modern design for the house and home. Here, every designer with ambition is longing to be given a little space. Constantly alive to new trends, its reputation is rapidly growing. Look out for the influence of Andrée Putman, France's First Lady of Design, in particular for her new editions for Ecart International. Stunningly displayed, they put most British furniture stores to shame. Besides Andrée Putman, there's the work of Philippe Starck (of Café Costes fame) and many other young designers. Interest is constantly generated with a series of design competitions so if the contemporary look is your scene, don't miss this department. It manages to make furniture appear lively, interesting and even, that rare thing, seductive.

Printemps is a good hunting-ground, too, for presents of every sort, especially at Christmas-time. It's probably the best place to start looking for reasonably-priced, attractive toys. Look out for scarves, perfume and a host of *petits trucs* and while you're about it take note of the selection of food, wines, fresh fruits and vegetables, spices and *charcuterie*, all of which whet the appetite for a visit to the terrace restaurant on the top floor. Renowned more for its *belle époque* decor than its food, it is still well worth the detour.

And if food is still on your mind after all that, outside, just beside it, is one of the best food street markets in Paris.

AUX TROIS QUARTIERS

17 boulevard de la Madeleine, 1er.
METRO: Madeleine.

Not to mince words, this store is frankly dull. It is the matron of the department store world: middle-aged, set in her ways, lacking the fun, the skittishness and the glamour of Printemps and Galeries. It caters to predictable, thoroughly conventional bourgeois tastes but the bourgeoisie aren't fools and they like their service to be polite and attentive — so polite and attentive it is. It is also blissfully uncrowded.

If you happen to be in the area and you need a scarf, a suitcase, some new perfume or maybe even a discreet cashmere sweater of reliable quality, you will not be disappointed. There is a fine selection of household linens and it is justly famous for its gloves and handkerchiefs. Choose them in peace and tranquillity and then enjoy a quiet cup of tea in the pleasantly restful *salon de thé* on the 4th floor.

Madelios is the annexe for men and it exudes the same air of contented respectability; it may be dull but it will never let you down, And men's clothing being less prone to the whims of fashion, it yields some very wearable items.

BAZAR DE L'HOTEL DE VILLE

55 rue de la Verrerie, 4e.
METRO: Hôtel de Ville.

More usually patronised by Parisians than by the tourist, BHV (as it is affectionately known) has an authentically Parisian air, albeit of a popular kind. Once described as being reminiscent of the late-lamented Gamages of High Holborn (of which it was said that 'many people come in but some never find their way out'), BHV is still one of the most difficult of department stores for the newcomer to suss out. It is notorious for having the best do-it-yourself department in Paris and the least helpful staff. Here you really need all your *hauteur* to get served.

Go there for every little *truc*, every conceivable and many scarcely conceivable gadgets. It is a *bricoleur*'s paradise: from garden shears to wallpaper stripper, from pre-cut timber to sophisticated home security you can find everything for the house and garden here.

Look out for an unimaginable selection of aids to maintain the body beautiful, a very Parisian necessity, gadgets to depilate, to curl the hair, to buff the nails, to tan the face and to cleanse the pores.

So brave the unhelpful staff; admire the best selection of *quincaillerie* in Paris; and if the rest of it is a little run of the *moulin*, never mind, it is very, very French.

And if your taste for shopping is irrepressible, it is worth noting that BHV (like its near neighbour Samaritaine) has a *nocturne* on Wednesdays, staying open until 10pm.

GALERIES LAFAYETTE

40 boulevard Haussmann, 9e.
METRO: Chaussée d'Antin.

Tour Montparnasse, 17 rue de l'Arrivée, 15e.
METRO: Montparnasse Bienvenüe.

Possibly now the prettiest of all the department stores with its fine glass dome and beautifully-organised departments. It is also the most luxurious, most expensive and most up-market of them all — it could be said to be to Paris what Bloomingdale's is to New York. The store offers a whole range of services: the busy visitor might like to park a heavy bag in the basement *consigne*, buy some theatre tickets, change some money, get a key cut, have a new skirt altered or even park a hired car — you can do all this at the Galeries.

If you feel you haven't got your eye in for what the current fashionable look is all about, there is no better place to start. Head for the two fashion floors and see what the big-name designers are up to. They are all there: from Kenzo to Rykiel, Comme des Garçons and Dorothée Bis, Dior, Ungaro, St-Laurent and Yohji Yamamoto, all beautifully labelled and well displayed. If you find a designer whose work you love you could always go to his own boutique later on.

There are also the Galeries' own-label clothes to look out for. These are marvellously authentic adaptations of the current look at much more bearable prices than the designer-labels. The Galeries are nearly always first off the mark in bringing out reasonably-priced interpretations of current fads; they were, for instance, the first to sell the components that add up to the Chanel look. Chanel-type gilt and pearl ear-rings are still to be found in the buzzing jewellery department, those immaculate braided and gilt-buttoned cardigans in knitwear, and those chain-handled quilted bags in the handbag section.

If you really don't have much confidence in your own ability to gather a little of Parisian chic about yourself, put yourself in the able hands of Jacqueline Murray who runs a totally free service called Mode Plus at the Galeries. In the privacy of a charming little salon you can tell the elegant Jacqueline Murray all about your lifestyle, your budget, the sort of look you'd like to aim at, and she'll help you get it all together. From the raft of designer and own-label clothes in the store she will select not just garments but all the accessories that turn the clothes into something special. Lest you feel this is all a little pressurising, remember you don't have to buy anything at all (though, I dare say you will need a fairly tough skin to be able to carry that through). If you find the service is what you need you can go back again and again — a record of everything you buy is kept up to date and they will look out for just the shirt to go with the skirt that goes with the jacket . . .

The ground floor is the place to look out for presents to take back home: the right piece of jewellery, the current taste in scarves, the T-shirt with just the right shape, the very latest belt.

The children's department is full of mini-chic, at a price, but do take a quick look at all the appurtenances the mini-set require. The satchels, the stationery, the toys — all are done with great panache and would make excellent presents. The best time to visit these departments is in the run-up to *La Rentrée* (the return to school after the summer holidays in September) always a big moment for the Paris stores.

Men, or women searching for presents for the man in their life, should pay a visit to Galfa Club, where their needs are catered for with the style we have come to expect.

If you still have energy to spare, the household department in the basement is a cook and home-maker's delight. Golden pottery from Provence, porcelain from Limoges, straw baskets, candles in all colours and shapes, gadgets galore, traditional bowls for holding coffee and dunking croissants — more temptations, more delights, more decisions.

Look in on the furniture and furnishings department as well. The standard here is exceptionally high and everything is beautifully laid out. Recently it was resplendent with roses blooming on everything from lampshades and china, to chintzes chintzier than you'd find in almost any English country house.

Galeries regularly has exhibitions on up-to-the-minute themes, so look in on these if you have any time left.

PRISUNIC

52 avenue des Champs-Elysées, 8e.
METRO: F. D. Roosevelt.

No aesthetic experience this. As you enter through the doors you may well have a slightly sinking feeling and wonder if it's worth the bother. Yes, it is. Keep going. Keep your tastebuds alert. There's lots of fairly down-market ordinary merchandise but almost every season there are some special numbers that you shouldn't miss. It might be a baby's dress, properly smocked, for a ludicrously cheap price, an irresistible cotton sweater in an expensive-looking cream, or a scarf that is just what you need to finish off this year's look. Prices are amazingly low, so keep your eyes peeled and you may be lucky.

If you have a car or the energy to cart home household bargains this is the place to buy some Provençal pottery, some French crystal, a fish kettle, some inexpensive but different plates and bowls, or the very latest can-opener. All come at rock-bottom prices.

There's quite a food department, too — not as exciting as shopping in a little local delicatessen but the mustards and olive oils, the cheeses and the spices are all well worth taking in.

Foodies with a waistline problem are trekking to Prisunic in droves to pick up some of Michel Guérard's lean-line specials: all are guaranteed to have less than 300 calories a serving, but with specialities like *poulet à l'estragon* on the menu nobody need suffer.

LA SAMARITAINE

rue du Pont-Neuf, 1er.
METRO: Pont-Neuf.

One of the oldest stores in Paris, it is still wrapped in an aura of times gone by. It reminds one irresistibly of the good old days when there were nice men to open doors, when parcels were always wrapped and *la politesse* was still the order of the day. The store itself is made up of several buildings, but your *hôtesse* will help you find your way around.

Samaritaine is most famous for its vast selection of proper working clothes: blue, tiny-check trousers, chefs' aprons, smocks and striped jackets, butchers' vests and maids' caps. Parisians with staff still buy their kit here; those without have been known to don a stiff white chef's jacket to wear themselves. And with workers' clothes, made in timeless shapes from classic materials in the time-honoured way, becoming newly chic, so a new generation, encouraged by the fashion gurus of *Elle et al*, is wending its way to Samaritaine.

Smart Parisian women buy paper overalls to slip over their Yves St-Laurent number whilst they put the finishing touches to the *sauce aux champignons*. Their younger offspring hunt down nightshirts just like *grand-père* used to wear and stop off to consult the resident astrologer on their way to look at the amazing collection of cats and dogs, birds and fish.

Housewives go for the thick linen sheets, just like the ones used in the grand, old-fashioned hotels, made in the Vosges mountains and selling at the sort of prices you may expect. In the basement there are some 60,000 (yes, 60,000) different products, all aimed at the world of *bricolage* or DIY, and, innovation, trained experts who will show you how to use the tools.

Parisians come to La Samaritaine for well-priced fridges and freezers and a reliable name for service. Tourists come for a whiff of real Paris and for one of Paris' most staggering views — don't miss the roof terrace bar on the 10th floor of Magasin 2 if you're there from April to September (it's closed for the rest of the year).

And remember that La Samaritaine, like BHV, has a *nocturne*, a late-night opening, until 10pm on Wednesdays.

FASHION

FROM HAUTE COUTURE TO PRET-A-PORTER

'Ze clothzes' as Clive James so memorably dubbed them in an irresistible television essay on the subject, are still one of the glories of Paris, as potent an ingredient in the overall image as garlic and baguettes. Haute couture, though often pronounced dying, or very sickly indeed, is currently looking surprisingly sprightly.

It is true that almost no couture house makes money on its haute couture collections alone. How could they, when there are roughly just 3000 women in the world who can pay the astronomical sums true haute couture commands? Haute couture provides the glamour, the gloss, the high-profile image that launches a thousand mass-market products. It is the vital heartbeat at the centre of the industry.

Why, you may wonder, would anybody pay the 50,000 francs and on and on upwards a couture dress commands? At its best a couture creation is a work of art, the sum total of a myriad of special skills, with that indefinable extra ingredient that transforms the merely well-made into a small miracle.

The couture dress is made to mould the client's body like a second skin, and every detail, from the button-holing to the seams, from the lining to the stitching, is so perfectly wrought that it seems a dreadful shame it can't all be seen. It is the result of hours and hours of handiwork and yet at its best it has the insouciant simplicity of a summer's day. To see a real couture dress is to be spoiled forever for mere run-of-the-mill fashion.

The haute couture *maisons* produce two collections every year, in January and July. They are sumptuous, hectic, dazzling affairs. *Un monde*, as *Paris* magazine put it, *fou, fou, fou*. There are the catwalks; the little gilt chairs; the champagne; the impossibly skinny, exotic girls; the kisses and the cries; the photographers; the crush and the famous clients sitting in the front row.

Once, these collections were strictly in-house affairs, with each house having a stable of house models who sashayed down the catwalk in clothes made specifically to their measurements. Today each complete collection is usually shown just once in all its glory. And no wonder; the costs are so exorbitant, even for these billion-dollar spinners, that once has to do.

Today, the collections are often held in a large hotel and the house models have given way to an international troupe of itinerant cover-girls who romp down one catwalk today and move onto the next tomorrow.

Invitations are restricted to fashion journalists, celebrities and rich, private clients. After the show the house is left with a full-colour video which usually takes some 15 days to process and for the next two or three months the video is shown to prospective clients, three or four times a week, at a specific time.

If you aren't a client but would like to see one of these video presentations you can — it isn't easy but it can be done. It helps if you are staying at a good hotel: the porter at the Crillon, the Plaza-Athénée or the Ritz could almost certainly fix it for you.

If you are well dressed and have the chutzpah you can always chance your arm by walking in off the street and asking in a polite but commanding voice for a ticket for one of the showings. Much will depend upon your appearance — if you're wearing jeans and sneakers you really would be wasting your breath. At Chanel, in Coco's time, it was strongly rumoured that the *vendeuses* had strict instructions to give way only to the thin: to be fat, said Mlle. Chanel, was not chic.

Of all the grand couturiers Yves St-Laurent is probably still the one riding highest. His shows are the most crowded, the most ritzy, the most frantic, and his creations some of the most copied in the world. Chanel is staging a big comeback: you have only to look at all those chain-handled bags, those immaculate cardigans and strings of pearls filtering through to the chain-stores to see how sought after is this house's impeccable feel for comfortable, casual elegance.

But each to his own *goût*. See some of the shows and decide for yourself. Here is a list of the names and addresses of all current members of the *Chambre Syndicale*, that gilded group whose talents inspire makers of clothes all over the world.

Remember that almost all the big names have opened boutiques of their own — often on the same premises, sometimes next door — where you can buy off-the-peg clothes. Prices will still be high, though nothing like as stratospheric as for haute couture, and you will get a little of the magic, of the flair, that goes into the handmade work of art.

HAUTE COUTURE

The magic names that belong to the *Chambre Syndicale de la Haute Couture* form one of the most exclusive clubs in the world. Currently there are just 23 members (with the fate of Courrèges, who no longer meets all the conditions, in the balance). There are stringent rules and regulations that members have to adhere to: a house must employ at least 20 skilled people in its own workshops; it must present a collection of at least 75 designs on a minimum of three live models twice a year, in spring and autumn, to the press; it must hold at least 45 showings for its private clients and, finally, it must announce publicly, in advance, the dates of each show.

CONTENTS

* Strictly speaking not all shops but also places to rest the feet, restore the spirits and engage the mind.

FROM HAUTE COUTURE TO PRET-A-PORTER

HAUTE COUTURE

PRET-A-PORTER

HAUTE COUTURE

BALMAIN

44 rue François-1er, 8e.
METRO: F. D. Roosevelt;
Alma Marceau.

Under the direction of Erik Mortensen, *jolie madame* can find here the reassuring *élan* that will flatter and never alarm. If it seems a little old-fashioned, well, that's what well-heeled women want for the daily round of shopping, lunching and dining — you wouldn't want it to date too soon, would you?

CARVEN

6 Rond-Point des Champs-Elysées, 8e.
METRO: F. D. Roosevelt.

A lower profile than some of the others with a style that sometimes seems to owe more to American showbiz than refined Parisian taste.

CHANEL

31 rue Cambon, 1er.
METRO: Madeleine.

Coco may long be dead, but her spirit lives on. Here Karl Lagerfeld goes on giving us the classic Chanel look that charms and beguiles. His tailoring, his soft knits and his silky blouses suit women of all ages. Fiery-eyed, ineffably French, model Inès de la Fressanges sums up the spirit of the house: all verve and zest and strong personality. No retiring violets here. American jetsetter Lynn Wyatt loves the braided suits, the whole Coco image reworked in the spirit of the times.

CHRISTIAN DIOR

30 avenue Montaigne, 8e.
METRO: Alma Marceau.

A grand old name, one of the greatest of all the houses and beloved of the Monaco princesses, who are nearly always in the front row at collection time. From the late Christian Dior came the famous New Look which turned fashion overnight into a subject on which all could pontificate. Today Dior's Marc Bohan still has an ineffable knack of making a woman look like a real woman; elegance and true chic are its hallmark. It has a particularly good off-the-peg boutique and a fine selection of reasonably-priced accessories like scarves and costume jewellery.

EMANUEL UNGARO

2 avenue Montaigne, 8e.
METRO: Alma Marceau.

Not to everybody's taste, Ungaro is noted for a very creative style that sometimes verges on the over-dramatic. Think of Anouk Aimée, almost his favourite client and a continuous source of inspiration, and you'll get the picture. An extrovert's dream, you'll be sure to be noticed and you certainly won't look like anybody else.

GIVENCHY

3 avenue George V, 8e.
METRO: Alma Marceau.

One of the most elegant houses of all, which will surprise nobody who remembers Audrey Hepburn's spectacular wardrobe in *Sabrina* and in her private life for more than 30 years. A favourite designer with those women, such as the late Princess Grace of Monaco, who prefer to be elegant rather than eye-catching.

GRES

1 rue de la Paix, 2e.
METRO: Opéra.

Mme. Grès, still wrapped in her immaculate turbans, is one of the grand old ladies of the haute couture scene. She it was who showed the world just what could be done with a length of silk jersey. The mistress of the art of draping, of cutting, and of subtle flattery, her exquisite taste still runs through the whole collection. For purity of line, for simplicity so exactly right it's almost breathtaking, the house of Grès is still supreme. There are those who feel that the prêt-à-porter, no longer under her direction, is less successful — see for yourself.

GUY LAROCHE

29 avenue Montaigne, 8e.
METRO: Alma Marceau.

For sheer charm Laroche is hard to beat — which may explain why he sells more haute couture models than almost anybody else. His prêt-à-porter is enormously successful all around the world: he understands the lifestyle of the rich young woman who flits from Palm Beach to Gstaad, and gives her the clothes she needs — ravishingly pretty rather than dauntingly chic.

HANAE MORI

17–19 avenue Montaigne, 8e.
METRO: F. D. Roosevelt.

This Japanese designer is different from all her other compatriots in being almost more Parisian than most Parisians. Her style is subtle, wearable, soft and flattering and her evening dresses have been acknowledged as among the best in Paris. She is enormously successful, with a flourishing line in ready-to-wear.

JEAN-LOUIS SCHERRER

51 avenue Montaigne, 8e.
METRO: Alma Marceau.

The grand designer for the grandest of lifestyles, an air of *luxe*, of voluptuous sophistication, envelops his shows. He loves the most expensive of materials and knows how to use them superbly. As for the rest of us, we would be all dressed up and with precious few places to go. Very, very French, he's best known for dressing Mme. Giscard d'Estaing and a host of the women behind Europe's most powerful men.

JEAN PATOU

7 rue Saint-Florentin, 8e.
METRO: Concorde.

Christian Lacroix, a recent winner of the supreme award in this gilded world, the Dé d'Or, is one of the brightest young stars on the scene, the latest darling of the fashion press. He sometimes cocks a snook at more conventional ideas of elegance and chic but has brought a breath of real fresh air into haute couture and attracted a new young clientele in the process.

LANVIN

22 rue du Faubourg Saint-Honoré, 8e.
METRO: Concorde.

In Jean-François Crahay's day, this was one of the most sought-after houses in Paris. Under Maryll Lanvin, an ex-American model who married Bernard Lanvin, it is producing pretty, wearable clothes but seems a trifle short on creativity and direction.

LECOANET-HEMANT

5 rue Lamennais, 8e.
METRO: George V, Etoile.

Who? I hear you ask. Yes, well . . . you may not know much about them yet but give them time. As the newest, youngest members of the *Chambre Syndicale* they haven't really had a chance to be put through their paces, but there are lots of ambitious plans in the pipeline.

LOUIS FERAUD

88 rue du Faubourg Saint-Honoré, 8e.
METRO: Saint-Philippe-du-Roule.

A lovely house producing clothes that almost any woman would long to own. Colour, line and sheer flattery are its strengths, as befits the designs of the most flirtatious of all the big names.

MUSEE DES ARTS DE LA MODE 107 rue de Rivoli, 1er.

METRO: Châtelet.

At last Paris has a museum where fashion freaks can go to indulge their passion. It seems scarcely credible that it has taken this long for Paris, long claiming to be the centre of the fashion industry in the world, to allocate some museum space to this, their most renowned industry. It isn't quite finished yet but what there is looks very promising: fashion photographs, paintings, clothing from the 18th century through to the 20th century as well as roomsets potently evoking the lifestyles to which these clothes belonged. Many of the grand old names of haute couture have contributed to the displays: how about Vionet, Poiret, Schiaparelli and Chanel to whet the appetite?

And when you've had a look at all those exhibits don't forget that it's a marvellous place to buy all those presents that you will need to take to the folks back home. Many of the couture houses have contributed their own accessories to the boutique: look out for scarves by YSL, witty costume jewellery (a wonderful Schiaparelli brooch by Cocteau), straw hats and berets, as well as old-fashioned paper dolls and masses of attractive postcards. It's all lodged in the newly transformed 18th-century Pavillon de Marsan of the Louvre.

NINA RICCI

39 avenue Montaigne, 8e.
METRO: Alma Marceau.

Gerard Pipart produces a very French, very sophisticated collection, the essence of *le style Parisien*. Nothing vulgar or *de trop* — ever.

PACO RABANNE

8 rue du Cherche-Midi, 6e.
METRO: Sèvres-Babylone.

One of the few of the grand designers to have his *maison* on the Left Bank, away from the perfumed *maisons* of the avenue Montaigne and the rue du Faubourg Saint-Honoré. This is something of a giveaway. Don't expect conventional chic: look for wit, originality and a sense of the theatrical. Sometimes it works; sometimes it doesn't, but it certainly makes things interesting.

PER SPOOK

18 avenue George V, 8e.
METRO: Alma Marceau,
George V.

This elegant Norwegian designs for the modern woman; he knows how to provide clothes for her busy, rushing life. The Per Spook woman does more with her life than shop: she works, she travels, dines out and drives, and the clothes he gives her will cope with it all. Favoured designer of the French movie set, the front row at his collections is often a movie-goer's dream — an ardent supporter has always been Jeanne Moreau.

PHILIPPE VENET

62 rue François-ler, 1er.
METRO: George V.

Most famous for his finely tailored, beautifully cut suits and coats. So subtle are they that it may take a while to appreciate the art that goes into them. For the older woman there could scarcely be a better, more flattering house to go to, but younger beauties, like Queen Noor of Jordan, go there to be flattered too.

PIERRE CARDIN

27 avenue de Marigny, 8e.
METRO: Champs-Elysées;
Clemenceau.

A grand, grand designer turned even grander businessman. Reputed to be the richest of them all, his *sorties* into chocolates and sheets, fountain pens and watches, seem to have left his collections without the inspiration they once showed, although the taste and the sense of line is as impeccable as ever.

SERGE LEPAGE

29 rue François-ler, 1er.
METRO: George V,
F. D. Roosevelt.

Said to be beloved by the potentates from the East, whose tastes and needs he understands. For the rest of us, he has yet to prove his worth.

TED LAPIDUS

35 rue François-ler, 1er.
METRO: George V,
F. D. Roosevelt.

Once a fully paid-up member of the avant-garde set, today he may not be the most original of designers, but he is one who knows well how to produce the kind of easy-to-wear clothes that both flatter and charm.

TORRENTE

9 rue du Faubourg Saint-
Honoré, 8e.
METRO: Concorde.

A flourishing house, though possibly with less of an international following than some of the others. Its clients seem mostly Parisian, of whom Mme. Mitterrand is probably the best known.

YVES SAINT-LAURENT

5 avenue Marceau, 16e.
METRO: Alma Marceau.

Since his earliest days working under Christian Dior, St-Laurent has scarcely ever been out of the limelight. He it was who gave us the Trapeze line, the safari look and who then showed us that women could look even better in a man's 'smoking'. Still probably the master of them all, certainly the most copied, his list of famous clients is long and glamorous, and topping them all is Catherine Deneuve, who scarcely misses a show. If you can't afford his couture there's lots prêt-à-porter.

PRET-A-PORTER

For most of us, though, the world of haute couture is as rarified as a Rembrandt — beautiful to look at but almost as out of reach. Do not despair, however, there is plenty of creative talent about and Paris has a way of attracting it.

After the *Grand Couturiers*, next in importance come the individual designers who show at the *Prêt-à-Porter* (affectionately known as the Prêt). Here the tickets are equally hard to come by; the scenes are as dramatic; the comings and goings of the fashion journalists and photographers even more frenetic; and the crush much, much worse.

The shows take place in October and March and the cream of young creative talent is on view. But the great difference is that most of the clothes on show will eventually trickle into the many boutiques scattered throughout Paris. You will be able to look and may actually be able to afford to buy.

Once upon a time most of the beau monde used to wend its way to the rue du Faubourg Saint-Honoré and the avenue Montaigne. Today, if you want to see where it's all at you can either take a trip down the designer floors of Au Printemps and Galeries Lafayette, or make for the two hottest fashion spots in Paris: the place des Victoires or the area round the rue de Grenelle, rue du Cherche-Midi and rue des Saints-Pères on the Left Bank.

The place des Victoires was pioneered by Kenzo and Thierry Mugler (both still in situ) and Françoise Chassagnac's modish boutique called simply 'Victoire' set the seal upon its status. Nowadays anybody wanting a fashionable outfit, and the shoes and accessories that will transform it into something special, could do a lot worse than head straight for the place des Victoires.

The rue Etienne-Marcel, leading away from the place towards the Marais, seems gradually to be becoming a mini outpost of Japan, so full is it of all the trendiest of the new-wave Japanese designers. Unlike Kenzo, who seems these days essentially Parisian, they have retained a strong Japanese identity. Go there for lots of minimalist chic; for great waves of black, white and grey; for masses of inspiration.

As the creative talent goes on burgeoning, and boutique space runs out, some of the brightest of the new stars are opening up in the Marais, Popy Moreni and Azzedine Alaia being amongst the most notable examples.

Over on the Left Bank, around the rue du Cherche-Midi, is another good hunting ground for the fashionably-minded.

Claude Montana and Emmanuelle Khahn (in the rue de Grenelle nearby), Sonia Rykiel, Anne-Marie Beretta, Dorothée Bis and Christian Aujard are just a few worth keeping an eye on.

And don't forget the highways and byways round the boulevard Saint-Germain where many a trendy boutique has put down roots — there you will come upon Missoni, Issey Miyake, Chloe, Kashiyama, Peggy Roche and others.

Wander round, make your own discoveries, look in on what the big names are doing. Here is a small selection of some of the most innovative, most genuinely creative of the new designers. Each has his own inimitable style and all add zest and diversity to the Parisian fashion scene.

ANNE-MARIE BERETTA

24 rue Saint-Sulpice, 6e.
METRO: Odéon, Mabillon.

Not so new, but still rising. A good name for women who like to look like women; who like their clothes to be intensely feminine but elegant and a touch original, too. And if you want something dramatic for a special occasion, she can provide that as well.

CHANTAL THOMASS

11 rue Madame, 6e.
METRO: Saint-Sulpice.

11 Forum des Halles, Grand balcon, 2e
METRO: Les Halles.

12-14 Rond-Point des Champs-Elysées, 8e.
METRO: F. D. Roosevelt.

Another of the pre-eminently feminine designers. The woman Chantal Thomass has in mind may be liberated enough in her lifestyle but she doesn't believe in showing it too much in her clothes. Go to her for a soft, romantic, infinitely beguiling style of dressing. If sometimes the style is a little coquettish, well, perhaps it is time to remind ourselves of these old-fashioned pleasures.

CLAUDE MONTANA

31 rue de Grenelle, 7e (for women).
37 rue de Grenelle, 7e (for men).
METRO: Sèvres-Babylone, rue du Bac.

Out of mere slithers of spaces, the architects have conjured up magic environments; fitting arenas for Montana's great talents. The master of how to handle leather, he, with Thierry Mugler, was one of the first to see the potential in large shoulders. A genuinely creative talent, his clothes are not necessarily easy to wear but they do convey class and style. Besides his slightly eccentric suits (one half brown, the other green) there are others which show more concern for tradition. And if you want a leather jacket, soft as handkerchief linen, there's no-one who does them better.

JEAN-CHARLES DE CASTELBAJAC

31 place du Marché Saint-Honoré, 1er.
METRO: Pyramides, Tuileries.

Jean-Charles de Castelbajac approaches fashion with an artist's eye, and no detail is too small to escape his attention. He often uses rare and innovative materials and he it was who invented the idea of the dress as *tableau*, which is presumably why he was approached to redesign the cassocks for the French clergy. He is another of the designers the timid and insecure should avoid. Castelbajac's woman is modern and unafraid — and a little streak of exhibitionism would not go amiss. When it comes to men, whom Castelbajac also clothes, the look is rarified, slightly dandyish, with more than just a touch of *le style Anglais.*

JEAN-PAUL GAULTIER

6 rue Vivienne, 2e.
METRO: Bourse.

Very *drôle.* When his latest boutique in the rue Vivienne opened, the crowds that came to inspect it were so deep they had to operate a queuing system. The image is very, very potent. The boutique itself is described by those who coin these things as 'new Baroque', but to the less knowing eye it looks more like a little bit of this and a little bit of that. The models in the shop are got up like ancient classical figures, contrasting strangely with the hi-tech mood of the videos set in the floor which show a running full-colour film of the complete collection. What, I hear you ask, about the clothes? Well, they take some wearing (after all, it's not everyone who looks her best in medieval hosiery) but, we are reliably told, they are amongst the most original, the most carefully constructed of the new generation. Above all, Jean-Paul Gaultier is never, ever dull.

KARL LAGERFELD

144 avenue des Champs-Elysées, 8e.
METRO: Etoile.

Besides the millions of dollars he's reputed to earn from masterminding the renaissance of Chanel, Karl Lagerfeld has his own stamping-ground, and here it is. Here he works out his own ideas: witty, spirited, contemporary, without the overwhelming influence of Coco to consider. One of today's most versatile designers (when he's not busy with Chanel or the Karl Lagerfeld collection, he turns his attention to fur and leather for Fendi), this is where you find pure, mainstream Lagerfeld.

MARITHE ET FRANCOIS GIRBAUD

38 rue Etienne-Marcel, 2e.
METRO: Etienne-Marcel.

This boutique looks frankly intimidating from the outside, so bleak and minimalist is the atmosphere as perceived through the windows. Apart from anything else it is hard to make out if it is for men or women — the answer, as I'm sure you've guessed, is that it's for both. One of the new breed of unisex shops, its four floors have created something of a sensation in Paris where the grand stone and metal staircase has become quite a parade ground for the famous and the wealthy, whose manner of dressing is thus theatrically displayed. There is a great deal of grey jersey, much black and white, and elegant boxfuls of what appear to be the chicest socks in Paris (they are white, grey or black, imprinted with Japanese characters in a contrasting white, black or grey). If your vision of Paris is all Maurice Chevalier and onion-sellers with Breton berets, this will be a splendid antidote.

PREMONVILLE ET DEWARIN

18 rue Saint-Marc, 2e.
METRO: Bourse, Montmartre.

With names like those how could they fail? Americans in particular seem to love the Gallic sound and Myrène de Prémonville, in the days when she was solo, must have found the name alone worth thousands of dollars. Besides the names there's lots of talent and the new double act belongs to the generation of young women designers homing in on the body beautiful and determined to show the female form at its very best. Lots of tailored suits to suit the new more fitted silhouette but done with this year's verve.

THIERRY MUGLER

10 place des Victoires, 2e.
METRO: Bourse.

One of the numerous Andrée Putman-designed boutiques, where the decor says as much as the clothes. Another proponent of the dramatic school of clothing — you couldn't wear a Thierry Mugler number and appear incognito. He was one of the first to give men and women those padded shoulders and his clothes are sought after by those who like couture quality with prêt-à-porter insouciance.

VICKY TIEL

21 rue Bonaparte, 6e.
METRO: Saint-Germain-des-Prés.

Ever since Elizabeth Taylor discovered her way back in the 60s and sashayed into First Nights in her creations, Vicky Tiel has had a steady flow of showbiz clients. Glamour is what she's known for, so glamour is what she gives. Think of Elizabeth Taylor — that says it all.

FOOD AND WINE

To go to Paris without a sense of excitement and adventure about food and eating is like going to Rome and missing out on the Sistine Chapel. Where to eat and what are matters of paramount importance to the Parisian. This doesn't meant that food has to be grand but it does have to be good. An impeccably cooked omelette is more to be savoured than a vulgarly sauced duck à l'orange. Quality is what it is all about. To the Parisian it really does matter that his baguette is crunchy, his vegetables plump and young, the meat well-cut, the fish absolutely fresh, the chocolate bitter and the coffee newly-ground.

So go to Paris with a sense of adventure. Linger in the bars and brasseries, wander round the markets and the food shops, see them as a unique chance to get under the skin of the ordinary people of the city, to feel something of what it must be like to be one of them. Here, I am willing to bet, is far more the stuff of memories than is to be found in any museum or gallery.

This section is not about restaurants, though dotted through the guide are a few pointers to some of the most notable. Paris is a city of countless bars and bistros, brasseries and fine restaurants and there are plenty of guides to help you find your way around.

It is about food to buy on the hoof, about markets to wander round, about some of the best places to find the freshest, most interesting food in Paris. Anybody with a passion for the subject — and it won't take many days in Paris before almost everybody gets caught up in the great national hobby — should make a point of buying *The Food Lover's Guide to Paris* by Patricia Wells, an inspirational book that goes into the subject in much more detail than I ever could in a single chapter: it will whet your appetite and make you long to go again.

Here in the meantime, for those not overly familiar with French, is a list explaining what some of the signs you will come across stand for. Remember that most food shops open somewhere between 8am and 8.30am but close down for a longish lunch-hour (some close from noon to 2.30pm; others from 1pm to 4pm — you'll have to take note as it can differ from *arrondissement* to *arrondissement*). They then reopen for a longish stint until 7pm or 7.30pm.

BOUCHERIE A butcher, more or less as we understand the meaning of the word, though not all sell pork or poultry. Watch out for butchers selling horsemeat (probably like most foreigners you will want to give it a miss): they will be called a *Boucherie Chevaline* and will have a horsehead sign over the door.

BOULANGERIE The baker where even today most bread is still baked on the premises; very often baked twice a day. Besides the ubiquitous baguettes, this is where you buy your croissants, your brioches, *pain au chocolat, religieuses, une amande* and all the other doughy delights you may require.

CHARCUTERIE This stands not only for the shop selling mainly pork products such as terrines, sausages, pâtés and smoked hams, but also for the produce itself.

CONFISERIE This is the confectioner and usually the sweets and chocolates will be made *à la maison*.

EPICERIE The grocer.

FROMAGERIE Where you buy your cheese.

PATISSERIE An essential stopping-off place for those who are picnic-bound: here you will find a vast array of delicious tarts and other sticky delights.

POISSONNERIE The fishmonger.

TRAITEUR A most useful shop this for the visitor. The nearest equivalent is take-away but Parisian *traiteurs* are take-aways with a difference. The standard is usually extraordinarily high but so, often, are the prices.

TRIPERIE As you may well surmise, this is the place for tripe, either *tout simple* or ready-prepared.

VOLAILLER This is where you buy your poultry and your game, although today many *boucheries* sell it as well.

CONTENTS

* Strictly speaking not all shops but also places to visit to rest the feet, restore the spirits and engage the mind.

BREAD

CHOCOLATE

COOKERY SCHOOLS

EPICERIES AND TRAITEURS

BREAD

No matter where you are in Paris you will almost certainly be able to find bread that is fresh, crisp and almost irresistible. However, there are two specialists that you should make a point of visiting if you possibly can.

LIONEL POILANE

8 rue du Cherche-Midi, 6e.
METRO: Sèvres-Babylone.

Poilâne bread has become a cult. The queues begin to stretch outside the little shop, in rain, in cold, in sunshine and in frost, from the first thing in the morning (he opens at 7am). Try it for yourself. He's most famous for his large, round sour-dough loaf, but try, too, the breads dotted with nuts or raisins, the *pain decoré* (large ones for celebrations can be ordered in advance) and the many other doughy delights. Don't worry if you're so overcome with hunger that you start to nibble before you've even left the shop — everybody does, it's part of the Poilâne mystique.

MAX POILANE

87 rue Brancion, 15e.
METRO: Porte de Vanves.

For some reason less famous than his brother, Max produces just as delicious bread made to the same ancient recipes handed down from their father and in almost the identical old-fashioned, traditional way. Compare the two and see if you can tell the difference. Here you may buy without the queues and you can also enjoy one of the most charming, truly authentic *boulangeries* in Paris.

CHOCOLATE

Chocolate in Paris isn't cheap but my goodness it is good. It is the sort of chocolate that chocaholics needs to steer clear of — once the fatal dip into those rich, dark, creamy bundles of temptation has been made, they are harder to resist than almost any others in the world. Chocolate in Paris is a high-quality product, and Parisians understand this and are willing to pay for it. Not for them the diluted, inferior brands that we sometimes go for over here, no, for them it must be nothing but the best. A box of chocolates makes a fine present if you are going out to dinner or to the theatre with French friends and any of the good shops will wrap it for you with infinite care if they know it is a *cadeau*. Here are just a few of the best chocolate addresses in town.

DALLOYAU

101 rue du Faubourg Saint-
Honoré, 8e.
METRO: Saint-Philippe-du-
Roule.

An old-established chocolate-house with an impeccable reputation. Best-loved seem to be the praline combinations, but all are worth trying — you've nothing to lose but your waistline.

DEBAUVE & GALLAIS

30, rue des Saints-Pères, 6e.
METRO: Saint-Germain-
des-Prés.

This is the shop where it all began, where chocolate was first dispensed as a tonic, a pick-me-up and a cure-all. Soon, however, the chocolate became more profitable than the pharmaceuticals they were intending to sell. Today they sell rich, dark, chocolates with an infinitely memorable flavour: the combinations of chocolate with praline, hazelnuts or almonds are nothing less than sublime.

FOUQUET

22 rue François-1er, 8e.
METRO: F. D. Roosevelt.

Another place to go for highest-quality chocolate — here they are all made by hand in a nearby *atelier*. Just to look at the selection is to see sweet-making so perfect as to be transformed into an art. If the chocolates are too calorie-laden you can always enjoy a cup of finest coffee and come away with a jar of Fouquet's very own mustard preserves or *confitures*. Beautifully packed, anything from Fouquet would make a splendid present.

LENOTRE

44 rue du Bac, 7e.
METRO: rue du Bac.

5 rue du Havre, 9e.
METRO: Saint-Lazare,
Havre-Caumartin.

49 avenue Victor-Hugo,
16e.
METRO: Victor-Hugo.

This sells quite simply some of the best chocolates in Paris — and in Paris chocolates are a serious business. The French are discriminating and demanding patrons and are willing to pay the price that the best chocolate commands. After all, if your idea of a chocolate is something made with all the skill of a consummate artist from the very best cocoa beans, vanilla and fine cocoa butter, then, *bien sûr*, you must expect to pay. So treat yourself; see what a truly consummate chocolate tastes like and ask for an assortment of the very best on offer. When you've found your favourite, you can go back for more. Watch out for opening times: rue du Bac and avenue Victor-Hugo are open on Sunday mornings (though rue du Bac is closed during August) whilst rue du Bac and rue du Havre are open on Mondays when avenue Victor-Hugo is closed. Try Lenotre for pastries too. His *gâteaux*, his meringues and his open flans are hard to beat.

LA MAISON DU CHOCOLAT

225 rue du Fauboug Saint-
Honoré, 8e.
METRO: Ternes.

More impeccable standards, more inimitable quality. Slightly more expensive, perhaps, than some of the others, but then there are those who think he is the best. All are handmade on the premises.

MARQUISE DE SEVIGNE

32 place de la Madeleine, 8e.
METRO: Madeleine.

There's something very sumptuous about the Marquise's offerings, redolent of plump creaminess and soft delights. Marvellously grand boxes for present-giving and, for the right occasion, look out for the heart-shaped versions filled with hazelnut and praline.

PETIT QUENAULT

56 rue Jean-Jacques-
Rousseau, 1er.
METRO: Les Halles.

Useful address for chocaholics who've always wondered why their *mousse au chocolat* or *chocolat marquise* never tastes quite the way it does in the classy restaurants — it's because they use Le Pecq cooking chocolate, that's why. Buy it here.

COOKERY SCHOOLS

A selection of cookery schools — after all, you may have been so inspired that you'll want to take home with you something of the wonders you have enjoyed.

CORDON BLEU

24 rue du Champ-de-Mars,
7e.
(Tel: 45.55.02.77.)
METRO: Ecole Militaire.

Probably the best-known name in the world of serious culinary instruction, and certainly one of the oldest, but did you know you could drop in for just a single afternoon's instruction in the classic techniques? It's been going since 1895 and takes food as seriously as you would expect from such an eminently Parisian institution. You'd be wise to book at least two or three days ahead and if you're really well-organised you should write ahead for the menus which are to be demonstrated, published a month in advance. The afternoon's demonstrations start at 2pm or 4.30pm. Though French is the language of instruction, non-French-speakers can learn an awful lot by simply watching.

ECOLE DE CUISINE LA VARENNE

34 rue Saint-Dominique, 7e.
(Tel: 47.05.10.16.)
METRO: Invalides.

Founded by an Englishwoman, Anne Willan, it has a largely American-based clientele. The year-long courses are highly thought of and are very expensive but there are demonstrations every afternoon from Monday to Friday (2.30pm to 7pm) which members of the public can attend and which are very reasonably priced. Often, distinguished chefs from some of Paris' most famous restaurants will impart some of their secrets before your very eyes. The demonstrations are run in French (though with English translations), and you come away, after tasting the results, with a complete set of instructions. In the summer and at Easter there are week-long courses.

MARIE-BLANCHE DE BROGLIE COOKING SCHOOL

18 avenue de la Motte-
Picquet, 7e.
(Tel: 45.51.36:34.)
METRO: Ecole Militaire.

For August and the first half of September, Marie-Blanche de Broglié teaches in her Normandy *château*. The rest of the year, courses are held in her Paris apartment. Everybody speaks well of the bubbling personality of the Princess herself and though she isn't always there, the courses, too, are highly recommended. There are single demonstrations, intensive 6-week courses or, for the short-of-time, 1-week residential courses held at her Normandy *château*.

PARIS EN CUISINE 78 rue de la Croix-Nivert, 15e.
(Tel: 42.50.04.23.)

METRO: Commerce.

An address for every genuine food lover to note. Run by an American food enthusiast, Robert Noah, this little company specialises in helping genuine food aficionados to learn more about their favourite subject. He'll put together almost any tour or course you want: he'll take you behind the scenes of many a Paris restaurant; he'll organise a wine tasting with experienced *sommeliers*; he'll help you learn the secrets of the *pâtissier*, or of the *chocolatier* or the *boulanger*; he'll take you to market or to school, to eat or to watch. You should contact him in advance and ask for his brochure to give you some idea of the range he offers.

EPICERIES AND TRAITEURS

A L'OLIVIER

77 rue Saint-Louis-en-l'Ile, 4e.
METRO: Pont-Marie.

As large and varied a collection of oils as can be found anywhere in the world. A l'Olivier specialises in oils from the olive: fragrant golden oils from Provence; green, fruity ones from Tuscany; robust oils from Greece, but go there, too, for oils made from sesame, walnut, hazelnut, palm and almond. In beautiful ceramic jars, in simple bottles or more humble tins, beautifully packaged and labelled, almost anything from A l'Olivier would make a splendid present.

ANDROUET

41 rue d'Amsterdam, 8e.
METRO: Saint-Lazare.

If you've ever wondered why there was all that fuss about French cheeses, head for Androuet. Try and get there for the mid-day or evening *dégustations* (noon to 2.30pm and 7pm to 9.30pm) where, for a reasonable sum, you can have a mini crash course in cheese-lore. It is quite an experience: tray after tray, in pre-arranged and carefully thought-out order, are brought before you. Each waiter explains (in French) where the cheese comes from; what sort it is; and how it is made and cared for. In between you sip wine and munch on crunchy baguettes.

If you already know what all the fuss is about and want to buy your own selection, Androuet is one of the most distinguished cheese shops in Paris. They take immense care not only to seek out authentic cheese-makers but also to keep the cheeses in perfect condition (a much more complicated business than I'd ever realised). Ask for help and advice, for the quality of the cheeses may vary according to the time of year (for instance during the summer many cheeses, including, say, Vacherin, will not be at their best). Real aficionados will ask for the *fromage fermier* or *au lait cru* — these are the small production cheeses, made in the time-honoured ways from raw (as opposed to pasteurised) milk.

CAVIAR KASPIA

17 place de la Madeleine, 8e.
METRO: Madeleine.

Sample upstairs the specialities *de la maison* and then, if your palate is pleased, go downstairs to buy some treats to cheer you up when you get back home. Caviar, smoked salmon, as well as proper blinis to help you serve it all in the authentic way.

LE COIN DE CAVIAR 2 rue de la Bastille, 4e.

METRO: Bastille.

Though you can go here for a fullblown meal, it is better (in my view) to use it to taste some of the caviar, the smoked fish, the blinis that you might want to buy to take home. Open continuously from 9am to 2am you can drop in and ask for a plate of mixed smoked fish products with blinis (smoked salmon, marinated salmon, salmon eggs and so on — quite a bargain). Or try the caviar (you can ask for as little as a single ounce). If you develop a taste for one of the world's great luxuries you can buy it to take away as well.

COMPTOIR LANDAIS

52 rue Montmartre, 2e.
METRO: Montmartre.

Aficionados of the rich and comforting specialities of the south-west should head for this little source of authentic *foie gras*, *confit d'oie* or *confit de canard* and the wickedly delicious confections with prunes and apples.

DEBAUVE & GALLAIS

30 rue des Saints-Pères, 7e.
METRO: Saint-Germain-des-Près.

You couldn't find a more charming place to buy your tea, your coffee, your chocolates or your vanilla. The almost perfectly preserved eighteenth-century front and interior gives you a real glimpse of the Paris that used to be (some of it will seem strangely modish: the marbled columns, the antique lights). Nowadays the chocolates no longer sell on their 'hygienic' qualities (the admirable aim of the original Sulpice Gallais) but on being quite simply delicious.

FAUCHON

26 place de la Madeleine, 8e.
METRO: Madeleine.

For *La Grande Bouffe* head for the place de la Madeleine and go first to Fauchon. This is the heart of foodie Paris. Some would claim that it's the gastronomic heart of the world. Fauchon's windows, in particular, are a sight that must be

seen: giant turbots stuffed with layers of spinach and sorrel, coated in sauce and then decorated with all the considerable skills the chefs can muster; stuffed chicken *en croute*; langoustines, crabs, pâtés and terrines. The colours and shapes are often so dazzling they seem more like still-lifes than food. For the Parisian of means, Fauchon is the *traiteur* par excellence. Venture inside and you will find wonderful things to take home: jars of mustard, small soufflés ready to cook in heat-proof jars, oils and vinegars to please the most fastidious palate, fresh *foie gras* and Beluga caviar, delicate *fraises-des-bois* and raspberries out of season, spice and condiments with exotic-sounding names. If you are buying just a few small presents, say a jar of peppercorns or a Fauchon mustard, you may well find the service somewhat disdainful but persevere (remind yourself, as you will probably need to several times on a serious shopper's tour of Paris, that they are, after all, there to serve *you*) for a little something from Fauchon makes a splendid present back home. Don't forget Fauchon's excellent cellar, its vintage wines, its rare spirits and the largest selection of giant bottles (including salmanazars, methuselahs and jeroboams) of champagne.

Across the road is the famous stand-up café where you can choose your own cake or patisserie and eat it at the bar with a cup of some of the best coffee in Paris. Choose from Jamaica Blue Mountain, pure Arabicas from Central America, brews from Brazil or Kenya, and, if tea is more to your taste, there are some 50 different varieties to choose from here.

LA FERME SAINT-HUBERT

21 rue Vignon, 8e.
METRO: Madeleine.

Another of the shops that those wishing to discover the mysteries of French cheeses should head for. Besides selling a vast range of cheeses of every sort (though it seems to specialise in country cheeses and raw milk cheeses matured in its own cellars) there is a little restaurant next door where you can sample several different sorts whilst nibbling bread from Poilâne and sipping one of the select group of wines on the menu. Besides the cheeses there are numerous dishes made with cheese — almost every evening the menu features a choice of *raclette*, cheese soufflé, cheesecake, etc.

FLO PRESTIGE

42 place du Marché-Saint-Honoré, 1er.
METRO: Pyramides.

61 avenue de la Grande-Armée, 16e.
METRO: Argentine.

Open until midnight every day of the week, this is the place to buy your picnic *de luxe*. A shop to change your concept of the take-away — go there for fine *charcutierie*, for *foie gras* and a beautiful selection of breads sold in portions as large or small as you like, for fresh cheeses and interesting salads, for poached salmon or delicately prepared chicken. You can also buy your bottle of wine, *une douceur* for afters, and all you need then is to head for your own patch of green and hope that the sun comes out.

HEDIARD

21 place de la Madeleine, 8e.
METRO: Madeleine.

Another must for anybody interested in food. The complete *epicier*, Hediard has faithful customers that come time after time just for its own blend of spices, its selection of teas and honeys, its rarified collection of exotic fruits and its beautiful fresh fruit purées (Parisian hostesses turn them into deliciously fragrant tasting sorbets). The fresh fruit purées, beautifully packaged in clear bottles, make excellent presents to take home. If you want an even more *recherché* present buy the Hediard vintage sardines: packed fresh from the sea (*never*, God forbid, frozen) in finest virgin oil with a little spice or salt, the sardines are then sealed into their tins. They should generally be stored for no more than four years so make sure to keep a check on the processing date which should be somewhere on the tin itself, or on the wrapper.

And if all that looking at food has made you hungry, troop upstairs to the small but elegant restaurant where you can enjoy a small but elegant meal in true Hediard style.

JO GOLDENBERG

7 rue des Rosiers, 4e.
METRO: Saint-Paul.

In the heart of the old Jewish quarter is this luxurious delicatessen and restaurant offering the sort of evocative food that every Jewish Momma knows how to make but doesn't always have the time for. Chopped liver, salt beef, smoked salmon, cream cheese and the bagels, the breads, the pickles and the gherkins. Warm, friendly and redolent of authentic Jewish community life, those homesick for a proper cheese-cake or an authentic chicken soup can try this restaurant. For the best atmosphere of all, go there for Sunday lunch.

LAJARRIGE BOUTIQUE

8 rue Meissonier, 17e.
METRO: Wagram.

The shop is open from 10am to 3pm, from 4.30pm to 8pm, whilst the restaurant opens at noon to 2.30pm and then again from 7pm to 9.30pm. Closed Sunday.

LAYRAC

29 rue de Buci, 6e.
(Tel: 43.25.17.72.)
METRO: Mabillon, Saint-Germain-des-Prés.

Open from 9am to 3am every day of the week.

LA MAISON DE LA TRUFFE

19 place de la Madeleine, 8e.
METRO: Madelaine.

LA MAISON DU MIEL

24 rue Vignon, 9e.
METRO: Madeleine.

MARIE-ANNE CANTIN

12 rue du Champ-de-Mars, 7e.
METRO: Ecole Militaire.

A marvellous idea this and part of a new trend of allowing one to taste before one buys, though when the products are as expensive as these are you don't expect, naturally, to taste without paying. Lajarrige itself is a restaurant which has now spawned this boutique where you may buy the products it specialises in: the *foie gras*, terrines, sausages, hams and *confits* from the south-west. The boutique itself has a small collection of tables where you taste the wares accompanied by bread (or toast) from the famous Lionel Poilâne. If you're travelling, think about the *foie gras* — you either buy it fresh and uncooked but vacuum-packed or made into a terrine. If *foie gras* is a treat new to you, sit yourself down at one of the tables, order a sampling, dip into this delicate pink liver and decide for yourself if it's worth the King's ransom it costs these days.

A marvellous source of take-away food in its own right (stop there, if you're in the district, for terrines and quiches, for salads and soups, for wine and a little something sweet to finish off with) but most of all worth knowing because of its extraordinary opening hours.

Not difficult to divine that this is *the* place to track down the freshest of truffles (from November to March is the season when you can expect to find them fresh, otherwise they will be dried or preserved in some way). Caviar, smoked salmon, truffles and *foie gras*, tinned pâtés and terrines — all things wickedly rich and expensive. At least most are small enough to fit easily into a suitcase to take back home.

Not to be missed — more honeys than you ever knew existed. It's been here since the turn of the century and the honeys are culled from La Maison du Miel's own hives as well as from hives throughout the world. If you thought all honeys were much of a muchness, stock on some of the miniatures and taste for yourself.

Any visit to Paris should take in at least one street market and I can hardly think of a better and more typical food market than the one in the busy, crowded rue Cler. Just off it is one of the newest of the distinguished cheeseshops in a city devoted to cheese. Opened by the daughter of Christian Cantin, who owns a famous cheese shop (at 2 rue de Lourmel, 15e), it is an enchantingly pretty but nonetheless very serious shop — all the proper cellars (a damp one for cows' cheese and a drier one for goats'), immense knowledge and much love go into making it what it is. I bought a large selection to take home to England and all were beautifully and immaculately packaged for the flight. If you seek it out, take the trouble to be adventurous: try the less familiar brands and if you've always thought goats' cheese was not your scene, give it a try here, you won't ever find it any better.

PASSIONS EXOTIQUES

27 rue Campagne-Première, 14e.
METRO: Raspail.

It may be hard to credit but the French are currently passionate about tea. Along with many other examples of Anglomania, tea-drinking has become something of a ritual in certain circles. It is taken very seriously and not just any old tea will do — the merits of Lapsang Souchong vis-à-vis Earl Grey are carefully weighed. One of the places where the tea-drinking Parisian might buy his tea is Passions Exotiques where some 60 different varieties (including some without tannin or, indeed, caffeine) are sold.

PETROSSIAN

18 boulevard La-Tour-Maubourg, 7e.
METRO: Latour-Maubourg.

The name alone almost says it all: Russian caviar, smoked salmon, *foie gras*, truffles, blinis, herrings, vodka and, for those who have learned to savour the happy partnership of *foie gras* and sweet golden-yellow wines, some of the best Sauternes in Paris. Those in the know wouldn't buy their caviar from anybody else.

PAUL CORCELLET

46 rue des Petits-Champs, 2e.
METRO: Pyramides.

Almost every *epicerie* is fascinating to the Englishman brought up on our familiar brands of groceries, but this one is more fascinating than most. To begin with there is always a fair selection of exotic spices, pulses, grains and *condiments*. Then there are more varieties of tea than most of us knew existed. Count the honeys, the mustards, the jams and see for yourself just how rich and adventurous the choice is.

SOLEIL DE PROVENCE

6 rue du Cherche-Midi, 6e.
METRO: Croix Rouge.

Another of those small shops that seems to be warmed by the sun of Provence, all those olives, glowing golden oils, honeys and aromatic herbs, sweet-smelling soaps and lotions remind one irresistibly of the golden South. Take home one of the scented honeys or a bottle of fruity extra virgin olive oil.

THAN BINH

18 rue Lagrange, 5e.
METRO: Maubert-Mutualité.

29 place Maubert, 5e.
METRO: Maubert-Mutualité.

If you haven't had a brush with Vietnamese culture and Vietnamese food, you've missed out on a great new Parisian experience. Here you'll find a whiff of Eastern magic; even if you have never ventured further East than Paris you'll sense its authenticity straight away. Here are the exotic fruits and vegetables, the kumquats, the Chinese cabbage, the bean-sprouts and the bamboo shoots. Here are the dried fish, the strange fungi, the spicy sauces, the noodles and the rice. Even if you aren't thinking of doing much cooking in Paris, you'll find lots of exotica to take home.

FOOD MARKETS

Every visitor to Paris should take in a stroll through at least one of the many open-air food markets here. Almost every district has one and they are an endless source of interest and insight into the hearts and minds of ordinary Parisians. Observe the care with which the housewife chooses her cheeses; watch the way the greengrocer lays out his rows of smooth purple aubergines, lines up his rosy tomatoes, piles up his golden apricots and sets out the fat fingers of asparagus; see the interchange between the butcher or the fishmonger as they and their regular customers discuss the purchase of the day — see the deep seriousness with which the business is approached. There is no better place to make purchases of your own. If you're going on a picnic (and with such a choice, who needs restaurants?) you can amble from the *boulangerie* to the *pâtisserie*, from the *charcuterie* to the *fromagerie*. The greengrocer can provide tomatoes and ripe peaches (though be careful not to choose them yourself or you'll unleash a stream of abuse) and somewhere there is bound to be somebody offering a vast selection of *plats froids*, all ready to be taken away.

Most markets are at their best and offer most choice first thing in the morning, from 8am onwards, but they go on bustling until the sacred hour of 1pm, when all Paris seems to head for somewhere to eat. They re-open at 4pm and round about 6pm are more feverish than ever as the homeward-bound office-workers stop off to buy their evening meal. By 7.30pm they are closing down after yet another busy day.

Here are just a few of the most famous of the open-air markets, but don't forget that if you aren't staying very close to any of them, there are lots more just waiting to be discovered. If you want a really thorough list you can contact the Mairie de Paris which issues a special list of them all in its free leaflet *Les Marchés de Paris*. Remember that all except rue de Seine/Buci and a very few of the smaller ones are closed on Sundays.

RUE CLER

Runs from avenue de la Motte-Picquet to the rue de Grenelle, 7e.
METRO: Ecole Militaire.

In this chic *arrondissement* you find a very chic street market which is nonetheless full of streetlife and bustling charm. The open stalls and the shops behind them sell everything from the finest vegetables to an immense variety of fish — everything that the foodie might need. Don't miss Charcuterie Gonin if you're doing serious shopping (as opposed to just imbibing the atmosphere) for here you'll find some of the most delicious takeaway food in Paris.

RUE DES BELLES-FEUILLES

Off the avenue Victor-Hugo, 16e.
METRO: Victor-Hugo.

Not worth the detour for the atmosphere alone but if you are seriously shopping for food here you will find some of the best produce in Paris — what else do you expect from this expensive little *quartier*?

In this colourful old part of Paris is one of the most charming, if one of the most expensive, of all the markets. If you're just soaking up the atmosphere you could hardly do better; if you're actually going to buy you'll be paying a bit over the odds. So many special shops and stands to look out for, it's difficult to list them all, but make for BOULANGERIE BOUDIN at 6 rue de Buci where I discovered something new to me, a delicious light pastry going by the name of *fougasse*; go to BOUTIQUE LAYRAC for marvellous ready-to-eat foods; stop at LA SPECIALITE DU CAFE (54 rue de Seine) for wonderful coffee and when you get tired have *un verre* at the TABAC DE L'INSTITUT at 21 rue de Seine. Or if you're feeling in need of something more substantial try LE PETIT ZINC at 25 rue de Buci, which always delivers in terms of authentic old Parisian atmosphere and some hearty regional dishes.

RUE DE SEINE/ BUCI

6e.
METRO: Odéon

RUE MOUFFETARD

5e.
METRO: Censier Daubenton, Monge.

One of the oldest street-markets in Paris (said to have been there since the 14th century), it stretches from the Carrefour des Gobelins to the rue de l'Epée de Bois and spreads out sideways as well. Wander down it, explore the sidestreets where you'll come upon a charming flower market and some exotic fare from the old French colonies. Though it attracts more than its fair share of tourists (age seems an irresistible attribute) it hasn't lost its bustling charm and you can still come upon tough restaurant owners bargaining with their suppliers, streetwise old Frenchmen insisting upon the best cut of beef and ordinary housewives dithering over which stall offers the plumpest tomatoes. At no. 102 there is

COUTELLERIE, offering every imaginable kind of kitchen knife. Wallow in the exotic Arabic delights at TRAITEUR ARA and the African specialities at LE VILLAGE AFRICAIN (just off the rue Mouffetard at 2 rue de l'Arbalete).

RUE PONCELET

17e.
METRO: Ternes.

Not on the main tourist beat, this market is chiefly worth visiting for that very reason. It boasts the usual selection of *boulangeries, pâtisseries, charcuteries et al* but in particular look out for Aux Fermes d'Auvergne where you will find authentic regional specialities from the Auvergne.

PATISSERIES

FINKELSZTAJN

27 rue des Rosiers, 4e.
METRO: Saint-Paul.

If a really scrumptious cheesecake takes your fancy head for this, one of the excellent pastry shops to be found in the heart of the Jewish quarter. Don't go there if you're worrying about your waistline, for the warm smells and the delectable sights

---

LADUREE 16 rue Royale, 8e.

METRO: Concorde, Madeleine.

This combination of tea-room and pastry-shop is right in the heart of one of the smartest shopping districts of all, so it's worth noting for when the feet begin to flag and the parcels need a rest. Stop and have a cup of tea or *café crème*, and ponder the relative merits of the array of delectable pastries spread before you.

will tempt even the most strong-minded. In addition to the traditional *pâtissier*'s wares, here you will find more unusual offerings as well.

LE MOULE A GATEAU

111 rue Mouffetard, 5e.
METRO: place Monge.

In this charming old street you'll come upon this typical, traditional *pâtisserie* selling all the things which has given French *pâtisserie* such a world-wide reputation. Besides the fruit tarts, the classic Pithiviers, the Madeleines and the *pain au chocolat* you can also buy small slices, enough for one, if you're just feeling hungry on the hoof.

PELTIER

66 rue de Sèvres, 7e.
METRO: Vaneau.

The fame of its special Princesse meringue cake filled with almonds, vanilla cream and little bits of nougat has spread far and wide, so perhaps you should find out for yourself what all the fuss is about. If almonds or the taste of nougat don't appeal there's a wonderfully rich Black Forest *gâteau* (but not like any you'll ever have tasted before, unless you've been very lucky) and some exquisite fruit tarts with the lightest, most delectable of pastry bases. And lots more besides — exquisite chocolates, sorbets and take-away dishes like no other take-aways you've ever come across before.

WINE

Here are a few of the most interesting wine shops that I've discovered. It seems odd that Paris, capital of the most famous wine-making nation in the world, should yield just a few truly serious wine merchants, but there it is. The ones that are good, however, are very, very good and are often full of old-world atmosphere to boot. If you're thinking of buying wine to take home, my advice would be to buy the best you can afford. British supermarkets have some of the most knowledgeable wine buyers in the world and offer incredible value when it comes to the inexpensive wines. So when in Paris why not try to learn a little more about this fascinating subject and seek out a few special bottles to save for a truly special occasion? It's worth remembering also that British wine merchants have always been great specialists in the wines of Bordeaux (referred to over here as Claret, although this term is not known in France and indeed, if used, could be confused with *Clairet*), and usually have a better selection at better prices than you'll find in France. So give the wines of Bordeaux a miss. Look out instead for wines from smaller vineyards which often don't produce enough for export; wines, say, from Burgundy or the undervalued wines of the

Loire. Remember that most people who go into the wine trade go into it because they love it and nothing pleases them more than a chance to expound on their favourite subject. So take your courage in both hands, tell them what you're looking for and how much you can afford to spend and I think you'll be surprised at the enthusiastic and charming help you'll be given. Many of them also speak English.

AU VERGER DE LA MADELEINE

4 boulevard Malesherbes, 8e.
MÉTRO: Madeleine.

Here you will find some of the rarest wines around, wines that you probably wouldn't find anywhere else. The shop itself is small but the real treasures are hidden in the cellars below, caves filled from floor to ceiling with bottles to excite even the most sophisticated and well-travelled of wine buffs. Though it has a wide range of French wines from almost every region, there is also a fine selection from other wine-producing countries. It's a good address to remember if you would like to track down a particular year or vineyard — possibly to celebrate a particular anniversary.

LA CAVE DE GEORGES DUBOEUF

9 rue Marbeuf, 8e.
MÉTRO: Alma Marceau,
F. D. Roosevelt.

The acknowledged king of Beaujolais, as even the most moderate drinker must be aware. Though obviously he sells plenty of the fragrant produce of this region, he also has many other choices on offer, some of which are exceedingly reasonably priced. Those anxious to learn more might be interested in his sample boxes of mixed selections.

CAVES DE LA MADELEINE

25 Cité Berryer, 8e.
(In a little passage off the rue Royale).
MÉTRO: Concorde,
Madeleine.

Steven Spurrier is the Englishman behind this interesting enterprise and he has made a considerable impact on the wine trade in Paris. Apart from his burgeoning little group of winebars (where you can extend your knowledge by many happy hours of sampling) here you can attend wine tastings, ask the English-speaking staff for help and buy from one of the best selections of Burgundies (in particular, look out for the 1983 wines from M. de Montille) in Paris. Nip along to his winebar The Blue Fox at the end of the passage if you're feeling peckish.

JEAN-BAPTISTE

48 rue de la Montagne-Saint-Geneviève, 5e.
MÉTRO: Cardinal Lemoine,
Maubert-Mutualité.

M. Besse looks as if he has come straight from central casting: there he goes with his wonderful old beret, chaotically surrounded by bottles of rare and wonderful vintages. A tiny shop, filled with treasures. Consult him before you buy, because it is hard to uncover all that the shop has to offer; he'll sell you anything from a bottle of table wine to a beautiful Burgundy, but you can be sure it'll be fairly priced.

LUCIEN LEGRAND

1 rue de la Banque, 2e.
MÉTRO: Bourse.

A couple of the most highly-regarded wine merchants in Paris, notable not just for their fine selections of interesting wines but also because the shops themselves are such a joy to visit. The oldest branch is at 1 rue de la Banque and there it

12 Galerie Vivienne, 2e.
METRO: Bourse.

is, still clad in its 19th-century apparel; still offering a choice of fine coffees, teas, confectionery, honeys, biscuits and other foods as well. Here you may buy wines specially bottled by M. Legrand's son, you may see one of the finest selections of Burgundies around, and you will find it a good place to seek out a good but inexpensive bottle. Out at the back in the Galerie Vivienne, an Englishwoman, Fiona Beeston, has been developing a fine selection of wines, mainly from Bordeaux (though now that prices have risen so high, she is beginning to offer a good selection from the Loire as well). Here you buy primarily by the case.

MAISON DU CHAMPAGNE

48 rue des Belles-Feuilles, 16e.
METRO: Porte Dauphine, Victor-Hugo.

This, you will have guessed, is the place for lovers of champagne to head for. It houses a vast and distinguished selection of champagne and a lot more besides, including cognacs, armagnacs and port. If you want to send a present to somebody, they'll deliver anywhere in the Paris area for a small extra charge, and they'll also despatch abroad.

LE PETIT BACCHUS

13 rue du Cherche-Midi, 6e.
METRO: Sèvres-Babylone.

Owned by Steven Spurrier and part of his little growing wine empire, this is chiefly known as a winebar where you may sip and watch the world go by. It is a very friendly wine-merchant as well and perhaps less intimidating than some of the older, grander establishments, particularly for those won don't have too much to spend.

RAINY DAYS

Years before all those smart neon-lit shopping malls began to proliferate in Paris, glass-topped arcades were where the serious shopper or the leisured *flâneur* went to shop or simply wander. Built in the early years of the 19th-century, they gave the Parisian a chance to indulge in the old-fashioned ritual of the *passegiata* — a chance to see and be seen. There they could be protected from the growing menace of the traffic, from the rain and the mud, they could window-shop or shop for real for anything from a brand new hat to a comforting patisserie.

Today the arcades are enchanting enclaves that the modern world seems to have passed by. The shops, *bien sûr*, have mainly been brought up-to-date but there are still the arching glass roofs, the marble floors, the brass lamps, the metal or stucco curlicues, the elaborate iron gates at either end that slam shut at 9pm.

There are some 99 such passages in Paris and here are details of just a few of them, for the inevitable day when the rain comes down and the winds begin to blow.

CONTENTS

GALERIE VIVIENNE

Entrances at 4 rue des
Petits-Champs, 5 rue de la
Banque, and 6 rue Vivienne, 2e.
METRO: Bourse.

This one of the most beautiful of all the passages in Paris and possibly the most lively. Admire the blue and beige mosaic-tiled floor, the soaring roof, the wrought-iron work and the bas-reliefs on high.

Some of the new arrivals, though, owe absolutely nothing to nostalgia — take JEAN-PAUL GAULTIER, for example, the newest arrival with an entrance in the rue Vivienne but with windows giving onto the *passage*. Bold, sharp and distinctly anti-establishment, his boutique has become a mecca for those who want to see the very latest look. Don't miss the six circular video-screens set into the floor.

Then move on to SI TU VEUX which is one of the most charming toy shops in Paris. Particularly likely to appeal to parents: soft, soft teddy-bears, miniature teasets, marvellous masks and puppets, dolls clothes and dolls to cut out. If you have children still in the party-going and party-giving set, it's a marvellous place to buy all those tiny presents that are *de rigueur* today, as well as strings of sweets and other surprises.

CAMILLE BLIN sells sophisticated, understated soft jersey clothes in subtle, off-beat colours and there is always an equally sophisticated selection of ivory and wood jewellery as well.

At KENT & CURWEN you could buy the sort of cricket sweaters that are some people's idea of what W.G. Grace wore to open at Lords — you and I know better but nonetheless they have captured something of the sporting English look. Lots of cashmere, ties that look as if they are the badge of some important club, striped blazers, cotton shirts and their own brand of T-shirt.

IXI:Z — do not worry, you do not have to know how to pronounce it in order to be able to buy its trendy brand of clothes, stationery and accessories. Marvellous matt black writing materials, satchels and briefcases as well as rather whacky clothes. CHRISTIAN ASTUGUEVIEILLE is your man if what you're after is some of the most avant-garde jewellery around. Leather bracelets, minimalist ear-rings, big splodgy black and white bracelets and necklaces (and when I say big I mean *big*) as well as giant red and white hooped earrings.

YUKI TORII sells a very different sort of Japanese image — his is fun and bright. It may lack the real innovation and the high sophistication of some of his compatriots but it is younger and jollier.

Rest your feet at A PRIORI THE: sink into a wicker chair, toy with a cup of China tea and watch the passing scene. Take a look at CATHERINE VERNOUX's individual brand of knits and separates and if you're a wine buff, don't miss LUCIEN LEGRAND FILLES ET FILS — there is one entrance for the restaurant and wholesale trade and one for you. Buy a case of fine claret or be tempted by some of their beautiful jars of jams and preserves.

GALERIE COLBERT

Runs off the Galerie Vivienne and has been recently renovated so that now the beautiful *faux marbre* columns, the bas relief decorating the curved archways and the beautiful light coming in through the rotunda windows can all be admired and seen in their full glory. Buy postcards or posters, or exact copies of objects in the collection of the Bibliothèque Nationale from the Bibliothèque's own boutique. Don't miss the marvellous GRAND CAFE COLBERT where you can sip some wine or a *café crème* in a cafe that seems not to have changed since the turn of the century, so artfully has it been restored.

GALERIE VERO-DODAT

19 rue Jean-Jacques-Rousseau, 1er.
METRO: Les Halles.

This is another very beautiful *passage*. Built by two *charcutiers*, Vero and Dodat, its painted ceilings, copper pillars and storefronts of rich mahogany make it a joy to behold.

Take in JEAN-CHARLES BROSSEAU's boutique if you're in the mood for a hat in utterly modern mood or want a chirpy shirt or a gutsy sweater. You may never have thought you wanted an antique doll but once you've seen those at

ROBERT CAPIA's shop at number 24 and 26 you'll wonder how you've lived so long without one.

R. ET F. CHARLES at no. 17 is an authentic *atelier* where stringed instruments of all kind are beautifully repaired.

IL BISONTE is very new and sells high-quality leather goods from Florence: look for a leather bag or a chic new belt, while GALERIE ERIC PHILIPPE specialises in turn of the century furniture as well as some good quality paintings.

Every good *passage* has somewhere to rest the feet. Here VERO-DODAT offers more than that, providing old-fashioned comfort in the form of a good old-fashioned restaurant serving French food of the sort that someone's *maman* used to make.

PASSAGE DES PANORAMAS, PASSAGE JOUFFROY, PASSAGE VERDEAU

116 boulevard Montmartre, 2e.
METRO: Montmartre.

These are three linked *passages* over in Montmartre. Here there have as yet been no grand restorations but old Paris lingers on all right, in the dim lights, the air of dilapidation and the old, shabby shops. Don't let that put you off, though, wander round and you will capture something of the atmosphere of the Paris that used to be, catching glimpses of the prosperous *mondaine* world that once inhabited these arcades. Start at the entrance to the Passage des Panoramas and you could be wandering back into the world of Zola's Nana. There's a shabby secondhand bookshop (but rummage around, you never know what you'll find) and soon you will come upon STERN, one of the proudest, oldest engraving houses in Paris. In its time it has elegantly engraved the coats of arms of some of the grandest houses in Europe onto stiff white cards, letterheads, invitations and visiting cards.

In the Passage Jouffroy, look out for PAIN D'EPICES, which seems to have two specialities: enchanting children's toys, music boxes, antique wind-up toys, miniatures for dolls' houses at number 29, whilst number 35 seems to cater for the new-fangled craze for all things pretty and sweet-smelling — anything from dried flower arrangements to candles for the dining-table and lotions for the bath.

At ABEL you can find the very umbrella to see you through the storm if you have left your own at home and besides umbrellas there are parasols and walking-sticks — the very props for a little saunter down the boulevard. AU BONHEUR DES DAMES will sell you delicious frivolities, the sort of inessential but charming little extras that turn bedroom and bathroom from functional boxes into enticing havens. Lots of frills and furbelows, all very feminine, if you see what I mean.

After that you will come upon the BOITE A JOUJOUX which sells the sort of jokes that some people seem to find life-enhancing and others just tiresome. The serious cinema lover should make a point of not missing CINEDOC. This is a gem of a find for the celluloid buff. Lots of posters, books and other memorabilia.

We come then to the Passage Verdeau, across the rue de la Grange Batelière, possibly the shabbiest of the three. There are few shops and a rather sad air of neglect but do go and look, for it has an atmosphere all of its own. There are also old and indeed antique cameras to be found at PHOTO VERDEAU and old postcards, books, magazines and posters at LA FRANCE ANCIENNE whilst adding to the general air of the old, shabby and secondhand is the LIBRAIRIE FARFOUILLE, which sells some truly marvellous second-hand books.

YET MORE PASSAGES

These then are just some of the arcades that might amuse you on a rainy day, but if you are in more modern mood and fancy some more modish clothes or artefacts, the tradition of building covered walkways is still alive and well. Head for the north side of the Champs-Elysées where there are many bright and noisy covered malls. Most have plenty of chic boutiques selling everything from clothes to jewellery, perfumes and scarves, and usually a choice of restaurants and snackbars as well.

At GALERIE ELYSEES at Rond-Point there is a branch of HEDIARD and, sign of the times, DUNE which sells electronic games and gadgets, friendly and unfriendly. Here you can buy your bullet-proof vest, your anti-attack equipment, your anti-rape whistle.

At Galerie Elysées 26 there are elegant mirrored ceilings (an attempt no doubt to reproduce the magical lighting of the old windowed arcades), a fascinating fountain, a branch of PRUNIER's restaurant, a marvellous confectioner called AMANDINE (marzipan lovers may gain several kilos in one glorious spree) and a gimmicky gadget shop called SOHO.

At GALERIE DU CLARIDGE there are two levels and more elegant clothes boutiques, as well as jewellers and a tempting *pâtisserie*.

ARCADES DU LIDO is possibly the oldest of the newer arcades and sits beside the site of the old Lido which has now moved further up the Champs-Elysées. Here you can clothe the men, women and children in the family and then revive yourselves at the Café de Paris with some of the best *tarte Tatin* in town.

GALERIE LES CHAMPS is a mixed bag of the good, the bad and the indifferent but anybody with a favourite child or godchild on their present list should make a point of looking in at LA PELUCHERIE where there can hardly be a soft toy it doesn't sell. Whether you go for a teddybear or a sweet-faced doll, I can't think of a child who wouldn't be thrilled with something from here.

Besides the modern versions of the old-style arcades, don't forget the glass and concrete complex of the FORUM DES HALLES which houses many a boutique, chainstore branch, restaurant, café and store — you could wander round for hours without even facing the great outdoors.

Then there is the PALAIS DES CONGRES at the Porte Maillot in the 17th *arrondissement* — not, in my book, an elevating place to shop but it does house a host of boutiques from bookshops to stylish men's outfitters, from delicatessens to wine merchants, from purveyors of children's toys to antique shops. If you are in the area and stuck for anything from a pair of shoes to a jar of pâté, you will be certain to find it here. Many of the goods sold are of high quality, it is beautifully organised and there are all sorts of useful services like banks and post offices.

Probably the most interesting place to shop in it is the group of stalls on level 2 going under the name of LES ARTISANS D'ART DU PALAIS DES CONGRES. Here artist-craftsmen from all over France have set up temporary stalls to sell their wares. As one artist finishes selling his latest output another seems to take over.

But be warned — should the legs be ready to flag and the flesh require a little reviving, the restaurants and snackbars here seem extortionately expensive and not very interesting.

Another soulless but convenient shopping emporium where the dedicated shopper can take in numberless boutiques (and, indeed, branches of Galeries Lafayette and Habitat) and never see the sky is the TOUR MONTPARNASSE in the rue de l'Arrivée in the 15th.

SOMETHING FOR MONSIEUR

Le look Anglais is all the rage. The point is not so much to reflect your personality or to be fashionable but to wear the right uniform. The uniform, of course, varies, depending upon the circles in which you move. For Monsieur BCBG (the French equivalent of our Sloane Ranger), the more English the uniform, the better pleased he is. The smartest Frenchmen of all go to the lengths of getting their suits made in Savile Row and buy their shirts from Turnbull & Asser, while for the average Frenchman, a uniform of navy blazer and grey flannels is *de rigueur.*

However, hard as he may try, the smart Frenchman never manages to look anything but, well, French. His Burberry, his Harris Tweeds, his Prince of Wales checks, do nothing so much as underline his Frenchness. He hasn't quite learned, as his English cousins know instinctively, that there is something called trying too hard. He can't bring himself to keep his clothes until they look old enough and comfortable enough to capture the truly English look. His cufflinks are too expensive, his tie too new, his suit too well pressed.

The one place where M. BCBG doesn't want to look English is when besporting himself upon a Mediterranean beach. Those leek-white limbs, those pallid colours, those non-descript swimming trunks — no, he can — and does — do much better than that. And here it is that French clothes for men come into their own. Here, their instinct for chic far outruns their Anglo-Saxon counterparts — the Englishman looking to perk up his wardrobe in Paris would do well to take a good look at their leisure clothes.

Besides our friend M. BCBG, there is a whole group of more forward-thinking Frenchmen and for them, *bien sûr,* Paris, too, has much to offer. Ever since Pierre Cardin, many moons ago now, took up the cudgels on behalf of the more modern Frenchman and decided that there could be more to masculine mode than depressing colours and monotonous shapes, the men's fashion scene has been as lively in its way as the women's. There is scarcely a big-name designer who hasn't brought out a *ligne masculine*, whether he be as mainline as St-Laurent or as way out as Comme des Garçons.

You see young Frenchmen swaggering down the boulevard Saint-Germain, slinging their *pulls* over their shoulder with all the studied chic of their female counterparts. You see them in their baggy cast-offs, their monochrome Japanese-style, their elegant mix of old and new, and realise that in Paris there is more than one way to make your sartorial mark. From the studied elegance of the *hommes d'affaires*, the conservative leanings of M. BCBG, to the casual chic of the young architect or forward-thinking executive, Paris can cater for them all.

CONTENTS

* Strictly speaking not all shops but also places to rest the feet, restore the spirits and engage the mind.

FASHION

TOBACCO

FASHION

AGNES B
6 rue du Jour, 1er.
METRO: Les Halles.

Agnès B for women has been a regular stopping-off place for many a fashionable woman but less well known is the shop at no. 6. Here men, too, may enjoy the relaxed but elegant approach to life so potently conveyed by Agnès B's clothes: roomy tracksuits; leather jackets; comfortable city suits, with something just that little bit different about them; and imaginative shirts to go with the kit. Excellent value.

ARNYS
14 rue de Sèvres, 7e.
METRO: Sèvres-Babylone.

Primarily aimed at men, this is a very expensive, very upmarket, very classic store. You may be sure that the taste is quite impeccable but it manages to be classic without being boring. Trousers are just a little easier, a little looser than you would find in a totally conventional store; there are some rough linen trousers in summer, some beautiful tweeds in winter; and jackets have the sort of style that means you could wear them anywhere. If you have the money and this is the sort of look you're after, you could hardly do better.

There's a range for women, too — if you're looking for a present for Madame what about a soft, soft cashmere shawl, or a chic weekend bag? None of it comes cheap, but all of it is eminently desirable.

ARTHUR ET FOX
40 rue Vignon, 9e.
METRO: Havre-Caumartin.

If you're feeling in the mood for a suit (and I'm not sure why you should, given that Savile Row still does the made-to-measure suit better than anywhere else in the world) Arthur et Fox offer a splendid compromise between made-to-measure and off-the-peg. They call it *à vos mesures* and what this means is that you choose the fabric and the style and try it on in a ready-made version. This is pinned and tucked until you are happy and then sent away for alterations. The British will feel utterly at home here, for the style of the house is based on rampant Anglophilia. Lots of lovely looking English-style fabrics, all at reasonable prices so everybody should be happy.

AU PRINTEMPS
Au Brummel department.
112 rue de Provence, 9e.
METRO: Havre-Caumartin.

Not the most beguiling of departments in which to shop but nevertheless a good way to get your eye in and see a great deal in one place. The merchandise itself is of good quality and you can see what most of the best-known names in masculine ready-to-wear are up to. Prices seem entirely reasonable and though you won't make a wonderfully *recherché* discovery you could well come away with a couple of shirts, some summer trousers (the leisurewear collection is usually particularly good) and a tie or two to remember Paris by.

CHARVET

28 place Vendôme, 1er.
METRO: Opéra, Concorde.

There is hardly a more distinguished label in the world of masculine apparel than that of Charvet. Probably best known for his shirts and ties (there's many an Englishman who if he buys nothing else makes a point of coming back with a Charvet tie) he will provide anything the smart man about town might need. Shirts are both ready-to-wear and made-to-measure, as are the suits. Then there are coats and raincoats, socks and ties, all in the very best materials. Some say the finest shirts in the world are those by Charvet.

CORTESE

63 rue de Passy, 16e.
METRO: Muette, Passy.

Some more relaxed, easy clothes to give a lift to any masculine wardrobe short on summer or leisure clothes. Nice, soft cotton trousers with easy waists, and jackets with a natural, nonchalant elegance. Get the assistant to help you put together a look and you'll wear it for a long time to come. Not terribly expensive.

DANIEL HECHTER

50 rue de Passy, 16e.
METRO: Muette, Passy.

115 avenue Victor-Hugo, 16e.
METRO: Victor-Hugo.

Forum des Halles, level 1, 4e.
METRO: Les Halles.

146 boulevard Saint-Germain, 6e.
METRO: Odéon.

50 Champs-Elysées, 8e.
METRO: F. D. Roosevelt.

13 rue du Faubourg Saint-Honoré, 8e.
METRO: Concorde, Madeleine.

One of the best names for the not too avant-garde man to look out for. If you want something that is interesting and a little different but that won't get you funny looks back home, you could hardly do better than pay a visit to one of Daniel Hechter's boutiques. He isn't cheap but he does have a knack of providing a kind of relaxed classicism so that his clothes look at once appropriate and yet up-to-date. You can find classic blazers next to soft, unstructured jackets, denims and grey flannels next to slightly baggy, good cotton trousers. Colours, too, are interesting without being alarming: a lot of navy, dark khaki and some sober checks. Wives with timid husbands will find Daniel Hechter a good place to wean them from their boring weekend gear.

DESFOSSE 19 avenue Matignon, 8e.
METRO: F. D. Roosevelt.

Should you, too, feel that you could do with a little Parisian finish, with a haircut or trim, a pedicure or manicure, a massage or a sauna, then Desfossé is the place for you. Here you will find a salon given over exclusively to the interests of the male, so should you wish for a few of those grey hairs to be discreetly darkened you may rest assured that no female customer will be there alongside you. Desfossé understands too that there are men who feel strangely ill-at-ease when far from a telephone, so should an urgent deal require your sudden attention you can buy and sell from the beauty couch itself. Inner man has no need to worry either — there's a bar at one end of the salon where you may lunch lightly and elegantly.

FACONABLE

25 rue Royale, 8e.
METRO: Madeleine.

This is the place to go for the sort of leisurewear that makes the Frenchman on holiday look so much together than his English counterpart. Everything from nicely cut cotton trousers to *le blouson* and light cotton shirts. Stick to the less *outré* colours and go for the navy blues, the khaki and the creams, and you could put together a whole holiday wardrobe that would take you anywhere. Smart swimwear and some wonderful pastel socks.

FRANCESCO SMALTO

275 rue Saint-Honoré, 1er.
METRO: Tuileries, Palais-Royal.

44 rue François-1er, 8e.
METRO: F. D. Roosevelt, George V.

5 place Victor-Hugo, 16e.
METRO: Victor-Hugo.

Though Francesco Smalto is Italian by origin (he came to Paris, via a master-tailor in Turin, when he was just 21 years old) he has become an enduring part of the menswear scene. It didn't take him long before he was applying his special knack and his acquired tailoring skills to a host of politicans, heads of state and the stars of screen and stage. It's easy to see why — he has that happy Italian knack of making good tailoring look entirely natural and unforced, but also pays strict attention to the craft. Today, if you want a new suit, whether ready-to-wear or made-to-measure, Francesco Smalto is the name to conjure with. Go to rue François-1er for couture and to the other addresses for ready-to-wear. There are snappy accessories to go with the suits: shirts, ties, the whole *ensemble*.

GALERIES LAFAYETTE

38–48 boulevard Haussmann, 9e. Galfa Club.
METRO: Chaussée-d'Antin, Havre-Caumartin.

If you feel the smaller boutiques are too trendy or too off-putting, a visit to Galfa Club in the Galeries Lafayette will be infinitely reassuring. Nothing too trendy, nothing too avant-garde, just a good selection of the big names in ready-to-wear and a fine way to see some up-to-the-minute menswear in one fell swoop.

GOLF AND GREEN

90 rue Saint-Dominique, 7e.
METRO: Latour-Maubourg, Invalides.

Men looking for bright leisure-clothes with a difference should look out for this small chain. The clothes have a touch of the Americas about them (that is, some of the colours are a trifle too bright and some of the checks a little too loud) but the range is on the whole attractive, clean and wholesome. It includes tartan cotton trousers with some nice subdued checks to choose from; good, simple, brightly coloured cotton cableknit sweaters; and lots of cotton shirts in stripes or plain, with a good classic look about them.

HEMISPHERES

22 avenue de la Grande-Armée, 17e.
METRO: Argentine, Etoile.

1 boulevard Emile-Augier, 16e.
METRO: Muette.

Something of a cult shop this, with an intriguing mix of old and new. It could be said to be to Paris what Hackett is to London, though besides the very classic English look there are some more eccentric offerings. There you will find the only jeans the smart Frenchman will wear: Levis 501; cashmeres in beautiful colours by McGeorge; Chester Barrie suits; Smedley polos and beautiful American parkas as well as finds from antique markets and junk shops all put together with style and panache. It is a unique shop and well worth the trek to the avenue de la Grande-Armée. But be warned — nothing in the shop is cheap.

KENZO

17 boulevard Raspail, 7e.
METRO: rue du Bac.

Kenzo is still probably the most French of all the Japanese designers to make their names and fortunes in Paris, and fans of his place des Victoire boutique might like to know that there is now an emporium specially for men. The new store is designery and more classic, but here men looking for ways of injecting a little bit of vitality into their wardrobes might like to make a start.

LANVIN

15 rue du Faubourg Saint-Honoré, 8e.
METRO: Concorde, Madeleine.

The imposing entrance shouldn't put you off. If you feel like investing in a really beautifully-made suit, a special shirt or even just a sweater, pay a visit to Lanvin, probably one of the best of the well-known couture houses when it comes to designing for men. Nothing here is cheap but all is eminently well made and infinitely desirable. You can buy off-the-peg or order made-to-measure.

MADELIOS

10 place de la Madeleine, 8e.
METRO: Madeleine.

The only really big store for men to be patronised by Monsieur BCBG, which will give you some idea of its style and taste. Here you will find soft cashmeres, good shoes, shirts and ties in discreet colours by the grand names, the whole panoply that contributes to the thoroughly 'English gentleman' look that Monsieur BCBG so craves. The quality is good, the tone sober and *bon* and if the general presentation lacks panache and enterprise, that is entirely in keeping with the tastes and attitudes of its generally conservative clientele.

MARCEL LASSANCE

17 rue du Vieux-Colombier, 6e.
METRO: Saint-Sulpice, Sèvres-Babylone.

66 avenue des Champs-Elysées, Galerie du Claridge, 8e.
METRO: George V, F. D. Roosevelt.

A good, unalarming shop for the visiting Englishman to look into. Rumoured to be a favourite with President Mitterrand, it purveys the sort of menswear that is just a little different. Good cotton shirts, some nice informal jackets, discreet suits and a nice line in soberly coloured sportswear.

MARITHE ET FRANCOIS GIRBAUD

Espace Bonaparte, 64 rue Bonaparte, 6e.
METRO: Saint-Germain-des-Prés.

After the cult of the 501s, something else had to come — it has. Black jeans are the current Parisian obsession among slick dressers and they don't come any more stylish than the ones to be found in Marithe et François Girbaud's latest boutique on the Left Bank. You may feel the price of being up-to-date is a little high, but this looks like being a style that will run and run. And apart from the trendy black jeans, look out too for impeccable linen and viscose-mix trousers, also in the inevitable black, as well as the chicest (and most expensive) 'battle' clothes in town.

MOTSCH

42 avenue George V, 8e.
METRO: George V.

Motsch is to Paris what Lock is to London, that is, quite simply, the best hatter in town. Like Lock it is much more

than a shop — it is an institution. Its reputation runs before it so that a hat from Motsch is a hat with a history, trailing memories of times long since gone by. Like many hatters, Motsch can no longer offer a silk top-hat but otherwise there is scarcely a *chapeau* that they couldn't provide. They take immense care in fitting hat to head and though it is one of the oldest hatters in Paris, it is becoming newly fashionable with the younger set who find that nothing is so chic as a good plain felt from Motsch.

The Renoma brothers cater for both men and women but in my view their clothes for men are rather more interesting than those for women. They seem to know just how to provide something up-to-date and interesting without going too far — not always easy in the world of *mode masculin*. For work or play there is always something to tempt the man whose wardrobe needs a little perking-up. What about a nice leather jacket (here, they never look as if they'd come straight from a motorbike), some beautifully-cut flannels, or even a jolly sweater for lounging about in at home? A good place to shop, in the peace and quiet of the 16th *arrondissement* away from the flurry of the big stores.

RENOMA

129 bis, rue de la Pompe, 16e.
METRO: Victor-Hugo, Pompe.

ST-LAURENT RIVE GAUCHE

12 place Saint-Sulpice, 6e.
METRO: Saint-Sulpice.

Yes, I know, we have St-Laurent Rive Gauche, too, but there is something about this particular branch that makes it a pleasure to shop in. Maybe it is just part of the Parisian charm, but this shop seems to have more of the genuine St-Laurent inspiration than the British imports. Anybody who has visited a St-Laurent shop will know that he isn't cheap, and if you are thinking in terms of a suit, you will need to be prepared spend quite a hefty sum. He does lovely leisurewear: nice informal jackets, good corduroys and flannel trousers and, if you want a souvenir without spending a fortune, you could always come away with something smaller like a shirt or a belt or even just a pair of socks with that famous logo on the package.

SCAPA OF SCOTLAND

6 rue de Grenelle, 6e.
METRO: Sèvres-Babylone.

This is the place for immaculate Oxfords, Shetland sweaters, tweed jackets, roomy raincoats and all the other *accoutrements* of the French idea of English style. The clothes are lovely: classic yet interesting and only made from the finest materials.

STRUCTURE

52 rue Croix-des-Petits-Champs, 1er.
METRO: Bourse, Palais-Royal.

A marvellously colourful boutique for men — and don't let that put you off. The style is uncompromisingly masculine: impeccable shirts, well-cut trousers, wonderful socks, but all in a glorious range of colours. It's not the place to buy your straight-down-the-line office suit but it is the place to indulge yourself in some informal leisure clothes. Pay Structure a visit if you're about to go on holiday; if you're going somewhere tropical; or if you just want to liven up your weekends. For women, it is the place to go to if you're looking for a special present for the man in your life. If you're in the area it's a place you can hardly miss — somehow its air of happy sunny colours seems to exude considerable warmth. Jolly assistants, too, and prices well in line with the quality on sale. Don't miss the shop if you're in Paris during sale time; they've become quite a feature and bargains are there for the taking.

WESTON

144 avenue des Champs-
Elysées, 8e.
METRO: Etoile.

97 avenue Victor-Hugo, 16e.
METRO: Victor-Hugo.

98 boulevard de Courcelles,
17e.
METRO: Courcelles.

It's not for nothing that Weston shoes have been called (by a Frenchman, *bien sûr*) the Rolls Royce of shoes. Made in the softest leather, beautifully worked in Limoges, Weston shoes are the most copied in France. So understated are they that it has been said that only those who wear them recognise them. Those who can bring themselves to pay the prices will not wear anything else. They come in sober colours like black, brown, maroon and navy blue though there are a few less happy versions such as the two-toned numbers and crocodile-skin shoes. Kit yourself out with moccasins for playtime, boots for winter and a sober pair for the office.

TOBACCO

A LA CIVETTE

157 rue Saint-Honoré, 1er.
METRO: Palais-Royal.

Since the 18th-century the gentlemen of Paris have been buying their pipes, their cigars and their tobacco here. Today, you too (those of you still not weened away from the noxious weed) may find the very finest products here: cigars preserved at just the right temperature in temperature-controlled humidors, everything from a simple cigarette to a fine Havana and all the essential appurtenances the smoker requires.

AU SIAMOIS

4 place de la Madeleine, 8e.
METRO: Madeleine.

Another of the grand addresses for the smoking classes — everything from a fine pipe to the best Havanas.

SERVICES

ACCOMMODATION

ELYSEES CONCORDE 9 rue Royale, 8e.
(Tel. 42.65.11.99.)
METRO: Concorde.

If hotels aren't your style and you'd like your very
own furnished apartment then Elysées Concorde
will be able to help. They'll find you anything
from a furnished single room to a plush five-
bedroomed apartment. If you want ancillary
services, like maids or cooks, laundry or TV
rental, they're all set up to organise that for you,
too.

Or try
FLAT HOTEL (Tel. 45.75.62.20)
Or
LOCATIONS ORION, (Tel. 42.66.33.26.)

If you're really stuck and you just want somewhere, anywhere, to stay, you'll get up-to-the-
minute advice on what's available by telephoning
43.59.12.12.

Or try the Tourist Office at 127 Champs-
Elysées, 8e. (Tel. 47.23.61.72.)

CLOTHES FOR HIRE: MEN

If you're caught on the hop by a sudden grand
invitation and don't feel like lashing out and
buying the kit, worry not, Paris has its equivalent
of Moss Bros.

AU COR DE CHASSE 40 rue de Buci, 6e.
METRO: Odéon.

Everything you might need for the grand soirée:
a 'smoking' and all the extras like shoes, appropriate ties, shirts, the lot. You have to leave a
deposit but once you've paid the fee you can hire
the lot for three days.

JEAN-JACQUES 36 rue de Buci, 6e.
METRO: Odéon.

Prices seem to be noticeably lower here than at
Au Cor de Chasse but as they are both so close,
it's probably worth sussing out the competition
and settling for whatever you like best.

CLOTHES FOR HIRE: WOMEN

If Madame needs to put on something of a show
and the grandness of the invitation is somewhat
unexpected she, too, can be fitted out.

EUGENIE BOISERIE 32 rue Vignon, 9e.
(Tel. 47.42.43.71.)
METRO: Havre-Caumartin.

You'll need to put down a deposit but then you
can hire a cocktail dress or a full-length evening
dress in a very up-to-date style and feel utterly
confident that you will hold your own.

TROC DE TRUC 37 rue du Colisée 8e.
(Tel. 45.62.08.00.)
METRO: Saint-Philippe-du-Roule.

Another address well worth knowing about if
your invitations turn out to be rather smarter
than you had imagined — hire something here
and you can rest assured you'll be turned out in
true Parisian style.

DRUGSTORES

Forget what the word drugstore usually means to
you — these are mini department stores. They're
not to everybody's taste, for they tend to be noisy,
bright, neon-lit and will do absolutely nothing to
remind you of the Paris of Maurice Chevalier
and Degas. They are all new and up-to-the-
minute. But they are useful: from 9am until
midnight at least, usually until 2am, drugstores
are the saviour of the insomniac, the forgetful or
just the plain chaotic. Here you can buy a last-
minute present, food for guests who have just
announced their arrival, books for the book-
worm, guides for those who've forgotten them,
cigarettes for the addicted, champagne for the
festive, toys for the kids — you name it, the
drugstores have it. There is make-up, films for
your camera, suntan creams and a host of
pharmaceutical goods (usually including a good
selection of homeopathic remedies), newspapers
and batteries, records and radios. Go here, too,
to satisfy late-night hunger cravings: they'll serve

a variety of hot and cold American-style delights of the milkshake and gooey banana split variety. They aren't to be recommended for your daily needs — for one thing prices tend to be higher (they have to be with the hours they keep and the sites they're occupying) and for another what they make up in usefulness they lack in charm. But at some time or another you'll need to know where they are — come the emergency that hits us all, they'll come up trumps.

DRUGSTORE DE NEUILLY 14 place du Marché, 92 Neuilly.
METRO: Pont de Neuilly.

This one is quieter and more agreeable than most.

DRUGSTORE DES CHAMPS-ELYSEES 133 avenue des Champs-Elysées, 8e.
METRO: Etoile.

DRUGSTORE MATIGNON 1 avenue Matignon, 8e.
METRO: F. D. Roosevelt.

DRUGSTORE OPERA 6 boulevard des Capucines, 9e.
METRO: Opéra, Madeleine.

DRUGSTORE SAINT-GERMAIN 149 boulevard St-Germain, 6e.
METRO: Saint-Germain-des-Prés, Opéra.

EMERGENCY MONEY EXCHANGES

Most banks are open from 9.30am to 4.30pm but you'll be infuriated from time to time by finding them shut just when you most need them. All the main railway stations (Gare d'Austerlitz, Gare de l'Est, etc) have exchange offices that are open for longer hours than the banks but they do not tend to be attractive places to change money. Firstly, once in Paris itself you don't tend to find yourself near any of the stations and secondly they are usually surrounded by jostling crowds of new arrivals grappling with their inadequate French. Save the nerves and go elsewhere. Here are a few of the places you could try.

CCF (CREDIT COMMERCIAL DE FRANCE) 115 avenue des Champs-Elysées, 8e.
METRO: Etoile.

Open from 8.30am to 8pm from Monday to Saturday.

UBP 154 avenue des Champs-Elysées, 8e.
METRO: Etoile.

Open from 9am to 5pm, Monday to Friday and from 10.30am to 6pm on Saturdays, Sundays and public holidays.

It tends to charge high rates so only come here in emergencies.

BARCLAYS BANK 33 rue de Quatre-Septembre, 2e.
METRO: Opéra.

Open from 9.15am to 5.30pm.

It is English-speaking and reputedly gives good rates of exchange.

BUREAU DE CHANGE 9 rue Scribe, 9e.
METRO: Opéra.

Open from 9am to 5.15pm, Monday to Friday.

LAUNDRY, REPAIRS AND OTHER SERVICES

ATELIER MAURICE DAB 1st Floor, 20 rue de Turbigo, 2e.
METRO: Etienne-Marcel.

A tiny workshop in the middle of one of the most fashionable shopping districts of all. Here M. and Mme. Dab will put your hems up or down, repair a broken zip, invisibly mend a torn jacket and generally provide the kind of service you thought had disappeared forever.

CLAIRE ET AGNES 42 rue de Passy, 16e.
METRO: Passy.

Take along your battle-worn umbrella and Claire and Agnes will return it to you like new. Better not, though, take along just any old umbrella because such workmanship doesn't come cheap.

CORDONNERIE VANEAU 44 rue Vaneau, 7e.
METRO: Vaneau, St François-Xavier.

When your shoes begin to show signs of strain, take them along to Cordonnerie Vaneau who will repair them as lovingly as if they were the Mona Lisa. A sentimental reminder of times gone by when shoe-repairing was a craft.

EXPRESS SERVICE 107 boulevard Haussmann, 8e.
METRO: Miromesnil, Saint-Augustin.

This is the address to note if you have an old and beloved handbag that is in need of a little care and attention. Handbags develop a patina with age and few of us can bear to part with them if they are of any quality — nice to know they can be mended.

Also try

MAROQUINERIE 35 rue de Châteaudun, 9e.
METRO: N-D-de-Lorette.

FAST INTERNATIONAL SERVICE 55 rue de La-Bruyère, 9e.
(Tel. 48.74.33.16.)

If you need help in a hurry, ring Fast International Service — they're said to be able to send a hairdresser round, to organise a babysitter, take your dog for a walk, fetch granny from the airport or do whatever else it is you urgently need done.

LAVERIE DU TEMPLE 27 rue Vieille-du-Temple, 4e.
(Tel. 42.78.41.50.)
METRO: Saint-Paul.

Open 8am to 12.45pm and then from 1.30pm to 7pm, Monday to Saturday. Closed the whole of August.

If you've run out of clean clothes and you're not staying with friends or in the sort of hotel that will do your laundry for you, then Laverie du Temple will come to your aid. They charge by the kilo and will wash and dry your dirty linen on the same day. You, I'm afraid, are left with the ironing.

SIDONIE LARIZZI 8 rue de Marignan, 8e.
METRO: F. D. Roosevelt.

Open 10.am to 7pm. Closed Sunday.

The queen, you might say, of the *haute chaussure* business, Sidonie Larizzi offers the marvellous service of making shoes to measure at prices that, for the quality and the effort involved, are really very reasonable. She'll make you a grand slipper to wear to a ball, or dye a shoe to match a silk dress. She'll give you a design in any height of heel as long as it doesn't ruin the line, and if you like the shape of a shoe but not the leather, why that'll be alright, she'll make it up for you in the material of your choice. There is also a selection of shoes that you can buy ready made. The same service that applies to shoes, she will extend to her collection of luggage, that is, you can order special colours, shapes and sizes.

TETE D'AFFICHE 5 rue Caron, 4e.
(Tel. 42.72.57.26.)
METRO: Saint-Paul.

Paris is one of the best places to buy modern posters and if you find one you can't resist and want it framed straight away, take it to Tête d'Affiche where they'll frame it quicker than almost anybody else, usually within 48 hours. You can browse through quite a selection of inexpensive posters there as well.

PHARMACIES

BRITISH-AMERICAN PHARMACY 1 rue Auber, 9e.
METRO: Havre-Caumartin, Opéra.

Open 8.30am to 8pm. Closed Sunday.

Comforting, familiar brands for those who have run out of or left behind their medical props.

PHARMACIE ANGLAISE DES CHAMPS-ELYSEES 62 avenue des Champs-Elysées, 8e.
(Tel: 43.59.22.52.)
METRO: F.D. Roosevelt, George V.

Open 8.30am to 10.30pm. Closed Sunday.

This pharmacy sells English and American proprietary brands and has English-speaking pharmacists who will dispense advice as well as potions.

PHARMACIE DES ARTS 106 boulevard Montparnasse, 14e.
METRO: Vavin.

Open 8am to midnight, Monday to Saturday; 9am to 1pm Sunday and public holidays.

Worth knowing if you need something after the other two are shut and you don't happen to be near the Champs-Elysées.

PHARMACY DHERY 84 avenue des Champs-Elysées, 8e.
(Tel. 45.62.02.41.)
METRO: George V.

Small but worth knowing about because it is open 24 hours a day, every day of the year.

THANK YOUS

Paris is a more formal city than London and the social rules are stricter. If you have been entertained for dinner, the theatre or a weekend in the country, it will need more than a thank you telephone call the following day — flowers would be splendid.

SAVART 8 Palais Bourbon, 7e.
(Tel. 45.51.78.43.)
METRO: Invalides, Varenne.

Taste in flowers, like in everything else, requires fine judgement and a sensitive nose for changing moods. M. Moulie of Savart could be said to be the Alain Senderens of the floral world. So trust your francs to him and he'll do you proud.

INTER MAGNUM
(Tel. 42.66.02.48.)

Flowers are lovely but *une bonne bouteille* is more reviving. If you're lucky enough to be treated to an invitation to a French home you will want to send a thank you present. One call to Inter Magnum and a bottle can be dispatched to any corner of France. Choose from a fine Beaujolais or a true champagne, from a glorious Marc to a white Burgundy. Remember that they'll add a service charge on top of the cost of the bottle.

THEATRE

HALF-PRICE THEATRE TICKETS place de la Madeleine, 8e.
METRO: Madeleine.

Open from 12.30pm to 8pm on Tuesday to Friday; 12.30pm on Saturday for matinees and from 2pm for the evening performance; and from 12.30pm to 4.30pm on Sunday.

Want to go to the theatre? It's worth knowing about the half-price ticket stand in the place de la Madeleine. Modelled on the idea started on Broadway, this little kiosk offers tickets at half-price daily.

TOURIST INFORMATION

AMERICAN EXPRESS 11 rue Scribe, 9e.
(Tel. 42.66.09.99.)
METRO: Opéra.

Open 9am to 5pm, Monday to Friday.

BUREAU DES OBJETS TROUVES (or, to put it another way, the lost and found office) 36 rue des Morillons, 15e.
METRO: Convention.

Open from 8.30am to 5pm Monday, Tuesday, Wednesday and Friday; 8.30am to 8pm, Thursday.

You'll need to cope with some paperwork here so if your own French isn't up to it you'd better try and rustle up a French-speaking friend to help you cope with the rigours of the chase.

TOURIST INFORMATION IN ENGLISH
(Tel. 47.20.88.98.)

TOURIST OFFICE 127 avenue des Champs-Elysées, 8e.
(Tel: 47.23.61.72.)
METRO: George V, Etoile.

Open 9am to 9pm, Monday to Saturday; 9am to 8pm Sunday.

TRANSPORT

Chauffeur-driven cars

MURDOCH ASSOCIES 59 avenue Marceau, 16e.
(Tel. 47.20.63.28.)

So you left the Rolls behind and now you need to arrive at Longchamp in style. This company will provide you with the Rolls or Mercedes of your choice, fitted out *comme il faut*.

DURAND & CIE 2 bis, rue de l'Eglise, 92 Neuilly.
(Tel: 46.24.37.27.)

If your style is a little more modest there is Durand & Cie who will hire you anything from a little *deux chevaux* to a Cadillac.

Hire a bicycle

PARIS-VELO 2 rue du Fer-à-Moulin, 5e.
(Tel. 43.37.59.22.)
METRO: Censier-Daubernon.

Open 10am to 7pm, Monday to Saturday.

If you (sensibly) didn't bring your car, can't face the métro and the sun is shining, you might like to think about hiring a bicycle. A marvellous way for the young and energetic to see the city. Paris-Vélo is the place to go to — they'll rent you one of their many bikes for one, three or any other number of days that suits you. Choose from simple models to more complicated and exotic five- or ten-gear bikes.

Hire a helicopter

HELICAP Heliport de Paris, 4 avenue de la Porte-de-Sèvres, 15e.
(Tel. 45.57.75.51.)

If a helicopter is more your style, try Helicap.

Hire a plane

UNIJET 217 rue de Faubourg Saint-Honoré, 8e.
(Tel. 45.63.11.58.)

A sudden emergency — the company's being taken over, somebody's ill — and you need to move fast. Unijet will get you there, and they operate a 24-hour service.

EURALAIR Aeroport du Bourget, zone Nord Aviation d'Affaires
(Tel. 48.35.95.220.)

If all the jets are out, try Euralair. They are used to providing aeroplanes of almost any sort at the drop of a hat. It'll cost you, of course, but then this is a service for those for whom time is money.

INDEX